D. James Kennedy is one of the most brilliant and eloquent defenders of Judeo-Christian values in America today. His new book, *The Gates of Hell Shall Not Prevail*, is an articulate apologetic of why people of faith should be involved in our culture and our political system.

Ralph E. Reed, Jr.
Executive Director
Christian Coalition

In *The Gates of Hell Shall Not Prevail*, D. James Kennedy has done a tremendous service to the body of Christ in exposing the agenda of secularists throughout our land. The myths brought forth by those with an anti-Christian agenda have been brought to life. Dr. Kennedy's forthright manner gives each of us a reason to hope as he calls upon us to engage the culture with the message of Christ. This is a must-read book.

Jay Alan Sekulow
Chief Counsel
The American Center for Law and Justice

This is an inspiring book—full of hope. It pulls no punches: the gates of Hell are clearly seen in all their horrific might as they energize today's darkest strongholds in American culture. Yet against that black backdrop the irresistible strength of Christ, working through committed believers, tears through and destroys the darkness in ways that will surprise and embolden every reader.

Marlin Maddoux
President, International Christian Media
and Host, *Point of View* radio program

For almost fifty years, I have been committed to helping fulfill the Great Commission, to helping take the Gospel to every person on Planet Earth in this generation.

More than any other country, America has the resources—money, manpower, and technology—to help finish this task given to us by our Lord, which is often referred to as the Great Commission.

That is why I am pleased to see this outstanding and timely book, *The Gates of Hell Shall Not Prevail*, by my good friend Jim Kennedy. I view him as one of the leading statesmen of our time. He is a scholar with a brilliant mind and a compassionate heart. He is a man of Christian principle and courage who boldly proclaims truth and error.

May God use James Kennedy and this great book to help the body of Christ, God's army, in this crucial, historic hour.

Dr. Bill Bright
Founder and President
Campus Crusade for Christ International

Every Christian in America should read this book!

Donald E. Wildmon
President and Founder
American Family Association

There are very few books that Christians must read. *The Gates of Hell Shall Not Prevail* is one such book. It's a practical volume that shows Christians how to deal with the culture and become more than conquerors. As soon as you read it, you will want your friends to read it.

Ted Baehr
Chairman
The Christian Film & Television Commission

THE GATES OF HELL
SHALL NOT
PREVAIL

D. JAMES
KENNEDY
WITH JERRY NEWCOMBE

THOMAS NELSON PUBLISHERS

Nashville • Atlanta • London • Vancouver

Published in association with the literary agency of Alive Communications, Inc., P.O. Box 49068, Colorado Springs, CO 80949.

Published in Nashville, Tennessee, by Thomas Nelson, Inc., Publishers, and distributed in Canada by Word Communications, Ltd., Richmond, British Columbia, and in the United Kingdom by Word (UK), Ltd., Milton Keynes, England.

Special thanks to Matt Johnston for his research assistance on rock music.

Library of Congress Cataloging-in-Publication Data

Kennedy, D. James (Dennis James), 1930-
The gates of hell shall not prevail / D. James Kennedy with Jerry Newcombe.
   p. cm.
   Includes bibliographical references.
   ISBN 0-7852-7686-6 (hardcover)
   ISBN 0-7852-7177-5 (paperback)
   1. Church. 2. Christianity—20th century. 3. Christianity—Forecasting. I. Newcombe, Jerry. II. Title.
BV600.2.K414 1996
262—dc20
                                                95-26217
                                                  CIP

Printed in the United States of America

3 4 5 6 7 - 00 99 98 97

Contents

To our wives, Anne Kennedy and Kirsti Newcombe,
for their tireless encouragement and patience,
without which this book would never have materialized.

Foreword

For almost fifty years, I have been committed to helping fulfill the Great Commission, to helping take the gospel to every person on Planet Earth in this generation.

More than any other country, America has the resources—money, manpower, and technology—to help finish this task given to us by our Lord, which is often referred to as the Great Commission.

That is why I am pleased to see this outstanding and timely book, *The Gates of Hell Shall Not Prevail*, by my good friend Jim Kennedy. I view him as one of the leading statesmen of our time. He is a scholar with a brilliant mind and a compassionate heart. He is a man of Christian principle and courage who boldly proclaims truth and error. I appreciate his position on our biblical heritage and how he constantly exposes the liberal agenda of those who oppose Christ. Jim Kennedy is a gifted, articulate, and patriotic American. I praise God that he is in the battle with us.

May God use James Kennedy and this great book to help mobilize citizens of this country and particularly the body of Christ, God's army, in this crucial, historic hour. Now is the time for action!

Dr. Bill Bright
Founder and President
Campus Crusade for Christ International

Other Books by D. James Kennedy

Abortion: Cry of Reality
Beginning Again
Chain Reaction
Character and Destiny: A Nation in Search of Its Soul
Defending the First Amendment
Delighting God: How to Live at the Center of God's Will
Education: Public Problems, Private Solutions
Evangelism Explosion
Foundations for Your Faith
The God of Great Surprises
The Great Deception
Help, God, I Hurt
Highway to Holiness
How Do I Get to Know God?
How Do I Live for God?
Knowing God's Will
Knowing the Whole Truth
Learning to Live with the People You Love
Messiah: Prophecies Fulfilled
Nation in Shame
Real Meaning of the Zodiac
Reconstruction
Spiritual Renewal
This Is the Life
Truth and Education
Truths That Transform
Turn It to Gold
What If Jesus Had Never Been Born?
What Is God Like?
Why I Believe
Wolves among Us
Your Prodigal Child: Help for Hurting Parents

Introduction

One day two men were sitting together on an airplane. As they talked with each other, it was revealed that one was a businessman. The second man said he was a representative of a worldwide organization with franchises in every country. "Really?" asked the first. "You must work for Coca-Cola." "No," replied the second, "we have far more field representatives than they'll ever have! We have more employees and more customers, if you can call them that." Now, the first man was definitely intrigued. "Microsoft?" "No—infinitely bigger." "The U.N.?" "Again, much bigger . . . and our worldwide assets far exceed the combined assets of the Fortune 500 companies." "Well, then I can't imagine who you work for! Tell me." The second man looked him straight in the eye and replied that he was a minister in the Church of Jesus Christ![1]

Think about it. The largest institution on the planet, the kingdom that contains more citizens than any country on earth, the association that has the most members is the Church of Jesus Christ! Not any one denomination within Christendom, but the collective body that professes to believe in the Son of God is the largest group of people on the globe. Christ's Church contains members from every country and every race, speaking a multitude of languages, from every socioeconomic strata. There's simply no other group, institution, or fellowship even remotely similar!

And yet the Church is also hated by many, mostly without cause. In our day, in our society, Christianity is under attack on all sorts of fronts—the media, academia, and the courts. Christian bashing seems to be at an all-time high. For example, a recent column by a member of the editorial board for the *Miami Herald*, one of the nation's leading newspapers, likened the Christian Coalition to the Ebola virus in Africa![2]

This book will examine the assault on Christ, with the purposes of encouraging believers in the midst of these dark days and providing information to help do battle in the "culture war." My goal is to show how, in the big picture, those who attack Christ and His Church are on the wrong side of history! The book will further show that despite this onslaught, the Church is growing like never before, mostly abroad, but also here in America, and is winning the victory! "The gates of Hell shall not prevail against it."

Overview

This book is divided into three parts, based on the teaching of Jesus in Matthew 16:18, wherein He said that He would build His Church and that the gates of Hell shall not prevail against it. The three points are:

1. He will build His Church.
2. The gates of Hell will attack the Church (implied).
3. The gates of Hell shall not prevail.

John Foxe, who wrote the classic work *Foxe's Book of Martyrs* (in 1563), said of Matthew 16:18: "The whole course of the Church to this day may seem nothing else but a verifying of the said prophecy."[3]

Here is an overview of the contents of the three parts of this book:

Part 1. Christ Is Building His Church

This section deals with the fact that Jesus Christ is building His Church. It deals with some important, incontrovertible facts, from which the attack on Christ can in no way detract. Here I'll examine the secure foundations of the Christian faith that no power of Hell can ever undermine. This includes the veracity of the Holy Bible, which is like an anvil that is constantly being hammered by critics of the Bible. But instead of the anvil falling to pieces, the hammers are demolished!

Part 2. The Gates of Hell

Here I will look at many modern-day "hammers" that are vainly trying to smash away at Christianity. This includes the attack on Christ in the media, in Hollywood, in "the public square," that is, the schools, the courts, and the culture at large. And I will even examine the attack on historic Christianity that comes from within the professing Church.

Part 3. The Gates of Hell Shall Not Prevail

In this final section of the book, I will put the present-day attack on Christ in historic perspective. And I will show how we as believers can effectively and Christianly respond to this assault. I'll also show how in the grand picture, Christianity is foreordained to triumph. So, onward Christian soldiers!

I pray that this book will be an encouragement to the body of Christ today, so that we will not be overwhelmed by the present and future onslaught against Christ, Christians, and the Church. The attack on Christ may indeed get worse. What this book shows happening today was inconceivable thirty years ago. What is inconceivable today may be reality three decades from now, as America seems to move away from God—unless God does a great work between now and then.

And there is some evidence that He is indeed working mightily in the land. Just as the early Church was not overwhelmed by the attack against them—an attack that was much more fierce than what we have known—we, too, can take encouragement that Christ will ever get the victory. In fact, He appears to be gaining the victory even now, when we consider the worldwide growth of the Church.

Christ Is Building His Church

Part

1

The Worldwide Expansion of the Church

*I will build my church; and the gates of hell shall not
prevail against it.*
—Matthew 16:18b KJV

Around the world, there are today nearly two billion professing Christians![1] Dr. Ralph Reed, the executive director of the Christian Coalition, writes: "How will our times be viewed by history? I believe these days will be remembered as a time of remarkable spiritual awakening. The greatest revival of religion in modern times is breaking out across the globe."[2] Indeed, the growth of the Church through the ages has started to become exponential in our time. To appreciate the present situation, let's put it all into historical perspective:

When Jesus Christ died and rose from the dead, there were some 120 believers who gathered in an upper room to pray, as He had commanded them. One hundred twenty meager souls were waiting to go out and spread the Word in a vast and teeming world. No one even took note of their existence.

Then Peter preached a sermon and there were three thousand who believed. Shortly thereafter, five thousand more were added to the number, followed by a great multitude of Jews and priests! Next came a time of persecution, and when it ended in A.D. 313 with the Edict of Toleration, there were about ten million professing Christians alive.[3] By the year 1000, this number had grown to fifty million.[4] By the end of the 1700s, most of the missionary impetus had stalled, yet the number had grown to 215 million professing Christians. That is an increase of 165 million in eight hundred years.

In 1795 the modern missionary movement began in earnest with William Carey. By the year 1900, the number had grown to five hundred million professing Christians. That is an increase of 285 million in one century. And then by 1980, just eighty short years later, that number had grown to 1.3 billion professing Christians. Then by 1990, that number had grown to roughly 1.8 billion—an increase of 1.3 billion people in the twentieth century alone![5] There is nothing even vaguely approaching this accomplishment in the annals of human history!

Thus, in a day when it seems like all Hell is breaking out against the Christian faith, we can rejoice in the work of our sovereign God. Of that number, no one knows exactly how many are truly born again and going to Heaven. Even if only a fraction of those who claim to be Christians are truly Christians, we're still talking about a very sizable population! When we look at the explosive growth of the Church worldwide, it makes us realize that, by God's grace, we *are* winning! My friend Dr. Bill Bright, founder and president of Campus Crusade for Christ, says, "Lately I have sensed that the body of Christ is on the verge of the greatest spiritual breakthrough in the history of Christianity."[6]

The Number of Bible-Believing Christians

As we look at these figures, keep in mind that we're talking about the growth of the Church in terms of professing believers of all denominations, whether Catholic, Orthodox, or Protestant. But the growth rate for evangelicals is also very high. Specifically, when we compare the number of "Bible-believing Christians" with the number of the world's population, we see rapid growth of Christ's Church. Dr. David Barrett, probably the greatest church statistician alive, supplied these statistics, indicating the ratio of Bible-believing, or evangelical Christians, to the total number of people in the world:

> One to ninety-nine by 1430
> One to forty-nine by 1790
> One to thirty-two by 1940
> One to twenty-four by 1960
> One to nineteen by 1970
> One to sixteen by 1980
> One to thirteen by 1983
> One to eleven by 1986

One to ten by 1989

One to nine by 1993[7]

And the number of Bible-believing Christians continues to grow at an extraordinarily rapid rate. Note how in the last twenty-five years, there has been a greater growth in the number of evangelical Christians than there has been in the last five centuries! David Barrett further states, "Today, 540 million out of 5.4 billion people in the world are Bible-believing Christians."[8] Today, just a few short years later, that number may be up to 700 million born-again Christians![9] What's more, despite the rapid growth of people on our planet, "the Kingdom of Christ is expanding even faster at over three times the rate of world population."[10] This is truly great news with far-reaching implications the world over!

It's hard for us to grasp this great news since it is happening in our lifetime; but, again, we're seeing the Christian faith growing at a much faster rate than it ever has before. More people are witnessing for Christ; more and more Christians are awakening to the privilege and responsibility and the joy that is theirs to share the gospel of Christ. More Christians are being trained to evangelize than ever before in history. And lives are being changed. For example, a violent man in Latin America who often used a knife as his weapon of choice saw the *Jesus* movie when missionaries showed it at an open-air meeting in his town. He was so moved by the film, he asked them if he could exchange his knife for a Bible!

Although most of the growth is taking place outside the United States, there is a great deal going on in this country. Seventy-eight percent of Americans claim to be Christians already.[11] We know, obviously, that not all of those who profess the faith are truly converted. Statistics can be misleading. Nonetheless, like church attendance figures, they indicate some measure of spiritual interest. Even if only one-tenth of those who claimed to be Christian were truly converted, that would still be *millions* of people—far outnumbering the committed humanists, atheists, agnostics, gays, and lesbians combined!

Yet the growth of the Church in America is "statistically invisible." A minister told me the other day that he had just led a man who was a member of another denomination to Christ. Notice that the man already was a professed Christian; he is today a professed Christian. Statistically speaking, nothing happened. It was a stealth conversion—invisible to the statistical radar. But, in reality, something tremendous happened. He was spiritually dead, but now he's alive. He was spiritually blind, but now he can see.

There are some encouraging trends in the American Church today. As of this writing, revival is currently sweeping across many of our Christian colleges![12] This could translate to great things for the future as many of these young people will be the future leaders in our churches. I'm also encouraged by the ever-growing Promise Keepers movement, where hundreds of thousands of men are committing themselves to live out their Christianity at home and in the workplace. God is doing a great work in our time.

George Barna, the church statistician, estimates that 36 percent of the American adult population are born-again Christians.[13] Barna qualifies, "Born again is defined as adults who say they have made a personal commitment to Jesus Christ that is still important in their lives today *and* believe that when they die they will go to Heaven because they have confessed their sins and accepted Jesus Christ as their Savior."[14]

Fair as the Moon, Clear as the Sun

A beautiful description of the Church was uttered centuries before it was officially inaugurated at Pentecost. We find this description in the Song of Solomon, which was written about 1000 B.C. Although the Song of Solomon has much to teach about human love between a man and a woman, it is also ultimately the story of the relationship of the heavenly Bridegroom and His earthly bride—the Church. Solomon writes,

> *Who is she who looks forth as the morning,*
> *Fair as the moon,*
> *Clear as the sun,*
> *Awesome as an army with banners?*
> *(Song of Solomon 6:10)*

That, I think, is one of the most glorious pictures of the Church to be found anywhere in the Scriptures.

We, the Church, are the bride of Christ. In the midst of the blackness of night of hopelessness, despair, and death, it is the Church that brings the hope of sunrise. Even in the most ancient of days, the Church was the morning star to give some hope of the coming morning to those who were lost in the darkness.

Even in the Old Testament when darkness still covered most of the earth, the Church was that moon, that fair moon that gave borrowed light to a needy and hopeless world—a world that could see nothing beyond that hole in the ground where life had little meaning and no hope. There was the Church, even back then, that was fair as the moon. That is, of course, an idealized picture of the Church. Unfortunately, there are many who would be seen merely as pockmarks on that moon; nevertheless, that is the picture God draws of the Church.

And yet there came a glorious day when the night was to fade away. In that bright and marvelous morning when Jesus Christ walked out of the tomb and the darkness of death forever faded away, the Church became clear as the sun.

Awesome as an Army with Banners

The Church is also an army—"awesome as an army with banners." We are the army of Christ. We sing "Onward Christian soldiers, marching as to war," although we too often sing it flippantly and without much thought. Nonetheless, we are exactly that—Christian soldiers in the army of Christ. He is the Captain of the well-fought fight that goes on before us. We are called to a great battle with the forces of darkness, with principalities and powers of the air.

We are called to go forth "awesome as an army with banners." We have a banner; it is the gospel. The Church has many banners. "Jesus Christ is Lord"[15] was one of the earliest ones. "He will never leave us"[16] is another. Others include "He always leads us in triumph,"[17] "He is King of kings and Lord of lords,"[18] and "He goes forth upon a white horse conquering and to conquer."[19] Have you noticed that when the armies of this world see their flag, their national emblem, lifted up, even soldiers who are fatigued will get new strength? So we, as the army of Christ, are to go forth in that way, and we should indeed strike fear into those who are the enemies of God, not because we take up a literal sword, but because we take up the Sword of Truth.

I believe that it is encouraging to see the Church down through the centuries, back a thousand years before Christ, when this Song of Solomon was first penned, up to that glorious resurrection morning, up through the centuries of Church history, on until today. And we look forward to the Church of the twenty-first century.

The Church in the Twenty-first Century

Since a new millennium is almost upon us, what will the Church be like in the twenty-first century? Well, I am not a prophet nor the son of a prophet. As one theologian has said, the future turns on so many tiny ball bearings that no one can prophesy it accurately who is not divinely inspired to do so. Yet, I believe there are some trends which, if they continue, will indeed result in a Church the likes of which has not been seen before.

The modern missionary movement began two hundred years ago. This force has had and will continue to have enormous consequences for the Church. For the first time, the gospel went out from the West until it traveled all around the world. A tremendous change has taken place only in recent decades as a result of the gospel's traveling around the globe.

In 1970, just twenty-six years ago, two-thirds of the world's Christians were in the West (U.S. and Europe), while the rest of the world's peoples had only one-third of the Christians.[20] Yet the non-West comprises two-thirds of the world's landmass and population.

In 1980 the ratio of Christians in the West to Christians in the non-West had radically changed to fifty-fifty.[21] By that point, sixteen years ago, half of the world's Christians lived in the other two-thirds of the world.

By 1990, 75 percent of the world's Christians lived in the two-thirds of the world that is non-Western.[22] In many of these places Christianity grows, even though the believers face horrific hostility and, sometimes, even martyrdom. For instance, many Islamic extremists are slaughtering Christians today, e.g. in Sudan.

So Christianity is no longer a Western religion. It is a world religion. In fact, the growth rate of non-Western missions is now reported to be five times that of Western missions.[23]

As we saw earlier, there has been in the last twenty-six years, the most incredible explosion of converts to Christ that the world has ever seen. In Latin America, the evangelical population is growing three times as fast as the general population.[24] In Africa there were ten million Christians in 1900; today there are over three hundred million Christians in Africa.[25]

In Asia the kingdom of Christ is expanding like never before. David Bryant, the director of the Concerts of Prayer ministry and author of the encouraging new book *The Hope at Hand: National and World Revival for the Twenty-first Century*, reports that in East Asia, a mass movement to spread Christianity began in 1980, when there were sixteen million East Asian Christians. Less than a decade later, that number had grown to eighty million![26] In China, about 25,000 are coming to Christ each day—despite intense persecution.[27] And there are thousands of Chinese Christians who are "praying for revival in the churches of America"![28]

Another encouraging development is that many Muslims are coming to faith in Christ like never before. Bryant writes that more Muslims have become Christians in the last ten years than in the last one thousand years![29] In Indonesia the number of Christians is so high that the Muslim government is "afraid to print it."[30]

It seems as if Jesus Christ is building His Church in our day like never before in history. David Barrett and Todd Johnson write that there are presently some five hundred million Christians in the world committed to fulfilling the Great Commission—five hundred million![31] Furthermore, they predict that the number of active "Great Commission Christians" by the year 2000 could well be one billion![32]

What is behind all these amazing developments? Well, for one thing, a greater commitment to prayer. Christians around the world are praying for revival and the expansion of the Church. For example, since 1989, when a "global prayer strategy" was initiated, millions of Christians from 180 nations have been involved in daily prayer for revival across the world. They spend at least five minutes when the sun rises in their area to pray for the spread of the gospel. Bryant says, "As the sun moves across each time zone, the torch of prayer is being passed around the clock, around the world."[33]

God is at work in a tremendous way. Indeed, the Church is going forth today as an army—"as an army with banners." That, I think, portends great things for the coming century. Jesus Christ is building His Church and the gates of Hell shall not prevail against it!

We have seen in the last fifty years of this century another phenomenon. It has been the era of the layperson. An increasing tens of millions of laypeople around the world have begun to share their faith in Christ. They have been equipped, trained, emboldened, and encouraged to go out and share the good news with others. This is another reason for the great explosion of converts around the world.

I believe that in this coming century the Church is going to do things people never dreamed it would do. For one thing, we are going to see the enormous growth of large churches in this country and around the world. I think of 135 years ago when Charles Spurgeon was the greatest preacher in the world. He said, as I read in the back of one of his commentaries, that around the year 1860 they had received the 4,225th member into the church, making that the second-largest church in Christendom. Did you grasp that? One hundred thirty-five years ago the second-largest church in the world had 4,225 members! Today, that would not be the second largest church in Ft. Lauderdale. We have churches with tens of thousands of members here in the United States, and in some other countries they put us to shame. There is a Presbyterian church with as many as 80,000 members in Korea and another church there with 800,000 members! God is doing some incredible things in our time.

Many smaller, inactive churches are going to close. Namely, those who have not been proclaiming the gospel—who have not been winning people to Jesus Christ. They are just withering away. But those churches (whatever size they may be) that have been faithful to the gospel, proclaiming the good news and training their people to do so, are going to grow, and it is not going to be uncommon in the twenty-first century to see churches that have ten, twenty, fifty, seventy-five thousand members in churches right here in the United States of America!

Another change that, if trends continue, will take place is that by the middle of the next century, most of the mainline churches in America will have disappeared. I predict that the historic "mainline" churches will be discovered to be "back alleys," dead-end streets. I am referring to those mainline denominations that have, by and large, become liberal, whose seminaries turn out ministers who do not believe the Bible—the kinds of ministers you will read about in Chapter 10, who don't believe Jesus said three-fourths of what is attributed to Him and now reveal that they don't even believe that He rose from the dead. Granted, there are some evangelicals in these mainline denominations, but many of the leaders espouse views that are far from biblical.

This kind of liberal unbelief, an ugly example of the attack on Christ in America, is a plague—a blight upon the Church—and it is going to fade away. A recent survey showed that by the middle of the next century, there will be two great religious forces in America, and far and away the largest one will be evangelical Christianity. Alister McGrath wrote, "In a 1990 survey of the 500 fastest-growing Protestant congregations in the U.S., 89 percent were found to be evangelical."[34] The other great religious force will be Roman Catholicism—maybe a third or a half the size of evangelicalism.

So there is going to be a tremendous growth in Bible-believing Christianity in the coming century. Evangelicals seem to be the wave of the future. As McGrath said, "Head and heart are being brought together in a movement that is looking forward to the future with a sense of expectancy and anticipation."[35] There will be an increase in the number of people who have been trained and have learned to witness, so that by the twenty-first century, there will be more and more missionaries traveling all over the world. And Christians who do not witness for Christ will be the strange ducks, the rare birds. Twenty-five years ago, 95 percent of the church members in America didn't witness to anyone. But by the middle of the next century, that figure may be almost reversed, as Christians increasingly realize that it is their responsibility and their privilege to share the gospel of Jesus Christ with others.

Another change I think we will see is that the Church will naturally exert a far greater influence in this nation, and others as well. This will lead, I believe, to tremendous changes in our culture, which has been written off by many as post-Christian. Well, they wrote off Christ, too, when they buried Him in the grave, but He rose again with power!

I believe the Church is coming back again after many, many decades of lethargy and sleep; it is rising from that sleep to be a responsible power. I believe we are going to see many of the most unfortunate and godless decisions that have been made in this country in the past few decades reversed, and America will be restored again to godliness—the kind of godliness that made us great. It isn't going to happen overnight. As we'll see so clearly in Part 2 of this book, there are still forces of evil and godlessness and immorality that are entrenched in the institutions of this nation because Christians have abdicated their responsibilities. But that, I think, will also change in time. In fact, it's already beginning to change.

Christians will have far more influence in public elections. I believe that in the twenty-first century, evangelical Christians will be the dominant force in elections in this nation. Those that would flaunt their disregard for moral and ethical standards will find it increasingly difficult, and finally impossible, to be elected to high office in this nation.

I believe the Church will also exercise more responsibility for the needy. As the nation retreats from the socialistic path it has been on for some time, the obligation will again be returned to the family, to local organizations, and to the Church. We will more fully exercise our responsibility and opportunity to minister to the poor, as the Church at one time did. That will give us the opportunity of bringing to them not only the physical necessities of food and clothing, but also the gospel of Christ that can feed their souls and clothe them in the white robes of righteousness.

I believe the Church is going to be more involved in education and discipleship. I spoke just recently in Detroit at a Christian college, and I pointed out to them that today such a college as theirs is rare in America. But stop and think. At one time *all* of the colleges in this nation were Christian colleges. I believe that though it will take years or decades, that is gradually going to happen again: Christians are going to take once again their place in the various spheres of national life and culture and have an influence on this society.

Another interesting thing is that one-third of all Americans today are involved in small groups, which is astounding. That is about eighty million people, and 60 percent of those are in the Church. Christians are going to find that much of their strengthening, their discipleship, and their spiritual growth will take place in these caring, sharing, praying, Bible-studying groups that are going to build up men and women to do the work of Christ better than ever before.

I believe that these are going to be exciting times. I think the twenty-first century will be *the* most exciting time to be a part of Christ's Church. The Church will, indeed, be "fair as the moon, clear as the sun," and it will be "awesome as an army with banners," and the banner over it is the love of Jesus Christ that we carry forth to a needy world.

Conclusion

So we see that Jesus Christ is building His Church around the globe—a development you won't hear about on the headline news. God forewarned us that the forces of Hell would attempt to thwart that expansion, but He promised that they would not prevail. Revelation 7:9 predicted centuries ago what we're beginning to see in our time more than ever before: ". . . and behold, a great multitude which no one could number, of all nations, tribes, peoples, and tongues, standing before the throne. . . ." Amen.

How Firm a Foundation

If in this life only we have hope in Christ,
we are of all men the most pitiable.
—1 Corinthians 15:19

In the last chapter, we got a glimpse at how Christ is building His Church in our time. Now, in the next few chapters, we want to look at some incontrovertible facts that show that Christianity is based on a deep foundation—a foundation that cannot be shaken by the very gates of Hell, try as they might.

Suppose for just a moment that Christianity were *not* true, then think what fools we would be! To constantly swim against the tide of society; to bear the brunt of prime-time lies and half-lies; to be portrayed on the silver screen as smarmy hypocrites; to be mocked, along with Christ, in "the song of the drunkards" (Ps. 69:12); to sometimes undergo direct persecution; and, as happens in many parts of the world, to be killed for the faith—and all for a *lie!* As Paul said, if only for this life we have hope in Christ, we are to be pitied above all men (1 Cor. 15:19)!

But the fact of the matter is that Christianity *is* true. Jesus Christ rose from the dead in human history, and there are strong historical evidences for that fact. Because Christianity is true, the Church can keep moving forward with the calm assurance that even though the forces of Hell may continue to buffet us, we know they shall not prevail! The purpose of this chapter, then, is to look at proofs for the truth of Christianity. We will focus primarily on Christ's bodily resurrection from the dead, but first we will begin with a quick overview of other evidences for the veracity of the Christian faith.

Messianic Prophecies Fulfilled

The Judeo-Christian Scriptures are unique in that in the Old Testament alone, there are over two thousand prophecies that have already come to pass. Nothing vaguely resembles this in any other book in the world. Consider the sacred writings of other religions: Twenty-six volumes that claim to be divine scriptures, or are claimed to be by their followers (since many of them make no such claim themselves), have no specific predictive prophecies. But the Old Testament has many specific predictions, which Jesus of Nazareth fulfilled.

I was sharing that with a woman recently, and she said, "Oh I don't believe in prophecies." That's because she was thinking of today's psychics. Our modern-day "prophets" are a joke! Predictions for 1994 made by psychics at the outset of the year included: that an earthquake would turn Florida into an island, that Whoopi Goldberg would give up acting and join a convent, and that a national lottery would be created to halve our taxes.[1] An article in the *Washington Times* points out that the psychics are getting their predictions wrong *repeatedly*: "In his annual review of would-be tabloid prophets, science writer Gene Emery found that not one of the approximately 100 predictions for 1994 that he studied had come true by late December."[2] Emery has been tracking these tabloid psychics' forecasts since 1978. They may be entertaining to read, but they consistently flop when they try to tell the future.

What a contrast with the Bible and specifically the messianic prophecies. The Old Testament contains 333 prophecies concerning the coming of Christ, which include 456 specific facts or details concerning the Messiah who is to come.[3] All of these prophecies were written between c. 1500 B.C. and 400 B.C., so you can see how difficult it would be to engineer this.

It was written that the Messiah would be crucified—"they pierced My hands and My feet" (a prediction made before the Phoenicians even invented crucifixion!) (Ps. 22:16b, c. 1000 B.C.). They prophesied He would be born in Bethlehem (Mic. 5:2, c. 720 B.C.). It was written that He would bear our sins and by His stripes we would be healed (Isa. 53:5, c. 750 B.C.). The Bible is without peer in this arena. Why? Because God divinely inspired the men at the time they wrote it. Holy men of God were moved by His Spirit as they penned Holy Writ (2 Peter 1:20–21).

A mathematician, Peter Stoner, had his graduate students calculate what the odds would be of any one person fulfilling just eight of these prophecies. He found the chance was one in 10^{17}—one in 100,000,000,000,000,000![4] Stoner gives an analogy to this:

> Take 10^{17} silver dollars and lay them on the face of Texas. They will cover all of the state two feet deep. Now mark one of these silver dollars and stir the whole mass thoroughly, all over the state. Blindfold a man and tell him that he can travel as far as he wishes, but he must pick up one silver dollar and say that this is the right one. What chance would he have of getting the right one? Just the same chance that the prophets would have had of writing these eight prophecies and having them all come true in any one man, from their day to the present time.[5]

If that isn't amazing enough, Stoner had his graduate students calculate the odds that any one person would fulfill forty-eight of these prophecies. The odds in that case were one in 10^{157}![6] And again, 333 prophecies were fulfilled in Jesus!

Former skeptical journalist turned pastor, Lee Strobel of Chicago, gives an analogy to the amazing predictions of Christ's suffering and crucifixion in Isaiah 53 written seven hundred years *before* the event: "That's like my trying to predict how the Cubs will do in the year 2693!"[7] The Christian faith is based on awesome evidence!

Uniformity of the Bible

The Bible is amazingly uniform, from Genesis to Revelation. It consists of sixty-six books, written by about forty different authors on two continents, written in two major languages over a span of about fifteen hundred years—yet with an amazing consistency from beginning to end.[8] This is all the more amazing, observes author James C. Hefley, when you consider that there was "no human editorial plan in writing the Bible."[9] It ultimately had the same author—God. Hefley says, "The 66 books [of the Scriptures] are a perfect whole, a purposeful revelation, a progressive proof that the Bible is more than the work of fallible men."[10]

The Claims of Christ

Jesus claimed to be divine. We lock up the people who make that kind of claim. He was either crazy, a deceiver, or He was telling the truth. As C. S. Lewis put it, He was either liar, lunatic, or Lord. His character and sanity would point to

His lordship. Lewis, the great Christian writer and professor at Oxford and later Cambridge, wrote,

> A man who was merely a man and said the sort of things Jesus said would not be a great moral teacher. He would either be a lunatic—on a level with the man who says he is a poached egg—or else he would be the Devil of Hell. You must make your choice. Either this man was, and is, the Son of God: or else a madman or something worse. You can shut Him up for a fool; you can spit at Him and kill Him as a demon; or, you can fall at His feet and call Him Lord and God. But let us not come up with any patronising nonsense about His being a great human teacher. He has not left that open to us. He did not intend to.[11]

The Resurrection

The evidence for the bodily resurrection of Jesus is compelling. Some historians have called it the best attested event in antiquity. It is an indisputable fact that the disciples of Jesus were emboldened and transformed from scared rabbits into courageous and bold witnesses who could not be hushed up. The Resurrection is so critically important because it is the cornerstone of the Christian faith. Take away the Resurrection and Christianity crumbles like a house of cards. Some of the liberal denominations have taken it away from their statements of faith (if they have one), and their churches are withering away—for their congregations instinctively know that there is nothing there but froth, and they will not tolerate being deceived. If Christ was not bodily raised from the dead in human history, Christianity would cease to exist.

The historical, bodily resurrection of Christ from the dead is unique among world religions. Confucius died and was buried. Lao-tzu wandered off and died with his water buffalo. Buddha rotted with food poisoning. Muhammad died in 632, and his body is cut up and spread all over the Near East. But Jesus rose from the dead! And by that resurrection from the dead He demonstrated that He was indeed the Son of God, with power. By His life, by His death, by His resurrection, He declares that He is God. Let's examine now the case for the resurrection of Christ.

The Evidence

Any case must deal with *all* of the relevant evidence. So, in dealing with the resurrection of Christ, we need to look at all the evidence.

It says in Acts that Christ "presented Himself alive after His suffering by many infallible proofs" (Acts 1:3). I want to examine seven pieces of evidence and seven theories that attempt to explain them away.

First, there is the Christian Church, which is the largest institution or organization that has ever existed on the face of the earth, with membership easily passing two billion people by the end of this decade.[12] Nothing comparable to it or even close has ever existed. The Grand Canyon wasn't caused by an Indian dragging a stick, and the Christian Church wasn't created by a myth!

Historians, secular unbelieving historians, tell us that the Christian Church began in Jerusalem in A.D. 30, the year Christ was killed, and that it began because the apostles began to preach that Jesus Christ rose from the dead. You strip everything else away from their preaching, their main message was that Christ rose from the dead (for example, see Acts 2:23–24).

Second, there is the empty tomb. Again, many adherents to many religions can travel to the place where the founder of their religion is currently entombed and say, "Here lies the dust of our esteemed founder." You cannot say that about Christ. He is not in the grave. He is risen.

For seventeen hundred years there was virtually no controversy that the tomb was empty. The Jews didn't deny it. The Romans didn't deny it. Nobody denied it until just recently. With our vast "rearview mirror" wisdom, we look back through more than nineteen hundred years and we decide, "Oh, the tomb wasn't empty." Too bad those who were there couldn't have been so smart.

Third, there is the Roman seal. The huge rock had a rope stretched across it; the clay was fastened to the rope and to the wall of the tomb, and the Roman seal was impressed upon it. If you broke that, you broke the seal. If you broke the seal, you "incurred the wrath of Roman law."[13] The penalty was death!

Fourth, there was the Roman guard. According to Professor Harold Smith, "A Watch usually consisted of four men, each of whom watched in turn, while the others rested beside him so as to be roused by the least alarm; but in this case the guard may have been more numerous."[14] These Roman soldiers were well trained. These people were experts in what they did. The penalty for leaving their post or for falling asleep at the job was death—and the death penalty was "always rigorously enforced."[15]

Fifth, there was the stone, weighing at least two tons, probably more. The opening would indicate that the stone would have to be at least seven or eight feet high. It took more than one person to move it.

Sixth, there were the post-Resurrection appearances. These are crucial. He appeared to one, then to another, then to two, then to three, and then to eight and ten and eleven and five hundred people at a time, over a period of about six weeks (1 Cor. 15:4–8). They saw Him, they heard Him, they handled Him. He fixed breakfast for them. He ate fish with them (John 21:7–14; Luke 24:42–43).

Connected to the appearances was the transformation of the apostles. One day they were cringing in an upper room for fear of the Jews, and soon after they were boldly upbraiding the Sanhedrin and proclaiming the resurrection of Christ. Consider also their martyrdom. They were crucified, crucified upside down, sawed in half, stoned to death, and killed in many other ways—all except John, who was exiled to the island of Patmos by Nero.[16] Why would they give their lives for what they knew to be false?

Seventh, there is the character of Christ Himself. Christ is universally acknowledged, even often enough by skeptics, to be a paragon of virtue, the most noble, moral, truthful, and ethical man the world has ever seen. The last thing Jesus would promote would be deception, including the deception that He rose from the dead.

Theories

As apologist Josh McDowell points out, some theories to explain away the resurrection of Christ take as much faith to believe as the Resurrection itself![17] He's debated the Resurrection with skeptics more than just about anybody alive. He writes,

> After more than 700 hours of studying this subject, and thoroughly investigating its foundation, I have come to the conclusion that the resurrection of Jesus Christ is one of the *most wicked, vicious, heartless hoaxes ever foisted upon the minds of men*, or it is the most fantastic fact of history. . . . A student at the University of Uruguay said to me: "Professor McDowell, why can't you refute Christianity?" I answered: "For a very simple reason: I am not able to explain away an event in history—the resurrection of Jesus Christ."[18]

Let's examine some of the theories put forth to explain away the resurrection of Jesus Christ.

The Fraud Theory

The first theory—which was and is the theory of the Jews—to explain away Christ's resurrection is called the Fraud Theory. Essentially, what the Jews are saying is that the whole thing was a fraud. We read: "Now while they were going, behold, some of the guard came into the city and reported to the chief priests all the things that had happened" (Matt. 28:11).

I have heard it said that after His resurrection, Jesus never appeared to anybody but believers. But it's not true. He appeared to the guard. They were so terrified by His appearance that they fainted and became as dead men. Then they came and told the high priest what had happened. Jesus appeared to James, his brother, who was skeptical. Jesus appeared to Saul, the persecutor. None of these was a Christian at the time.

The Bible continues: "When they had assembled with the elders and consulted together, they gave a large sum of money to the soldiers, saying, 'Tell them, "His disciples came at night and stole Him away while we slept." And if this comes to the governor's ears, we will appease him and make you secure.' So they took the money and did as they were instructed; and this saying is commonly reported among the Jews until this day" (Matt. 28:12–15) . . . and until this day, nearly two thousand years later.

Let's consider how that stacks up with the evidence. First of all, there is the Christian Church. Does the Fraud Theory give a plausible reason for the Church? The Church was founded by the apostles who preached the Resurrection. If the Fraud Theory were right, then they knew they had stolen the body and planted it in the rose garden. But they went ahead and proclaimed that He had risen from the dead.

But something happened to the disciples that changed them in a moment, from men of cowardice to men of heroic courage.[19] They said the reason for their transformation was that they had seen Jesus risen from the dead. To say that they stole the body and made up a resurrection doesn't make sense; that view does not reflect the realities of human nature. For example, when two criminals are charged with the same murder, even when they have previously been friends, they will almost invariably accuse the other of pulling the trigger. But the disciples didn't change their story one bit, although they had everything to gain and nothing to lose by doing so. The apostles continued throughout all of their lives to proclaim that they had seen Him risen from the dead. Their speaking out led to torture and execution, but none of them ever sought to save his own skin by revealing the "fraud."

Dr. Principal Hill, who wrote *Lectures in Divinity*, which was popular in the nineteenth century, has shown the absurdity of the Fraud Theory perhaps more succinctly than anyone else:

You must suppose that twelve men of mean birth, of no education, living in that humble station which placed ambitious views out of their reach and far from their thoughts, without any aid from the state, formed the noblest scheme which ever entered into the mind of man, adopted the most daring means of executing that scheme, conducted it with such address as to conceal the imposture under the semblance of simplicity and virtue. You must suppose, also, that men guilty of blasphemy and falsehood, united in an attempt the best contrived, and which has in fact proved the most successful for making the world virtuous; that they formed this single enterprise without seeking any advantage to themselves, with an avowed contempt of loss and profit, and with the certain expectation of scorn and persecution; that although conscious of one another's villainy, none of them ever thought of providing for his own security by disclosing the fraud, but that amidst sufferings the most grievous to flesh and blood they persevered in their conspiracy to *cheat* the world into *piety, honesty and benevolence*. Truly, they who can swallow such suppositions have no title to object to miracles.[20]

How true that is. No, the Fraud Theory will not stand up to the evidence.

The Swoon Theory

A second theory to explain away the Resurrection is the Swoon Theory. This is the theory of the Christian Scientists. The Swoon Theory is the idea that Jesus never really died. It's interesting that until the 1800s nobody ever thought that Jesus hadn't died; everybody believed He had.

I think it is significant that the people who put Him to death were "in the business." What was their trade? Their business was taking people who were alive and making them into people who were dead. That is what they did for a living. They'd go home at night and say, "Well, I did three today, honey." They were experts at what they did.

But what the Swoon Theory says is that Jesus didn't really die; He merely swooned and then, being placed in the fresh coolness of the tomb, He revived. That does not live up to the facts. Here is a man who had been scourged, which often killed people in and of itself. His hands and feet and His side had been pierced.

In the Philippines, some people have had themselves "crucified" on Good Friday. They will sometimes stay up there for three, four, or five minutes, and then—not having been scourged, not having been up all night, not having gone

without food for hours, not having had their side pierced—they are taken down
and to the hospital, where they very nearly die!

Jesus, we are supposed to believe, having been placed in the cool freshness of
a tomb, revived. But if a person has gone into shock, should you put him in a cool
place? No way! That would kill him. Instead, you cover him with blankets and
try to keep his body temperature up. So the cool freshness of the tomb may sound
nice on a hot day, but if you are in shock, that is the last thing you want. In fact,
if He were not dead when they put Him into the tomb, that most certainly would
have killed Him.[21] But, supposedly, He stays there for three days, and then He gets
up on mangled feet, hobbles to the door of the tomb and finds this stone weighing a
few tons. Then, with mangled hands, He places His hands against the flat side of the
rock and rolls it away. Then He overcomes the Roman guard of armed men. After
that He takes a seven-mile hike to Emmaus and chats with the fellows on the way.
Then He treks almost a hundred miles to Galilee and climbs a mountain. There He
convinces five hundred people that He is the Lord of life!

The Swoon Theory has received a fatal blow by David Friedrich Strauss, a
nineteenth-century German skeptic who wrote about the life of Christ. He didn't
believe in the Resurrection, but he knew that the Swoon Theory was utterly
ridiculous. Listen to what an unbeliever says about the Swoon Theory:

> It is impossible that a being who had stolen half dead out of the
> sepulcher, who crept about weak and ill, wanting medical treatment,
> who required bandaging, strengthening and indulgence and who, still
> at last, yielded to his sufferings, could have given to the disciples the
> impression that he was a conqueror over death and the grave, The
> Prince of Life, an impression which lay at the bottom of all of their
> future ministry—such a resuscitation could only have weakened the
> impression which he made in life and in death and at the most, could
> only have given it an elegiac voice, a lament for the dead. But could
> by no possibility have changed their sorrow into enthusiasm, have
> elevated their reverence into worship.[22]

And with Strauss's critique, other than among the devoted Christian Scientists, the Swoon Theory has swooned away.

The Spiritual-Resurrection Theory

Then there is the view of the Jehovah's Witnesses, which is the Spiritual-Res-
urrection Theory. This theory also seems to be gaining currency with some

theological liberals today. They say that Jesus' resurrection was not physical, it was spiritual, and that He was just a spirit. But the Bible directly refutes this: "Now as they said these things, Jesus Himself stood in the midst of them, and said to them, 'Peace to you.' But they were terrified and frightened, and supposed they had seen a spirit" (Luke 24:36–37).

Yes, say the Jehovah's Witnesses, they were right. What they saw was a spirit. Not so fast. Luke continues,

> And He said to them, "Why are you troubled? And why do doubts arise in your hearts? Behold My hands and My feet, that it is I Myself. Handle Me and see, for a spirit does not have flesh and bones as you see I have." When He had said this, He showed them His hands and His feet. But while they still did not believe for joy, and marveled, He said to them, "Have you any food here?" So they gave Him a piece of a broiled fish and some honeycomb. And He took it and ate in their presence. (Luke 24:38–43)

This is not to mention the fact that if Jesus were just a ghost or spirit, then what about the body? Well, the body is still in the tomb. What about the disciples who ran to the tomb when they heard that Jesus had risen? They would have gotten there, and the stone would have been in front of the door, and Jesus would have still been in the tomb. The Jehovah's Witnesses have managed to take care of that, too, with the same disregard of anything the Scripture or history teaches, and they simply say that God destroyed the body. He evaporated it, so it just disappeared. But there is nothing in the Bible that says anything whatsoever about that!

The Wrong-Person Theory

Fourth, there is the view of the Muslims. This is the Wrong-Person Theory. I doubt very much if you ever heard of this because, other than the Muslims, I don't know of anybody that believes it. But the Koran says of Jesus, "They slew him not nor crucified, but it appeared so unto them" (Surah 4:157). They believe that on Good Friday, God provided a substitute for Jesus who was crucified in Jesus' place. (Some Muslims believe Judas was that substitute.) But the eyewitness accounts say that *Jesus* was crucified. Second, there was Mary, Jesus' mother, standing for hours at the foot of the cross, looking at Him and weeping over her dying son. He says to her, "Mother."

According to the Wrong-Person Theory, she was confused—as were Pilate, the Sanhedrin, and the disciples. Everybody was confused, including Jesus—because He went to the disciples after He rose from the dead. I wonder who it is they think appeared to the disciples and said, "Behold My hands and My feet"?

Another fatal flaw to this theory is that it doesn't coincide at all with the *character* of Jesus. He was a man of impeccable integrity, but according to this theory, He would be a fraud, a deceiver. Furthermore, if this theory were true, then the tomb would still be occupied; the substitute's body would still be in the tomb. But what about the guard? What happened to them? When the early Christians declared Jesus risen from the dead, they could have easily countered what they said and just showed them the tomb with the Roman seal still affixed. This theory doesn't fit any of the known facts in this case.

The Hallucination Theory

Fifth, there is the Hallucination Theory, that all of the disciples simply had hallucinations when they saw Him risen from the dead. Psychologists have pointed out that hallucinations are idiosyncratic; that is, they are very personal and private, and people don't have collective hallucinations.[23] Jesus appeared to the people in the morning; He fixed breakfast with them. They hallucinated having breakfast! He appeared at noon; He walked with them to Emmaus; He appeared with them at supper time several times; He appeared inside; He appeared outside, and He even appeared to five hundred people at one time. Not only did they see Him, but they heard Him, talked to Him, handled Him, and watched Him eat. They could not have been hallucinating these things.

Not to mention the other evidence, because having thus hallucinated that Jesus was alive and had appeared to them, they ran to the tomb and hallucinated that the tomb was empty, the guard was gone, the stone was rolled away, and the grave clothes were empty. Then they began to preach that Jesus rose from the dead. If that were the case, then this hallucination would be contagious. They declared, "You, Sanhedrin, you have taken with wicked hands and you have slain the Prince of life and glory, and God has raised Him from the dead." So, the Sanhedrin ran down to the tomb, and they had the same hallucination. They, too, hallucinated that it was empty.

And the Romans, seeing the tumult, went down and checked things out and talked to the guard. The guards all had hallucinations that the tomb was empty. This is all ridiculous, obviously. It doesn't deal with any of the evidence.

The Wrong-Tomb Theory

And there is the theory that suggests the women went to the wrong tomb. But again, we must deal with the evidence.

If this theory were correct, then the women went to the wrong tomb, and Peter and John ran to the wrong tomb; then the rest of the disciples came, and they went to the wrong tomb. Joseph of Arimathea, who owned the tomb, naturally would want to see what happened, and yet he, too, went to the wrong tomb. Of course, the Sanhedrin also were concerned, and they went to the wrong tomb. And then, of course, the angel came down and went to the wrong tomb, but what does an angel know about tombs?

Of course, all the while there were the guards saying, "Hey, fellows, we're over here!" They, at least, were at the right tomb. But again, this obviously is a wrong theory, and it doesn't answer any of the facts.

If the women and everybody else went to the wrong tomb and they started proclaiming Christ risen from the dead, what would the Sanhedrin do? Why, they would go to the right tomb. They would tell the soldiers to roll back the stone. They would say, "Bring Him out." Then they would hang His corpse up by the heels in the town square in Jerusalem, and they would say, "There is your glorious Prince of life! Take a good whiff of His rotting corpse." That would have been the end of Christianity right then and there.

The Legend Theory

Lastly, there is the Legend Theory. This is the idea that the "myth" of Christ rising from the dead just sort of gradually grew up over the decades and centuries. This view was popular in the nineteenth century. That was back when they said that the Gospels were written in the second or even the third century, by people other than the apostles. But all of that has collapsed in the last thirty or forty years, and even the late Bishop John A. T. Robinson of England, one of the most blatant critics, wrote a book pointing out that the conservative scholars were right all along and that the Gospels were written by the men whose names they bear and in the times we have said they were written.[24] Robinson said, near the end of his life, that he believed all the Gospels, including John, were written before A.D. 70.[25]

Furthermore, as stated above, secular historians point out that the Church began in A.D. 30 in Jerusalem, because that is when the apostles began preaching the Resurrection. Jesus and the Resurrection were the central thrust of their teaching. So there was no time for mythmaking or legend spinning. As Peter said, "For we did not follow cunningly devised fables when we made known to you the power and coming of our Lord Jesus Christ, but were eyewitnesses of His majesty" (2 Peter 1:16). John, speaking of Jesus, the "Word of life," said, "That which was from the beginning, which we have heard, which we have seen with our eyes, which we have looked upon, and our hands have handled, concerning the Word of life . . . we declare to you" (1 John 1:1, 3b).

What's more, we know how all the apostles died. They were crucified and stoned and cut up.[26] All this was done to them for believing a supposed legend that hadn't even yet developed, and that wasn't going to develop for another one hundred or one hundred fifty years! That's absurd! It doesn't deal with any of the facts. It doesn't deal with what the Sanhedrin and the Romans would have done.

Josh McDowell says there are eighteen different first-century pagan writers who present more than a hundred facts about the birth of Christ, His life, teachings, miracles, crucifixion, resurrection, and ascension.[27] This is no legend that built up over the centuries. It began at the beginning.

The "Miracles-Don't-Happen" Theory

Some people begin with the assumption that miracles don't happen; therefore, Christ could not have risen from the dead. But this doesn't explain any of the facts. It's also circular logic. It's merely a presupposition that disallows the possibility of the Resurrection. Who's open-minded here? Surely not the person who rejects the Resurrection out of hand because they *know* miracles don't happen. How can anyone know they don't happen? It's an illogical assumption.

But Christ *Did Rise from the Dead*

The truth is that Christ rose from the dead. The greatest problem mankind has ever faced, generation after generation, century after century, millennium after millennium, has been solved by Jesus. Death has been with us since the fall of man, and always people have asked, "If a man dies, will he rise again?" Jesus Christ has given us irrefutable evidence that the answer is yes. The greatest efforts of the most brilliant, unbelieving, skeptical minds of the last two thousand years to disprove the Resurrection have all come to naught. There is not one of them that could stay afloat in a debate for fifteen minutes when the evidence is given a fair examination.

There are other evidences I could discuss at length if space permitted. I will mention one briefly. It is the transformation of the Sabbath from the Jewish Saturday to the Christian Sunday. The Resurrection took place amidst Jews who were committed and zealous Sabbatarians. How is it that suddenly the Christian Church changed from observing the seventh-day Sabbath to celebrating Sunday as the Lord's Day? Because the Resurrection of Jesus Christ from the dead happened on the first day of the week.

Conclusion

The great conflict between God and the devil, between Jesus Christ—who is building His Church—and the forces of Hell—which are out to tear it down—has already been settled. The apostle Paul had to deal with a first-century false teaching in the church at Corinth. Some of the members of that church were claiming that there was no resurrection of the dead, which would imply that Jesus had not risen from the dead. Paul then wrote the following words, which have assured tens of millions of Christians down through the centuries:

> And if Christ is not risen, then our preaching is empty and your faith is also empty. . . . And if Christ is not risen, your faith is futile; you are still in your sins! Then also those who have fallen asleep in Christ have perished. If in this life only we have hope in Christ, we are of all men the most pitiable.
>
> But now Christ is risen from the dead, and has become the firstfruits of those who have fallen asleep. (1 Cor. 15:14, 17–20)

Changed Lives

One thing I know: that though I was blind, now I see.
—John 9:25b

In the last century, in Britain, there was a skeptic who said to a converted drunkard, "Surely you don't believe those Bible miracles, such as Christ turning water into wine." The ex-drunkard replied, "If you think that's a miracle, come to my home and I'll show you how Christ changed beer into carpets, chairs and even a piano!"[1] Christ had come to dwell in the heart of that converted drunkard and had transformed his inward life and his outward circumstances as well. As the Bible says, "Therefore, if anyone is in Christ, he is a new creation; old things have passed away; behold, all things have become new" (2 Cor. 5:17).

As the kingdom of God advances, more and more lives are changed. Despite the anti-Christian bigotry we find in our culture, despite the anti-Christian stereotyping that goes on in the movies and in prime time, more and more people are coming to Christ and seeing their lives transformed. This is another example of the evidence that Christianity is true. Why? *Because it works!*

Changed Lives in Jesus' Day

From His time to the present, Jesus Christ has been active in the supernatural work of transforming human hearts. To put the matter in economic terms: Jesus Christ changes many societal liabilities into societal assets. Church history reveals a long list of people whose hearts He has changed. The Bible vividly portrays some of the lives Jesus transformed while He was on earth.

Mary Magdalene was a new woman when Jesus cast out seven demons from her (Luke 8:2). Mary was privileged to be the first to see Jesus after He had been raised from the dead.[2]

Zacchaeus gave away half of his income after meeting Jesus. He had formerly been involved in a dubious but lucrative position, which he forsook to follow Christ.[3]

Simon Peter, an impulsive man, often acted before he thought; the Lord changed him into a powerful Christian leader.[4] At the end of Peter's life, when he was to be executed by crucifixion, he insisted that he be crucified *upside down*, which is more excruciating, for he did not feel worthy to be killed in the same manner Jesus had been.[5]

Two brothers, John and James, nicknamed "Sons of Thunder,"[6] presumably because of their explosive tempers, went on to become loving disciples.

A first-century skeptic, doubting Thomas, wasn't present when Jesus first appeared to the disciples; he boldly declared that he wouldn't believe Jesus was risen until he saw and touched the Lord. But when Christ reappeared eight days later, Thomas bowed, declaring "My Lord and my God!" He went on to serve as the first known missionary to India and was slain with a dart.[7]

A demon-possessed man lived among tombs and regularly broke the chains with which men tried to bind him. His mind and life were restored by Jesus.8

Saul of Tarsus was a murderous, religious persecutor of the faith; Jesus transformed him into Paul the apostle, the great Christian missionary.[9] He was an outstanding first-century "Christian basher" until Jesus took hold of his heart.

Converts throughout the Centuries

Throughout the centuries, Christ has changed countless men and women for His glory. The list includes men and women whose lives have literally altered the course of history.

Saint Augustine of Hippo was a man who in his youth pursued every lust imaginable,[10] but he went on to become one of the greatest Christian thinkers in the history of Western civilization. Augustine introduced a view of history "which would long dominate Christian society in the West."[11]

St. Patrick was sold into slavery in Ireland, later escaped, was converted to Christ, and then returned to Ireland as a missionary.[12] The people who get drunk on March 17 to celebrate St. Patrick's Day do poor homage to this great man who first brought Christianity to Ireland.

Theodora was a pagan actress and dancer until Christ changed her heart. She went on to marry Emperor Justinian and exert a godly influence on him and the Byzantine Empire.[13]

St. Anselm of Canterbury left home because of his stormy relationship with his father, but later he became a dedicated Christian.[14] His intellectual arguments for the faith have reached down through the centuries to our own.

St. Francis of Assisi was disowned by his father when Francis made a vow of poverty.[15] The peace-loving nature of Francis was such that he was able to secure an audience with the Muslim leader, Saladin, to attempt to bring about a peaceful ending to the Crusades.[16]

Martin Luther thought, like just about everyone else in his day, that you could work your way into Heaven, until he understood that Christ's finished work on the cross is the sole key to our salvation.

St. Teresa of Avila's life was purposeless, until she consecrated herself to Christ and became a spiritual reformer and writer.[17]

William Wilberforce was an upper-class member of Parliament, whose life could be summarized as one of trivial pursuit until he met Jesus Christ. He went on to play a critical role in the abolition of the slave trade in England, and in the formation of important missionary societies.[18]

George Mueller often got drunk as a youth but was converted to Jesus Christ and went on to establish Christ-centered orphanages for thousands of abandoned boys and girls.[19]

Adoniram Judson sneered at the faith of his parents, preferring instead to embrace rationalism—until he came to the realization of how bankrupt that philosophy was in the face of life's realities and in the face of death.[20] Judson went on to become one of America's greatest missionaries.

Felix Mendelssohn, the great German composer of Jewish descent, was searching for God but didn't think he would find Him within the Christian Church; however, in the process of putting on the stage production of Bach's *St. Matthew Passion*, he discovered God in the Christ of the Passion. "And to think," said Mendelssohn, after the resounding success of the *St. Matthew Passion*, which had been hidden away for more than a hundred years, "that it should be . . . a Jew who [has] given back to the people the greatest Christian work."[21]

Peter Marshall was a young man from Scotland who seemed to have no purpose in life, until he met Christ one night. He came to America and went on to become one of our greatest preachers and the chaplain to the Senate. His wife, Catherine Marshall, immortalized his story in the book and the movie *A Man Called Peter*.[22]

Malcolm Muggeridge was a witty journalist and the editor of the English satirical magazine, *Punch*. He was also a "fellow traveler" during the heyday of Stalinism. In the words of author Lloyd Billingsley, Muggeridge felt that the Soviet Union "had a future, whereas Britain and the West had only a past." He became the Moscow correspondent for the liberal British newspaper, *Manchester Guardian*. Before leaving for the workers' paradise, he and his wife "cheerfully burned their bridges"—destroying diplomas and their marriage certificate and other vestiges of bourgeois society. But when they arrived in Soviet Russia, they were soon disillusioned. Eventually he realized that man cannot bring utopia on earth. Muggeridge became a Christian and used his writing skills to bring glory to Christ.[23]

Nicky Cruz, a violent gang member in New York City who swung baseball bats at the heads of his enemies, wanted to kill David Wilkerson, a country preacher who felt led to evangelize gang members. Wilkerson eventually led Cruz to Jesus Christ. Their story is told in Wilkerson's book *The Cross and the Switchblade*.[24] Today the life mission of Nicky Cruz is to proclaim the good news of Jesus Christ, who changed this former gang member from the inside out and set him free.[25]

Chuck Colson, former special counsel to President Nixon, went to jail for Watergate-related crimes. The headline of the *Wall Street Journal* on October 15, 1971, declared:

NIXON HATCHET MAN
CALL IT WHAT YOU WILL, CHUCK COLSON
HANDLES PRESIDENT'S DIRTY WORK[26]

But Jesus Christ got hold of Chuck Colson and made him into a new man. Today Colson is a prison reformer through Prison Fellowship, the Christian ministry he founded in the 1970s, and he is one of the greatest Christian writers and speakers of our time.

William J. Murray, whose mother is the notorious atheist Madalyn Murray O'Hair, found the Christ his mother hates so much. Interestingly, Madalyn Murray O'Hair was the first guest on *The Phil Donahue Show*.[27] One of the defining moments in her life, when her atheism became solidified, was when she ran outside during a thunderstorm and defied God, "if there was one," to strike her dead right then and there. He chose not to. "You see, you see!" she exclaimed, "I've proved irrefutably that God does not exist!"[28] Note that she was pregnant at the time, and inside her was William J. Murray, one of the Lord's future servants! After being exposed to vehement atheism all his life, Murray came to a realization: *"There has to be a God because there certainly is a devil. I have met him, talked to him, and touched him. He is the personification of evil."*[29] Soon after this insight, Murray discovered Christ through reading the Gospel of Luke.[30] Today he is a powerful evangelist and also an advocate of allowing God back into the public schools—this is the very man who, as a boy, had been at the center of *Murray v. Curlett* (1963), one of the key Supreme Court school-prayer decisions.

John Perkins was a black minister who was the object of racial discrimination and hatred. Having grown up in utter poverty in rural Mississippi, Perkins was devastated when his older brother was killed because of the color of his skin. He hated white people and eventually fled to California to start a new life, where he discovered he didn't hate all white people—just the ones back in Mississippi. His son became a Christian through child evangelism at a mostly white church, and this led John Perkins to become one also. He eventually felt a call to return to his native Mississippi to help his people in the name of Jesus Christ. His ministry almost cost him his life during the Civil Rights movement, when an overzealous sheriff nearly beat him to death and forced him to mop up his own blood. But because Jesus Christ had made him a new man, Perkins could forgive him and all those involved in the dehumanizing practice of segregation. Perkins founded the Voice of Calvary, a multifaceted Christian ministry that meets spiritual and physical needs of the poor. To this day, Voice of Calvary has an outreach in Mendenhall and Jackson.[31]

Jeff Fenholt played the original Jesus in the sacrilegious musical *Jesus Christ Superstar*, which purposefully leaves out the Resurrection. Fenholt toured the U.S. and recorded the album, which sold approximately fifteen million copies in the United States. Fenholt later became a vocalist involved with Black Sabbath, a rock group with even an anti-Christian name. Although he was outwardly successful, inwardly he felt a "deep emptiness."[32] He has since come to embrace, as his Savior and Lord, the Jesus Christ of the Gospels—not the fictionalized Jesus he used to portray on the stage. Today he is a singer and speaker for the Lord.[33]

Carol Everett was a former abortionist who set out to make a million dollars in the abortion field and was well on her way to achieving this goal. She used to encourage promiscuity among young people, as this was good for business. But numerous employee-related problems led her to seek counseling. In the providence of God, and unknown to her, the counselor who helped her was a Baptist minister, who shared the gospel with her. After her Christian conversion, her eyes were opened to the grisly trade she engaged in. Today she is "playing for the other team," as a strong advocate for Christ and for the pro-life position. She wrote the excellent book *Blood Money: Getting Rich off a Woman's Right to Choose*.[34]

Johnny Hart, cartoonist and creator of the enormously successful *B.C.* and *Wizard of Id*, was angry at God after the death of his mother. He resorted to drinking to cope with the loss, and he also dabbled in the occult, using a Ouija board to try to contact his deceased mother.[35] But God used Christian television (including my program, thankfully) to bring Johnny to Himself. Today Johnny Hart is at peace with God and with himself. Many of his panels creatively proclaim the gospel. When one adds the combined circulation of *B.C.* and *Wizard of Id*, Johnny becomes the most widely syndicated cartoonist in the world.[36]

Sy Rogers is a former homosexual who was so immersed in the gay lifestyle that for about a year and a half, he dressed up and lived as a woman. He worked in a clerical job in an office in the Washington, D.C., area, and it was assumed by his employer and colleagues that he was a woman. He wrote, "Achieving much-desired acceptance in my role as a woman, I was considered attractive and even popular in gay circles."[37] Meanwhile, he was undergoing the lengthy counseling needed for a sex-change operation at Johns Hopkins Hospital. However, that institution announced they would no longer perform that procedure. Through a series of events, Rogers became a Christian and was freed from his homosexuality and his desire to dress like a woman. He got involved with Exodus International and with helping homosexuals come out of that lifestyle through Christianity. Today Sy Rogers heads an outreach in the country of Singapore, ministering to the numerous transsexuals there.

Marcia Montenegro taught astrology and served on the Board of Astrology Examiners in the city of Atlanta, which licenses astrologers. She was chairperson of that board for three years and was very active in the Metropolitan Atlanta Astrological Society. She lived by her charts and made decisions based on the movements of the planets. Marcia honed and practiced her craft and was interviewed by numerous media outlets, including CNN, as a spokesperson for astrologers. Despite all this, she began to feel an inexplicable urge to go to church—an urge that she fought for months. She finally gave in and was eventually converted by reading the Gospels, and she became released from what she calls "the bondage of astrology." Today she shares her testimony in churches and in print, and she's disappointed to find so many professing Christians reading horoscopes.[38]

Richard Lumsden, biology professor and former dean of Tulane Graduate School, dogmatically taught evolution to his classes, until one day a student politely asked him a number of pointed questions. She asked him questions such as: "How does evolution fit with the fundamentals of information theory?" "Aren't the odds of random assembly of genes mathematically impossible?" "Last month you showed us how mutations were genetic disasters. How, with regard to natural selection, could mutations randomly produce new and better structures, improved species?" "Where exactly in the fossil record is the evidence for progressive evolution, the transitional forms between major groups?"[39] Initially Lumsden dogmatically defended evolution, trying his best to answer her questions. But after an honest evaluation of the issues, he concluded that evolution was scientifically bankrupt: "I realized that the origin and diversification of life by evolution was a mathematical, physical, and biochemical impossibility, that the evidence for it was at best circumstantial, and a lot of what we really knew about biology was outright contradictory to the hypothesis."[40] Dr. Lumsden became a reluctant creationist first and later a Christian; today he teaches creation at two Christian institutions.[41]

I could go on and on with examples of lives transformed by the gospel. You yourself probably know all sorts of people whom Jesus Christ has changed—former alcoholics, former drug users, former pornography addicts, former homosexuals, former skeptics, former thieves, former murderers, former churchgoers who knew about the Lord but never knew Him personally. People from all walks of life. People from every socioeconomic stratum. The gospel of Jesus Christ transcends culture and race. Jesus Christ is alive and at work *today*, as millions can testify, giving people who were dead in their sins a new life, a chance to start all over again. I should know—*I* was one such person.

The Gift of God—My Changed Life

At one time, I was far away from God, immersed in the sin and pleasures of the world. But one Sunday morning, after having attended a party until late the night before, I was awakened by a preacher on my radio alarm clock,[42] whereas there had been music on that radio station the night before. Not interested in spiritual things, I was about to spring out of bed and change the station, but he said a few things that caught my attention. In striking contrast to what the world thinks—to what *I* thought—the preacher declared that the Bible says, "The wages of sin is death, *but the gift of God* is eternal life in Christ Jesus our Lord."

I will never forget that first day I heard that amazing statement from the book of Romans (6:23). I was astonished that this radio preacher had the audacity to say that God wanted to give me Heaven as a gift. I thought the man must be mad. Being, of course, a great authority on theological matters—at the age of twenty-four—I figured that he didn't know what he was talking about! After all, who was he but a doctor of theology, a pastor of one of our nation's great churches, with a worldwide radio ministry! How could that compare to my vast theological knowledge!

But how well I remember that day—within a week of hearing that radio preacher—when I first discovered the truth about myself, when the Holy Spirit opened my eyes to see myself as I really was. I was arraigned before the bar of God's judgment. Justice accused me, and the scales tipped precipitously against me. The angels were impaneled as juries and brought in a sentence of death against me. The Judge looked me sternly in the face and said, "I pronounce that you shall die. Do you have anything to say for yourself before the sentence of eternal death is pronounced on you?" For the first time in all my self-righteous life I was speechless! The Judge brought down His gavel, and the sentence was pronounced. Eternal death descended on me, and I stood on the scaffold of God's judgment. I felt the black cap of eternal death placed on my head, about to be pulled down over my eyes. My heart pounded within my breast and my knees grew weak. I abandoned all hope as I was about to sink into everlasting perdition. Suddenly, I heard a cry, a voice, that said, "Stay! Let not that man descend into the pit." I looked and there came running One whose face was flecked with blood, whose hands were pierced, who said, "Surely he deserves to die but the spear pierced My side instead. Surely he deserves to descend into the pit, but there in the blackness of midday at Calvary, I descended into the pit for him. All that he deserves I have properly taken. Now let him go free."

That day my life was transformed. I rose, went forth, and followed Him. My heart for these past forty years has overflowed with gratitude and love for Christ. For I know that within my soul there is a certificate that says, "The gift of God is eternal life in Christ Jesus my Lord."

My conversion to Christ and all the conversions mentioned above are similar to the healing of the blind man in John 9. Jesus encountered a man blind from birth, and He gave him the gift of sight. But the healing was done on the Sabbath, so it caused a controversy among the Jews, to whom a violation of the Sabbath was an egregious offense. Some thought Jesus a sinner because He healed on the Sabbath; others asked how He could do this apart from the power of God. When they asked the formerly blind man about this, he gave them a beautiful straight-forward testimony: "Whether He is a sinner or not I do not know. One thing I know: that though I was blind, now I see" (v. 25). Every true Christian can echo that last sentiment: "Though I was blind, now I see."

Through the years, I've seen hundreds, even thousands, come to Christ at the Coral Ridge Presbyterian Church in Ft. Lauderdale, where I serve as senior pastor. All of them have a story to tell in one way or another. Some are more dramatic than others, but as long as they truly come to Jesus Christ, they are on their way to Heaven. I think of a man whose whole family rejoiced when he was converted. His daughter told my wife, "I've got a new daddy! And I like him better than the old one." Of course, some of the finest testimonies are from those who grow up in a Christian home and love and serve the Lord faithfully all their lives, without ever going the path of the prodigal son. It doesn't matter *how* you come to Christ; what matters is *that* you come to Christ!

Distortions of Christianity

Unfortunately, throughout the ages, the devil has distorted Christianity so much that the gospel has often been obscured. People, even lifetime churchgoers, often don't have a clue what real Christianity is all about. So what exactly *is* Christianity? Sometimes, the "Christianity" being attacked by our culture today is such a false, twisted caricature that it bears little resemblance to the true faith. And indeed it ought to be attacked! Therefore, I want to devote the rest of this chapter to the purpose of clarifying what true Christianity really is.

Law and Gospel

Suppose that you lived in a rural area one hundred years ago, when horses and buggies were common. One day you came into the city and discovered that most people were putting the buggy in front of the horse and saying, "Giddyap, horse, push, push." And somehow they couldn't get the horse to push the buggy at all. You would think to yourself, *How incredibly stupid can these city folk be?* And you would be right.

The vast majority of people in America today have the gospel just that backward. They have totally reversed it and they wonder why it won't work—why it just won't go.

The Bible contains two basic elements, like a horse and buggy. It contains law and gospel. And unless we get these in the proper relationship it never will work. We must look carefully at the relationship of the law to the gospel in the New Testament. How do they fit together?

The proper relationship between the two—as taught by the early Church and by Augustine—is the great rediscovery that Martin Luther made that so changed the world. D. T. Niles said that in all other religions good works are "in order to," whereas, in Christianity, good works are "therefore."[43]

Even in the Ten Commandments, God said, "I am the LORD your God, who brought you out of the land of Egypt, out of the house of bondage." *Therefore*, He decrees, "You shall have no other gods before Me" (Ex. 20:2–3). Having first been brought up and brought into God, *therefore* we do these things.

In all other religions people are doing good deeds (or what they perceive as such) in order to somehow get to God. "The world has many religions," said

George Owen, "it has but one Gospel."[44] I hope that you'll let that sink in. There are hundreds of religions in this world; there is only one gospel. Only Christianity is good news.

People say, "Well, all religions are the same." When they say that, they're simply saying, "I am ignorant of the nature of religion altogether, and I really know nothing about it," because Christianity is antithetical to all of the pagan religions of this world. In all other religions, humans are endeavoring to reach up and somehow find God. In fact, that's what the word *religion* means. It means "to bind oneself to." Only in Christianity is God reaching down to humans. The Lord reaches down to find fallen and helpless humanity. God Himself does what is necessary for us to be reconciled to Him.

All of the religions of the world could be boiled down to one two-letter word. This is the essence of the message of every pagan religion in the world: "Do." "Do this," "do that," "don't do the other." And because people are blinded to the truth of the gospel and do not see that the basic message of the Bible is the gospel, they think that Christianity is also simply "do"—"do this" and "don't do that."

But the basic message of Christianity is not "do," but "done." "It is done" were the last words of Christ before commending His soul to the Father. It is done! It is finished! It is complete! It is enough! *Tetelestai* is the Greek word Jesus said when He breathed His last. This Greek word was often used in economic transactions, meaning "paid in full." Jesus Christ paid the penalty for our sins. The atonement is completed, and now all who trust in Him may freely have eternal life.

William Culbertson said that every religion in the world that he knew anything about says this, "Something in my hands I bring." That's what they're all doing. I bring these good works, these acts of piety, these prayers, these churchgoings, these temple visits—whatever they may be. Only Christianity says "nothing in my hands I bring; simply to the cross I cling."[45]

This is the meaning of grace. It is a wondrous gift given to those who have nothing to pay, those who do not deserve it at all. And here we are, undeserving, receiving that gift of eternal life, which we could never purchase on our own. That is the wondrous meaning of grace. The reason people have such difficulty in understanding this is because it's foreign to anything that they know. This world does not operate on grace; it operates on the basis of merit, on the basis of justice. Quid pro quo, this for that; you do this, you get that.

Consider the trial of Julius and Ethel Rosenberg, the famous couple accused as two Soviet spies who gave away our atomic secrets. They were convicted for espionage by the jury and were sentenced to death. Their lawyers said to Judge Kaufman, "Your honor, all my clients ask for is justice."

And Judge Kaufman replied, "What your clients have asked for, this court has given them. What you really mean is, what they want is mercy, and that, this court is not empowered to give."[46]

But that is precisely what our God—the Judge of all the earth—is able to do: grant us mercy. That is the wondrous news of the gospel.

How Good Is Good Enough for Heaven?

I remember twenty-five years or so ago, my wife and I were invited to a dinner at the home of one of our church families. There must have been about ten or fifteen people present. There was a long table at which I was invited to sit near one end; my wife was seated near the other end. Across from me was the mother of the hostess who said to me, "Oh, Reverend Kennedy, I am so happy to be seated across from you because I've always wanted to ask a minister a question."

And I said, "Well, fine, I'll be glad to try and answer it. Don't make it too hard or I'll have to get up and go ask my wife. But what is it?"

She said, "How good does a person have to be to be good enough to get into Heaven?"

Well, now, that's a question that many people ought to ask themselves. So many do not even bother to do so, but at least this woman had the intelligence to realize that if one was going to get into Heaven by being good, then one should intelligently ask how good is good enough. What is the passing grade in this course? Is it 70 or 75 or 80 or 60 or 50 or what is it?

And I said, "Oh, is that your question? Well, that's easy."

Her face broke out in a huge smile. She said, "Do you mean you *know*?"

I said, "Of course. That's the simplest possible question."

She said, "You'll never know how relieved I am. I have been worrying about that for years."

I said, "Well, you'll never need to worry about the answer to that question ever again, because from this day forward, you will know."

She said, "Oh, I'm so glad I came. What is it?"

I said, "Jesus said it very clearly, very understandably. He said, 'Be ye therefore perfect, even as your Father which is in heaven is perfect'" (Matt. 5:48 KJV).

The smile left her face. She looked like one of those cartoon characters that had been hit by a skillet. Her face just sort of fell onto the table and she sat there silently for a long time, and then she said, "I think I'm going to worry about that more than ever."

And I said, "Well, dear lady, I did not go into the ministry to make people worry, but far from it—to deliver them from their worries." And I was happy to share with her the gospel of Jesus Christ, that while none of us is perfect, and none of us has lived up to God's standard, and all of us have fallen short, Jesus Christ came to do what we have been unable to do.

And so the law shows us the helplessness and hopelessness of our condition. The law declares to us that if we offend in one point, we're guilty already. In fact, the law would even take us to the end of the trial, that we might see the outcome of our judgment. Would you like for me to tell you how your encounter with the judgment of God will come out? Christ has already told you. He says, "You are condemned already."

There it is, a preview of coming attractions. You already know the end. If you are trying to gain admission into Paradise by keeping the law and doing good works and being the best person you can be—then let me tell you that the verdict is already in. You have failed. You have flunked! Your grade is F, and the declaration of the Judge is, "Depart from Me, you cursed, into the everlasting fire" (Matt. 25:41). But again, Christianity is good news. Jesus died for us, in our place, and offers us the free gift of eternal life. Thus, God has made salvation available to us by His grace, which is unmerited favor.

Two Options—Life or Death

There are two groups of people. Those who are trying to work their way into Heaven and those who have trusted in Christ alone for the salvation of their eternal souls. In which group are you? You cannot escape, my friends. There are some decisions that are impossible not to make. This is one of those. You will decide this day. You cannot avoid it.

There are some decisions in life with two options. While we are deciding which of those options we will choose, we discover that we are already in one of them. For example, your car stalls on a railroad track, in the path of an oncoming train. Two options now loom before you. You can leap from your car and save your life, or you can stay in your car and try to save both life and auto. As you weigh the dangers and gains involved in those two options, the inevitable fact is that you have already chosen one: you are in your car and the train is still coming!

Today you likewise have two options: life or death. But while you consider the choices, you have already chosen one, for you are already in that state of death into which every soul was born. And the judgment train of God is coming! You must choose.

The gospel is the greatest offer ever made. I tell you that the day will come when the offer will be recalled and the time of grace will end forever. But now, the sun of His grace is shining, and the offer of His love and mercy waits for you. There are some who have feebly accepted that offer, but they lack the assurance that they are going to Heaven. But He promises in His word through His servant John: "These things I have written to you who believe in the name of the Son of God, that you may *know* that you have eternal life" (1 John 5:13, emphasis mine).

Dear one, have you ever truly yielded your life to Christ? Have you ever truly surrendered yourself to Him? Won't you come to Him and yield your heart? Say, "Lord Jesus Christ, melt this cold, hard heart of mine. I want You as my Savior, and I want to be Your child. Lord Jesus Christ, I yield myself to You. I open my heart. Come in and cleanse and melt and woo my heart to Yourself. Bind me with bonds of love to Your side. Help me, henceforth, from this day forward, to love You supremely, to serve You faithfully until I come to see You face-to-face. In Your name I pray. Amen."

If you prayed that prayer in sincerity, you have begun the greatest adventure on which you could ever embark. And I would strongly urge you to begin to pray and read the Bible every day. If you've never read the Bible before, start with the Gospel of John (the fourth book of the New Testament).

I also urge you to get involved with a Bible-based, Bible-believing church. If you would like a free book to help you become established in the Christian faith, write to me and ask for *Beginning Again*.[47]

Once we know Jesus as our personal Lord and Savior, our "thank-you" to Him for His gift of salvation will be to serve Him in every area of our lives. Good works will naturally flow from our lives, as good apples grow naturally on a healthy apple tree.

Conclusion

The many lives transformed by the gospel in centuries past and in our own day are another link in the chain of evidence that Christianity is true. Why? Because it works. Granted, this is a subjective type of link compared with other links in the chain of evidence. But if you know the Savior, you know Him personally. No matter what skeptics might say against Him, you know deep down that they don't know what they're talking about! All I know, said the formerly blind man, is that I was blind, but now I see!

The Anvil of God

But the word of the LORD endures forever.
—1 Peter 1:25a

Years ago I saw a painting that I have never forgotten. It was a painting of a large anvil. Around the anvil on the floor lay shattered, smashed hammers and, underneath, these words from the Bible: "The word of the LORD endures forever" (1 Peter 1:25a).

"God's Anvil" is an appropriate metaphor for the Word of God, which has endured the attacks of innumerable skeptics and unbelievers and yet still stands, unscathed, in spite of the onslaught of the ages. When the attacks against the Bible, against Jesus Christ, and against the faith are put into the larger, historical perspective, we can be confident that the present attacks will ultimately fail, as they have in the past. "Hammer away, ye hostile hands. Your hammers break, God's anvil stands."[1] Indeed, "the word of the LORD endures forever."

Kings and Tyrants

God, in a supernatural way, has sustained His Word down through the centuries against attacks from all classes and ranks of men. Numerous kings and tyrants, with the scepter of state in one hand, have taken up the hammer of unbelief with the other and have attempted, with government power, to smash the anvil of God.

King Herod

One of the early kings who tried to thwart God's Word was Herod, who was sometimes called "the Great." Herod the Great heard that the wise men had said the One who would rule Israel was to be born; he gathered them together to inquire where this would be. "So they [the magi] said to him, 'In Bethlehem of Judea, for thus it is written by the prophet:

> But you, Bethlehem, in the land of Judah,
> Are not the least among the rulers of Judah;
> For out of you shall come a Ruler
> Who will shepherd My people Israel. (Matt. 2:5–6)

Thus said the prophet, declaring the Word of God.

King Herod then took up the hammer of his might and sent forth his soldiers to destroy that promise and to nullify the prophecy. They killed all of the children two years old and younger in all of the environs of Bethlehem. The king thought he had nullified the prophecy of the Word of God. But God warned Joseph in a dream, and Joseph took the child and Mary and fled to Egypt. The prophecy came to pass; the Word of God was fulfilled; He who was to rule His people came forth out of Bethlehem!

Diocletian and Julian

Writer James C. Hefley observes, "No book has weathered so many storms and survived as has the Bible."[2] One of the worst cases in history of the attempt to destroy the Bible came at the hands of the Roman emperor Diocletian early in the fourth century. He had his soldiers destroy every copy of the Scriptures they could find. Dr. James Montgomery Boice, who founded and headed the International Council on Inerrancy,[3] points out: "It was actually a capital crime to possess a copy of the Bible at one time, but the Bible survived."[4] Julian the Apostate was another emperor who tried to stamp out the Bible. While Constantine (who ruled A.D. 312–337) had allowed for religious freedom in the Roman Empire, Julian (who ruled A.D. 361–363) tried to turn the Empire back to paganism and away from Christianity. He tried to stamp out the Bible, but providentially his reign only lasted a short time.[5]

Attacks on the Word of God are not new, and God seems to almost delight in turning the tables on the critics of His Word. Eventually they are proven wrong, and we find the Bible was right all along. In the long run, faith will always win in the conflict with unbelief. The Bible and Christianity will always stand the test of time. Indeed, throughout the ages, the Bible has proved itself indestructible.

Skeptics and Critics

David Hume, the famous Scottish philosopher, whose name is synonymous with skepticism, believed he had undermined faith in philosophy and religion. Through his scathing attacks, Hume felt that the foundations of religion would most certainly be destroyed and the Bible would soon become an ancient artifact. But shortly after his death, David Hume's house in Edinburgh became the headquarters of the Scottish Bible Society, which published tens of thousands of copies of the "hated" book! "Hammer away, ye hostile hands. Your hammers break, God's anvil stands."

In the spirit of David Hume, there have arisen in the last two centuries what have been called "higher critics"[6] of the Bible. These unbelievers use the Bible against itself. They attempt, by carefully searching the Bible, to find anything to use as an axe to destroy Scripture. I find it very interesting that at the beginning of the nineteenth century, as this movement began, something else of note was occurring. That something is known as modern archaeology. These two movements grew up simultaneously and had a significant effect on both science and religion.

One was based upon theories spun in studies and locked-in libraries around the world. The other was based on firsthand facts dug up by people with spade and shovel, axe and pick, who uncovered the past right before their eyes.

The remarkable thing is that, on the one hand, the higher critics very quickly came to their conclusions, which they no doubt had already reached before they began their studies: that the Bible was an unreliable, unhistorical, and mythological book and that you could almost be sure that most anything it said on any historical subject was not to be taken seriously. Biblical criticism, said Abraham Kuyper around the turn of the century, had degenerated into "biblical vandalism."[7]

At the same time, archaeologists were coming to very different conclusions. Many of them began as unbelievers, skeptics who were convinced by the higher criticism: people like Professor Sayce of Petri (the greatest of the Assyriologists), Sir William Ramsay, and D. J. Wiseman. When literally holding in their hands the cold facts of history, they finally concluded that the Bible was indeed a remarkable book. The more facts they uncovered from the ground, the more convinced they became that the Scriptures were indeed the Word of God, accurate in all its details. Vernon Grounds writes, "By means of this science [archaeology] the supernatural accuracy of the Bible has been overwhelmingly demonstrated in recent times."[8]

The archaeologist's spade picks apart the carping of the higher critic; the Word of God is again seen to be true. It is a wondrous thing that Christians are not called to a blind faith, which is faith without evidence. Rather, we are called to a faith in a Word that has been examined more than any other book in the history of the world. Every word, syllable, letter, and accent of that book has been scrutinized by hostile critics for centuries. Still it stands; the Word of God holds true, that all Scripture is given by inspiration of God. Jesus said, "Heaven and earth will pass away, but My words will by no means pass away" (Mark 13:31).

The Bible as History

German journalist Werner Keller published a best-selling book in the mid-1950s on this issue, The Bible as History. This classic book has sold more than ten million copies and can still be found in bookstores. Keller writes of the biblical archaeologists:

> For a century now, American, English, French, and German scholars have been digging in the Middle East, in Mesopotamia, Palestine, and Egypt.... In Palestine, places and towns that are frequently mentioned in the Bible are being brought back once more into the light of day. They look exactly as the Bible describes them and lie exactly where the Bible locates them.... These breathtaking discoveries, whose significance it is impossible to grasp all at once, make it necessary for us to revise our views about the Bible. Many events that previously passed for pious tales must now be judged to be historical. Often the results of investigation correspond in detail with the Biblical narratives. They not only confirm but also illumine the historical situations out of which the Old Testament and the gospels grew.[9]

To write his book, Keller did a massive amount of research on the various archaeological findings related to the Bible. He traveled to "the libraries of many lands" to dig deep into the scientific journals which were known among the archaeologists, but not necessarily the laypeople. After poring through all the research known at the time, Keller concluded:

In view of the overwhelming mass of authentic and well-attested evidence now available, as I thought of the skeptical criticism which from the eighteenth century onward would fain have demolished the Bible altogether, there kept hammering in my brain this one sentence: "The Bible is right after all."[10]

That "the Bible is right after all" is widely held among many scholars today. Norman Geisler, a seminary professor, and William Nix, an educational consultant, put it this way: "Much of the Bible is historical and as such is subject to historical investigation. The most significant area of confirmation in this regard has come from the field of archaeology."[11]

"The Assured Results of Higher Criticism"

Before archaeology disproved many of their unbelieving, armchair theories, higher critics of the Bible tried to make mincemeat of the historical reliability of the Scriptures. Their unproven hypotheses were condescendingly known as the "assured results of higher criticism."

For example, they said it was obvious that Moses could not have written the Pentateuch because writing had not even been invented in his day.[12] But the spade of the archaeologist has been the frustration of the higher critic—it was discovered that writing existed long before Moses.[13] Recent discoveries have indicated that writing was flourishing on the earth fifteen hundred years before Moses was born.[14] This "assured result of higher criticism" was shattered on the floor!

The "Mythological" Empire of Assyria

Then there was the perverse joy the critics had with the biblical stories about the empire of Assyria and with its capital, Nineveh—the land to which Jonah the prophet was sent. They said that it never existed; that all of the supposed kings of Assyria and Nineveh were simply mythological characters of the mythological empire of Assyria, which never existed anywhere but in the fertile minds of the writers of the biblical myths! How did they know that? Very simply: none of the secular historians ever mentioned Nineveh of Assyria or any of its kings. Therefore, whenever the Bible is thrown into conflict with secular historians, it is obvious to any "intelligent" person that the Bible is wrong and the secular historians are right! Why is that obvious? It is obvious when one begins with the presuppositions that supernaturalism cannot be and that there is no God; therefore, there cannot possibly be an inspired Scripture.

But then came Sir Henry Layard, who boarded a boat at Mosul and floated down the Tigris River to excavate at Nimrud. He and his men began to dig. They found a brick on which was inscribed the name of Shalmaneser III—one of the "mythological" kings of the "mythological" empire of Assyria. Layard sent the brick to a museum in London where it was examined carefully and declared, with absolute certainty, to be fraudulent. It could not have really been Shalmaneser because, you see, he never existed. He was never the king of Nineveh and of Assyria because such an empire never existed!

Soon after, British Major Henry Crewsicke Rawlison did a most impertinent thing. He had the temerity to dig up the whole city of Nineveh.[15] The results proved to be extremely embarrassing to the "assured results of higher criticism," for there in the great library of Nineveh were thousands of inscriptions dealing with all the various kings of Nineveh and the whole history of the Assyrian empire. Again, another of the "assured results of higher criticism" crumbled!

The "Imaginary" Hittites

The skeptics then turned their attention from the Assyrians to the Hittites.[16] The Bible mentions the Hittites forty times. Who are the Hittites? Again they were an "imaginary" people who dwelled in the midst of the pages of the Old Testament. They never really lived, said the "assured results of higher criticism." Then in 1905, Dr. Hugo Winckler uncovered the city of Boghas-Keui in central Turkey[17]—the former capital of the "mythological" empire of the Hittites. In recent times, other discoveries have shown that the Hittite empire was more vast in scope than anybody had ever conceived it to be—even larger than we would have gathered from the writings of the Bible.[18] It was apparently the largest kingdom of its day. Yet, for decades the skeptics were saying that it never existed. Another assured result bit the archaeological dust.

The "Impossible" Battle of Jericho

Then there was Joshua, who fought the battle of Jericho and commanded the people to walk around the city for seven days—after which the walls fell down! That was a nice story for Sunday school and it even made a nice song. Of course, as every "intelligent" person knew, it never really happened.[19] However, Professor Garstang, a great archaeologist, arrived at the site of Jericho. He spent six years laboriously uncovering one layer after another of the city until he uncovered ruins from the time of Joshua.

So amazing were Garstang's discoveries that he wrote a startling statement, which he and two other archaeologists signed and sent out to the amazed critical world. In it he said this: "There remains no doubt that the walls fell outward so completely that the attackers would be able to clamber up and over the ruins in the city."[20] Furthermore the city was subsequently burned, even as the Old Testament declares.

A few decades after Garstang's work, the biblical account was again challenged, this time by archaeologist Kathleen Kenyon, who dated the city's ruins in such a way that they couldn't square with the time of Joshua's conquest.[21] But Kenyon's research was later disproved by archaeologist Bryant Wood, director of the Associates for Biblical Research, who said that there was "remarkable agreement" between the biblical account and the archaeological evidence. Wood learned that "extensive ceramic remnants and carbon-14 samples contradict Kenyon's dating of the city's fall, and other evidence converged to support the biblical account."[22] He wrote up his findings in the *Biblical Archaeology Review*.[23] As Werner Keller said, "The Bible is right after all."[24]

The Birth of Jesus

There were attacks by skeptics on the New Testament as well. The birth of Jesus has been a familiar target. Luke was declared to be a faulty historian in three main points concerning his account of the birth. First, said the scholars, there was no such thing as a census taken in Rome. There was no historical record of it. Second, Quirinius was not the governor of Syria in B.C. at the time Christ was born, but rather, as Josephus declared, in A.D. 6.[25] Third, people did not have to return to their ancestral homes for enrollment as Luke had declared. This was obvious; it was the "assured results of higher criticism," and "we're sorry, but you will just have to tear that page out of your Bible. For that, you see, is just not true."

But the spades of the archaeologists continued to turn. They found that the Romans did indeed have censuses. They began with the emperor Augustus and continued every fourteen years. It was discovered that Quirinius was governor of Syria twice, the first time beginning in 7 B.C. A papyrus was discovered in Egypt that contained these fascinating words: "Because of the approaching census, it is necessary that all those residing for any cause away from their homes should at once prepare to return to their own governments in order that they may complete the family registration of the enrollment and that the tilled lands may retain those belonging to them."[26] It was precisely what Luke had declared! Once more, "the assured results of higher criticism" crumbled into the dirt.

Over and over the Bible has been confirmed by archaeological discoveries. Sometimes there have been temporary discrepancies between the Bible and archaeology. I say *temporary* because as they kept digging, the alleged contradictions were resolved. Dr. Clifford Wilson—a retired biblical archaeologist, retired professor at Sydney University in Australia, and author—said on our recent television special about the reliability of the Bible that he's repeatedly seen how accurate the Scriptures are:

> The further I've gone [in archaeology] the more I've become convinced as to the remarkable unique accuracy of the Bible as the world's most wonderful textbook. Now I didn't always think that. I used to have all sort of reservations. . . but you wait a while, you keep digging, and you find it's the Bible that has the answers! . . . The Bible is recognized by archaeologists not necessarily as a spiritual book but as a good book of history.[27]

Indeed, the great Jewish archaeologist Nelson Glueck declared: "It may be stated categorically that no archaeological discovery has ever controverted a biblical reference."[28]

Several years ago, *Time* magazine had an important article entitled "How True Is the Bible?" wherein they discussed the condition of the Bible after two hundred years of attacks by critics. They stated,

> The breath, sophistication and diversity of all this biblical investigation are impressive, but it begs a question: Has it made the Bible more credible or less?. . . After more than two centuries of facing the heaviest scientific guns that could be brought to bear, the Bible has survived—and is perhaps better for the siege. Even on the critics' own terms—historical fact—the Scriptures seem more acceptable now than they did when the rationalists began the attack.[29]

The Bible Will Be Vindicated

If there are any legitimate objections to any detail in the Word of God, give it enough time. The Bible will be vindicated. The critics may harp away, but in the end they will be proven wrong. More than a hundred years ago, one of the greatest preachers of all time, Charles Haddon Spurgeon, made a very wise observation, paraphrased here by Dr. James Montgomery Boice:

If you want to be thought very wise today, but look very foolish in about fifty years, attack the Bible. Point out all the errors. But if you're willing to be thought foolish now, obscurantist, fundamentalist or whatever, but believing that in fifty years you will be vindicated, stand with the Bible.[30]

Critics Transformed into Believers

Sometimes there are those critics who set out to tear down the Christian faith—because they perceive it as myth—who become believers once they look at the preponderance of the evidence. They then become strong apologists for the faith they once tried to destroy. Let's examine a few such people.

Sir William Mitchell Ramsay

Another skeptic, the erudite Sir William Mitchell Ramsay, was a famous authority on the ancient world. He was born into a home of wealth, skepticism, and atheism. He was well educated at Aberdeen and Oxford. He was determined that he would see the Word of God demolished by his wit. Unlike the philosophers who contemplated religion from ivory towers, he would go to the source. So, with the spade of the archaeologist—a field in which he was well trained—he would prove the Bible to be nothing more than the carefully constructed myth of ambitious monks of the second or third century.

Ramsay decided, after much study, that the Achilles' heel of the New Testament was the book of Acts. It included the three missionary journeys of Paul, with detailed accounts of names, places, and offices throughout the Roman world. He went to the Near East and began his work. The critical world was excited. Never had anyone been so prepared as was Sir William Ramsay! Indeed, there must have been some Christians who were somewhat intimidated by what might come from this great undertaking to destroy the Scripture.

That was in 1881. For fifteen years he labored indefatigably, following the route that Luke laid out in the book of Acts. At last, he wrote in 1895 the important book *St. Paul the Traveller and Roman Citizen*. Ramsay had found Luke to be an infallible guide, a prince of historians, accurate to the minutest detail. He declared, "I take the view that Luke's history is unsurpassed in regard to its trustworthiness. . . . you may press the words of Luke in a degree beyond any other historian's and they stand the keenest scrutiny and the hardest treatment."[31]

That was just one of many books. For forty years Ramsay continued his studies, excavations, and book writing—all to the increasing dismay and chagrin of the unbelieving world, but to the delight of Christians. Finally, Sir William Ramsay committed his life to the Christ of the Scriptures that he had found to be unfailingly sure.

General Lew Wallace

Rarely does a general get together with a colonel to discuss theology, but that is precisely what happened one day some time after the Civil War on a train passing through the Midwest. The colonel was Colonel Robert Ingersoll, the most famous skeptic and unbeliever of his day, who traveled through the country lecturing against the Bible. On this occasion he asked the general, Lew Wallace, a writer with great literary skills, why he didn't use his skills to demolish the "myth" presented in the Bible—show Jesus Christ for who He really was: merely a man among men.

The general thought that it was a good idea, and so some time later, he began to gather all the historical materials he could find. As he searched, he found himself growing ever more astonished. He was amazed to discover that this Galilean peasant, reared in an obscure town called Nazareth, out of which no good thing could come (John 1:46), having never received any education, having never attended school, with no degrees or background of any sort, suddenly emerged from total obscurity, walked up on a mountain and delivered the most astounding statement on human ethics the world had ever heard.

The general's amazement increased as he followed the life of Jesus of Nazareth. At last, at the cross of Calvary, like the centurion, Wallace bowed the knee and received Christ as his own Savior and Lord. He wrote his book in 1880. It did not present Jesus as merely a man among men, but as the incarnate God, dwelling among men. The book? *Ben-Hur: A Tale of the Christ*. His book presents Christianity in a positive light, and the death of Christ is the key to the resolution to one of the main conflicts in the story—Ben-Hur's leprous sister and mother are healed because of the Crucifixion. One of Wallace's fictional characters says this of Christ's kingdom:

> There is a kingdom on the earth, though it is not of it—a kingdom of wider bounds than the earth—wider than the sea and the earth, though they were rolled together as finest gold and spread by the beating of hammers. Its existence is a fact as our hearts are facts, and we journey through it from birth to death without seeing it; nor shall

any man see it until he hath first known his own soul; for the kingdom is not for him, but for his soul. And in its dominion there is glory such as hath not entered imagination.[32]

The novel glorifies Jesus Christ and is a far cry from Ingersoll's original vision! The classic movie, based on the novel, is also sympathetic to Christianity. It won the Academy Award in 1959 as the best picture of the year; it also received a total of eleven Academy Awards, which is still the record. How's that for a movie based on a book whose author originally set out to disprove Christianity?

Frank Morison

Another skeptic who set out to write a book *against* Christianity ended up writing a positive book on the faith, after he did his homework. Earlier this century, Frank Morison, a British journalist who was also a trial lawyer, set out to write a book to disprove Christianity in general and the Resurrection in particular.[33] Morison writes: "When as a very young man, I first began seriously to study the life of Christ, I did so with a definite feeling that, if I may so put it, His history rested upon very insecure foundations."[34]

But as Morison studied the facts, he concluded that he could not write the book he intended; he ended up with a very different volume than the one he set out to pen. The name of his book is *Who Moved the Stone?* He entitled his first chapter "The Book That Refused to Be Written." As he studied the evidence for the resurrection of Christ, he found it compelling. He wrote in the preface of that book,

> This study . . . is essentially a confession, the inner story of a man who originally set out to write one kind of book and found himself compelled by the sheer force of circumstances to write quite another.
>
> It is not that the facts themselves altered, for they are imperishably in the monuments and in the pages of human history. But the interpretation to be put upon the facts underwent a change. Somehow the perspective shifted—not suddenly, as in a flash of insight or inspiration, but slowly, almost imperceptibly, by the very stubbornness of the facts themselves.[35]

One hundred ninety pages later, Morison concludes: "There may be, and, as the writer thinks, there certainly is, a deep and profoundly historical basis for that much disputed sentence in the Apostles' Creed—'The *third* day he rose again from the dead.'"[36]

Lee Strobel

In our time, there lives a man who also wanted to disprove Christianity, a man who was moved by Morison's book among others. He is Lee Strobel, a former atheist and journalist, who was the legal affairs editor for *The Chicago Tribune*, having graduated from Yale Law School.

As a journalist, Strobel had a "get-the-story-at-any-cost" mentality. He also had a mean streak, relishing the power he wielded in such a position: "What I really savored was making big shots dance to the newspaper's tune." For example, he intentionally postponed calling a prominent businessman until Thanksgiving Day, just before the family feast, to inform him that the paper was going to run a major story the next day on how the man was under investigation for fraud.[37]

But Lee Strobel's wife, Leslie, went to church one Sunday morning. He was taken aback, asking quickly, "You didn't give those guys any of our money, did you?" She soon became a Christian, and this led Strobel to do a historical search on Jesus. He wanted to debunk Christianity once and for all: "No Resurrection, no Christianity,"[38] which is theologically correct. He meticulously engaged in the type of careful research that had made him a respected reporter. But the more Lee Strobel studied, the more convinced he became of the veracity of Jesus Christ. He, too, became a Christian, and today he is a minister of the gospel at one of the nation's largest Protestant congregations, Willowcreek Community Church in the Chicago area. He specializes in helping skeptics find faith in Jesus Christ.

Conclusion

Try as they might, our present-day critics who hammer away at Christ, the Church, the Bible, will not succeed in the long run. The anvil of God will endure forever. The Word of God has endured through all the ages, and it will endure the present attack on it from all sides. Here is how author A. Z. Conrad put the immortality of the Bible into perspective:

There It Stands

Century follows century—
There it stands.

Empires rise and fall and are forgotten—
There it stands.

Dynasty succeeds dynasty—
There it stands.

Kings are crowned and uncrowned—
There it stands.

Despised and torn to pieces—
There it stands.

Storms of hate swirl about it—
There it stands.

Agnostics smile cynically—
There it stands.

Profane, prayerless punsters caricature it—
There it stands.

Unbelief abandons it—
There it stands.

Thunderbolts of wrath smite it—
There it stands.

The flames are kindled about it—
There it stands.

The arrows of hate are discharged against it—
There it stands.

Radicalism rants and raves against it—
There it stands.

Fogs of sophistry conceal it temporarily—
There it stands.

The tooth of time gnaws, but makes no dent—
There it stands.

Modernism tries to explain it away—
There it stands.

An anvil that has broken a million hammers—
There it stands.[39]

The Gates
of Hell

The Hammers

If the world hates you, you know that it hated Me
before it hated you.
—John 15:18

Have you ever visited the catacombs in Rome? To climb down in there and imagine a group of committed Christians in centuries past praising God, huddled in secret for fear of their lives, is a thrilling experience. But what is most noteworthy about the catacombs is that they bespeak the victory of Christianity against one of its most terrible enemies—the Roman Empire. The catacombs serve as a reminder that the gates of Hell shall not prevail against the Church. The Caesars are long dead and the empire with them, but the Church continues!

We saw in the last chapter how the Bible is like an anvil that doesn't crumble, despite the blows of a hundred or even a thousand hammers. In this section of the book, we will look at some of the present-day hammers that are trying to pound away at the Bible, at the Church, and even at Jesus Christ Himself. Indeed, there is an attack against things Christian in America. We see it in the movies, on TV, in the schools, in the universities, in the public arena, in the courts, and even within some church circles. As Pat Buchanan once said, Christian bashing has become a popular indoor sport in America.[1]

But the biggest losers in the long run will be the unrepentant anti-Christian bigots, who will one day stand before the very One they mocked. In the attack on Christ, the other side may be successful in a few ways: they may cause individuals to lose their eternal souls; they may lead Christians astray, rendering them ineffective; they may even lead whole cultures astray or cause nations to perish (as did Nazi Germany). But no matter what fleeting success the devil may have,

Christ's kingdom will stand. Sometimes you hear this expression: "God said it. I believe it. That settles it." I think a better variation of that is: "God said it. That settles it. P.S., I believe it. P.P.S., If you're smart, you'll believe it too!"

We're Winning

We saw in the first part of this book that the main spiritual conflict has *already* been settled. God has won. He defeated Satan when Jesus hung on the cross and rose from the dead—period. It's only a matter of time before the effects of that victory are felt completely; as Paul reminded the Roman Christians, "And the God of peace will crush Satan under your feet shortly" (Rom. 16:20). The delay between the promise and the realization of that promise reminds me of what happened in the U.S. after the Emancipation Proclamation went into effect after the Civil War. There were many blacks in the South still living in virtual slavery. The *effects* of the liberation of blacks in this country weren't necessarily felt right away, but in time they were. In the same way, this world has not yet seen the complete triumph of Christ over Satan, but it will! It's just a matter of time. And that's the point of this whole book: God has won, Satan has lost. The gates of Hell shall not prevail!—come what may in our nation.

Unfortunately, in the context we find ourselves today, it is often easy to lose sight of the fact that the gates of Hell shall not prevail. They seem to be doing quite well today, thank you.

Humans now have channels of communication open to them that were previously unheard of, but we find these great tools often being used against the Christian faith. As of this writing, plans are in the works for a $100-million film starring Arnold Schwarzenegger that will present the Crusaders as exceptionally cruel and barbaric and even cannibalistic.[2] In contrast, the Muslims will be presented as the good and kind ones, no doubt; ironically, the Muslims sparked the Crusades by invading the Holy Land and by not letting Christian pilgrims worship in peace there.[3] On another front, novelist Gore Vidal recently wrote a blasphemous book, *Live from Golgotha*, which (among other things) portrayed Paul and Timothy as homosexual lovers. He said of Christianity that it is "the greatest disaster ever to befall the West."[4] The religion of Jesus Christ helped shape this culture and this country, and yet today there is a strong backlash against Him.

After the Oklahoma City bombing in April 1995, the media sometimes lumped together various Christian groups—guilt by association—with those responsible for creating the climate that led to the bombing. *Time* magazine, for example, insulted the Christian community in an article called "Outcasts Digging in for the Apocalypse." Talking about antigovernment groups of the "radical right," reporter Philip Weiss pontificated: "Their coalition included well-known elements of far-right thought: tax protesters; Christian home-schoolers; conspiracy theorists influenced by the John Birch Society's fear of one-world government."[5] Christian home-schoolers? Who is *Time* magazine trying to kid? It's unconscionable to me that the anti-Christian bigots of this country would use such a terrible tragedy as the explosion in Oklahoma City to promote their own agenda. In reality, the Christian faith *was* involved in Oklahoma City—after the bombing, to help pick up the pieces! For example, the churches of that city worked together in providing relief for the bombing victims. The Red Cross (which has Christian origins)[6] was right there, as was the Salvation Army (a Christian denomination). Billy Graham came to provide spiritual solace for the victims' loved ones. In short, where were the Christians in the Oklahoma City tragedy? They were right there in the trenches, helping the suffering.

We live in a time when crime is on the increase, when the social fabric of our nation is unraveling at the seams. Yet, as Gary Bauer, head of the Family Research Council in Washington, D.C., points out, to hear the cultural elite talk, you'd think that the problem in our culture occurs somehow whenever Christianity is on the rise. The moral problems we see every day are a result of a culture running away from faith, running away from reliable standards of right and wrong.[7] Keep in mind: when religious liberty is inhibited, religious instruction is stopped; religious knowledge diminishes, and ungodliness, immorality, and crime accelerate. Hence, there is a connection between all of the horrid crimes we see out there and the kind of religious instruction the people in the country receive (or don't receive).

Christian Bashing

Ironically, in our age, which thankfully stands foursquare against bigotry and prejudice, we find an intensifying bigotry and prejudice directed against Christians, Christ, or the Church. For example, the prominent newspaper where I live reflects this dichotomy. On the one hand, the paper editorially takes a stand against bigotry and prejudice; yet, on the other hand, it harbors within its pages columns by one of the most virulent, anti-Christian bigots I've ever had the displeasure of reading. A man, who, it seems, can hardly go a fortnight without angrily lashing out at one Christian or another. While some of the assault against us is based on our own sins and misdeeds, much is not.

The Christian bashing of our culture is actually relatively new (for our country). Take the example of Hollywood. Up until about twenty-five years ago or even less, films about Christians were virtually always presented in a positive light, and

Jesus Christ was only mentioned reverently. But today, Christ—the spotless and holy Christ, the only perfect and pure person ever to grace this planet—is Himself held up to unbelievable and savage mockery.

If you are anything other than the most casual observer of our times, you will have noticed an increasing tempo of anti-Christian propaganda, even in this nation that was founded as a Christian republic.[8] More and more Christians are being pilloried, but this should not shake our confidence, because we know the gates of Hell shall not prevail—the hammers of the enemy will crumble.

The entire history of the world is simply an unfolding of the great conflict between Christ and Satan, between Christ and Antichrist.[9] Scripture says of the devil: "He is filled with fury, because he knows that his time is short" (Rev. 12:12b NIV). The conflict between Christ and Satan, and all of the devil's minions who have risen up over the centuries to bring people into darkness and tyranny, continues apace unto this day. We, in fact, may live at the very end of the ages, at the climax of this long struggle that might soon reach its dramatic finish by the return of Jesus Christ to planet Earth.

The ancient world that Christianity conquered—not by force but by love— was transformed by the gospel. The ancient sins of abortion, abandonment, slavery, homosexuality, promiscuity, polygamy, bestiality—which were practiced and also endorsed by many of the philosophers of ancient times—disappeared virtually entirely under the influence of Christianity.[10] It should not be surprising, therefore, that when the modern "sophisticated" secular humanist opposes Christianity, there appear in his or her wake the same vile sins that besmirched the ancient, pagan world.

Thus, more is at stake for the future of our nation than our religious liberties. The battle we are engaged in is of vital importance because we could actually be plunged into another five-hundred-year Dark Ages. It could happen. The world got along for millennia without America, and it can get along without America again. The ten tribes of Israel were so assimilated into their neighboring nations that they disappeared almost entirely. The Roman Empire was dissolved before the oncoming pagan hordes, and America can go the same way. Ravi Zacharias, a missionary to North America from India, said America could slide into total anarchy or be taken over by Islam. Either that or we could have spiritual revival.[11] In short, there's a great deal at stake in this battle for the soul of America! Even if America goes, Christ is still building His Church, so other nations will take over for America as the center of Christianity.

Dr. James Dobson also has alerted us to the fact that we could become almost completely secularized, as has happened in Western Europe. He warned,

Remember that Great Britain was deeply religious through the 1940s. Its culture was greatly influenced by Christian thought and values. Perhaps 60 to 70 percent of its population went to church each week. . . . Today only *three* percent of Britons consider themselves to be deeply committed believers. For them, the civil war is over. Traditionalists lost. . . . The culture has been redesigned from top to bottom by secular humanists, and they did it primarily by influencing the younger and more vulnerable members of their society.[12]

Thus, there is a lot at stake in the conflict between Christ and the spirit of antichrist in our culture, not the least of which is the eternal condition of millions of souls. I'm not saying these things will happen. What I am saying is, let us realistically entertain the possibility so we can do what we can to prevent it from occurring, before it's too late.

A Quick Overview of the Attack on Christ in America

While the forces of Hell shall not prevail against Christ's Church, they seem to be having a field day in our time! Here's a brief overview on how this attack against Christ is being waged on various fronts in our day; these are some of today's prominent hammers that are pounding away at Christianity:

Hammer 1: The Media

We live in an information age, yet in reality there is a great deal of *dis*information in our society on matters that touch on Christianity. Christians are routinely presented as buffoons or bigots, while the important contributions of the Christian Church to our society are either ignored or are divorced from their Christian roots. The main character of a recent made-for-TV movie, for example, was a devout Christian who was so strict in his religious convictions, he killed his mother, wife, and children for being "insufficiently pious."[13] So those watching TV and listening to radio get a very distorted picture of the Church. Programming (both news and entertainment) that bashes Christian values and teaching often permeates the airwaves.

But the gates of Hell shall not prevail!

Hammer 2: Movies and Pop Music

Movies in recent years have often been anti-Christian. Hollywood regularly portrays Christians and the Church in false stereotypes. For example, in the remake of *Cape Fear* by Martin Scorsese,[14] an evil psychopath was a Bible-quoting "born-again Christian." What was at one time totally beyond the imagining of Americans—to publicly ridicule the Lord Jesus Christ Himself—has become a regular occurrence in film. Secular rock music joins the fray in the attack on Christ and often leads the pack. Numerous rock groups directly attack Christianity or praise Satan in deliberate anti-Christian diatribes. The number one song a few years ago was "Losing My Religion."[15]

But the gates of Hell shall not prevail!

Hammer 3: Hostility in the Public Arena

In the last few decades, there has been a systematic effort to remove any vestige of Christianity in our public life. In the name of *pluralism*, a hostile *secularism* attacks any expression of Christian ideas or beliefs in public. Christmas nativity scenes are routinely banned from public property, even when paid for with private funds. Painted crosses on water towers are scrubbed off. Even the words *John 3:16* (whose meaning escapes many people) have been banned from public stadiums. We see Christian bashing in the universities, private and public, including those with Christian roots! Christianity is systematically excluded in public schools, so much so that even *history* is often distorted, lest little Johnny hear about Christianity. This anti-Christian bigotry is even taken to ridiculous lengths. For example, recently a small kindergarten student "was chastised for writing 'I love you God' on her tiny palm."[16] We also see Christian bashing in the arts. Art that directly blasphemes Jesus Christ—such as the picture depicting Him shooting up heroin or the crucifix submerged in the artist's own urine—is not only produced in our day but is *funded* by the taxpayers! Think about what's going on in our culture: It's not OK for a picture of Jesus to be displayed in public—*unless* that picture is submerged in urine! That's how far we've come.

But the gates of Hell shall not prevail!

Hammer 4: Oppression: Distortion of the First Amendment

An unhistorical interpretation of the First Amendment underlies much of our church-state conflict. This misreading of the First Amendment has led to the stripping away of any public expression of Christian views and beliefs. Because of the ACLU and other groups, the First Amendment—originally created to ensure our religious freedom—has now been turned into a club of oppression. So we end up with such twisted decisions as:

- A guilty verdict in a murder trial was thrown out of court because the prosecution quoted from the Bible.

- The Supreme Court ruled that the Ten Commandments can't be posted in the public school classroom, lest little Johnny read them and obey them.[17]

- Christian pro-life activists are now on the same level as the Godfather, according to the Supreme Court. The stringent RICO laws designed to halt the mob are turned on Operation Rescue activists who are trying to protect human life (albeit in a misguided way).[18] When this Supreme Court decision was first reported, one media wag said, "Mother Teresa, meet Michael Corleone."

The separation of church and state, which is not even in our constitution, has now been misconstrued to mean the separation of *God* from the state. Thus, the so-called "constitutional separation of church and state" has turned the establishment clause of the First Amendment into a search-and-destroy mission for any vestige of Christianity in the public arena.

But the gates of Hell shall not prevail!

Hammer 5: Unbelief within the Church

There is an attack on Christ from within the Church, and virtually all of those involved in this phenomenon reject the Bible for what it claims to be, the Word of God. Some self-described "Bible scholars," for example, recently ruled on the sayings of Jesus, concluding that He said very little of what the Gospels say He said. The results of this now notorious "Jesus Seminar" were widely touted in the media, but often without proper rebuttal by qualified conservative scholars.[19] Thus the Christian bashing we find in our culture at large is not restricted to those outside the Church.

But the gates of Hell shall not prevail!

And on and on it goes. These five "hammers" comprise the next five chapters of this book, five common examples of contemporary Christian bashing.

Sometimes it seems like all hell is breaking out against Christ and His Church these days. Recently I read that a law had been passed in Canada, which, according to the article, forbids ministers from preaching the gospel on television. A number of studios were invaded, records confiscated and equipment taken, and some ministers thrown into jail! (Jay Sekulow, the Christian constitutional attorney, has now opened a branch of the American Center for Law and Justice, the ACLJ, in Canada—the CCLJ—to fight this case.)[20]

The attack on Christ today occasionally goes to ludicrous extremes. Take for example the Mississippi man who tried to sue the Bible! The *Washington Times* writes that he "was asking $45 million in damages from Oxford University Press and others on the grounds that the Bible is hearsay that oppresses blacks and homosexuals."[21] Fortunately, he discontinued his lawsuit because he ran out of money.

The Agelong War against Christianity

What we are witnessing in our time is the agelong war against Christianity—a war which has been sometimes cold and sometimes hot. I want you to know that it has become red-hot again.

Even people who are not Christians can see what's going on today with our culture's Christian bashing. The perceptive syndicated columnist Don Feder, who is an Orthodox Jew, wrote,

> White Christians are about the only easy target left. . . . Christian bashing (in all of its raw ugliness) is: 1) ridiculing conservative Christians as benighted and sheeplike; 2) suggesting there's something sinister about political ideas based on scriptural standards or 3) implying that clergy forfeit their constitutional rights when they don a clerical collar.[22]

Elsewhere, in the context of responding to the film *The Last Temptation of Christ*, Feder observed: "As a Jew, I doubt I can be accused of sectarian bias in the controversy at hand. I do not believe in the divinity of Jesus Christ. I do believe in respecting the faith of those who regard him as their savior."[23]

Would that more non-Christians in the media thought like Don Feder. But such is not the case. In recent television programs and motion pictures, Christians have been held up as bigots, as censors, as intolerant, as narrow minded, as ignoramuses. They are portrayed as those who are a threat to freedom, those who are a threat to the very well-being of our lives. For example, Showtime's movie *Flight of Black Angel* featured a fundamentalist Christian who was an Air Force pilot. He "goes berserk, murdering his family and shooting several of his fellow pilots."

His ultimate goal, which was not achieved, was to nuke the world beginning with Las Vegas. He states: "I'm doing [God's] work. Everything [on earth] must be destroyed. . . .[I'm] bringin' the light of heaven [to] the diseased, the unclean, the corrupt, the liars."[24] Christians today are routinely portrayed in a bad light with a few exceptions now and then, such as the television show *Christy*. These pitiful, last-gasp efforts of Satan may distract us, but they won't slow us down: Christ is building His Church.

The World Hates Christ and Christians

Jesus Himself said that the world would hate us. Why? He said, "If the world hates you, you know that it hated Me before it hated you" (John 15:18). The world hates Jesus Christ, which is one of the most astonishing facts in history! Here is a world sunk in its sin, in rebellion against God, deep in every form of immoral, anti-God behavior, already condemned by God[25]—simply waiting to fall off the precipice into perdition.

Then, the sinless, holy Son of God, lovingly and compassionately comes to live the perfect life that we cannot and to die an atoning death in our stead, taking upon Himself all the vileness of our sins and becoming sin for us. Then held up between Heaven and earth upon a cross, the wrath of His own Father is poured out upon Him in our place. He dies in our stead and purchases for us eternal life, which He freely offers to every last one of us—sinful sons and daughters of sinful fathers and mothers—if we will but trust in Him.

For this anguish, this agony, this trouble of coming into this dark world, He is requited with hatred. That is astonishing! He Himself answers the question why. Christ says, "They hated Me without a cause" (John 15:25b). His only desire was for our good; His only purpose was that we should live "happily ever after." And for that, the world gives Him its hatred. The Scripture says that the world is at enmity with God.

Jesus is the only perfect human being who ever graced the planet, yet rarely can we even sit in a restaurant without hearing His name dragged in the mud. To hear people curse with His name is always like a dagger in my heart. Why do they do it? What ill has He done to them? He seeks nothing but their well-being. Why do they hate Him? They hate Him without a cause, because they are depraved and their hearts are at enmity with God. Thus, they oppose any furtherance of His gospel. They work hard at squelching Christianity and especially the public expression of anything Christian. The result of this hostility is the attack on Christ in contemporary America.

A Repeated Pattern

But the world has always thought itself rid of Christ and His Church, only to be disappointed again as God has continued to fulfill His promise and Christ has continued to build His Church. The very gates of Hell—with all of the demonic forces and all of the efforts of unbelievers—have failed to stop the Church. That has been true since the beginning.

The world of unbelief nailed Christ to the cross, saw Him drop His head in death, saw His body taken down from the cross and placed in a tomb, saw the stone sealed in front of the tomb, saw a cohort of soldiers placed in front of it—and the world of unbelief said, "Well, that is that! So much for Jesus Christ!" But in spite of their satisfaction, three days later, on that bright and halcyon Sunday morning, the stone rolled away from the tomb, and Jesus Christ walked out into the light of morning! And the world has never been able to put Him back in the tomb again.

For three centuries, all of the might and all of the weight and all of the animosity of the Roman Empire came crashing down on the neck of the young Christian Church. But, as was inevitable, the attack on Christ in ancient Rome failed. Christ builds His Church and the gates of Hell cannot prevail against it!

More centuries passed and darkness descended upon much of Christendom. And yet during this time, barbarians—most of our ancestors—were slowly converting to Christianity. Over time, their cruel, pagan ways were being abandoned. Meanwhile, some major parts of the gospel were being obscured. At some points, it seemed that the light of the gospel was flickering at best. Then, suddenly, when it seemed that the truth would be lost forever, there broke forth with blazing splendor that great spiritual renewal called the Reformation. The gospel of justification by faith in Jesus Christ spread across Europe and made an incredible impact on the world.

Several more centuries passed. Again the darkness descended upon England. Deism held sway and unbelief was rampant. Faith was formal and nominal at best. It seemed like the true gospel would almost be forgotten. Morals were at an all-time low. Suddenly, the bright flash of John Wesley and George Whitefield was seen across England and there was again a great quickening and revival of faith. The whole landscape of England was changed; its morals were restored and the gospel again became a force to be reckoned with in England.

A great revival took place in the American Colonies in the 1700s. But toward the end of that century, it seemed that faith was failing again. Then suddenly the Second Great Awakening took place. Once more tens of thousands of people were swept into the kingdom of God and the life and faith of America were renewed.

During the so-called "Enlightenment," when some of the philosophers believed they had logically overturned the existence of God, one of the freethinkers,
Voltaire, made an interesting prediction. The great Frenchman was quite sure
that within a hundred years, Christianity would be a thing of the past. And yet,
after his death, his printing press and his house in Geneva were purchased by the
Swiss Bible Society for the printing and promulgation of that Bible Voltaire so
much despised![26] Who reads Voltaire today? Not many, but there are hundreds
of millions around the world who will read the Bible this very day!

In our own time, in the late 1960s, *Time* magazine heralded on its cover these
three ominous words: "God Is Dead." It seemed that the unbelievers were
gleefully gathering for the funeral. But within a decade the same *Time* magazine
proclaimed on its cover these words: "The Year of the Evangelical." It would seem
that evangelical Christianity in America had grown to such proportions that it was
now a force to be reckoned with in this nation—and that even presidential
candidates saw that they must seek the support of Christians if they would rule
in this land of ours.

In our own time, we've also seen that the Church in Russia, Eastern Europe,
and China has undergone intense persecution. Yet despite the most incredible
onslaught against Christianity and the blood of millions of Christian martyrs,
there are more followers of Christ in these countries today than there are of Karl
Marx!

The Second Coming Won't Be Like the First

I can't help but believe that those who continue to attack Christ fail to see
the eternal peril they are in. They hold in their minds some distorted picture of
a poor, helpless Jesus who wouldn't hurt a fly rather than the Christ who is
revealed in the Bible. They fail to see the contrast between His first and second
comings:

- The first time He came He was despised and rejected; the second time He
  will be glorified and admired in all them that believe.

- He came to hang upon a cross; He will come to sit upon a throne.

- He came into the darkness of night illumined only by the brightness of a
  star; He will come again in the glory of a day where the glory of the sun will
  be eclipsed by His brightness.

- He came to be seen by only a few; when He comes again He will be seen
  by all.

- He came in weakness; He will come in power.

- He came in humility; He will come in majesty.

- He came to be judged for us; He will come to be our Judge.

Jesus shall reign! The gospel of Christ will continue going forth in victory. Every weapon devised by man to destroy the gospel has utterly failed. Nothing can stand before it. And I am sure the pagan philosophies and religions of this nation and of the entire world will crumble before the advent of the gospel of Christ. He who sits upon the white horse that goes forth conquering and to conquer will continue until every nation, tribe, and tongue on this earth shall offer their praise to the Savior.

The Church Is on the Offensive

When Peter confessed that Jesus was the Christ (the Messiah), the Son of the Living God, our Lord told him that He was building His Church and the gates of Hell shall not prevail (Matt. 16:13–18). He didn't say that the gates of *Heaven* shall prevail against Satan. He said the gates of *Hell* shall not prevail against the Church. What's the difference? Who is on the offensive versus who is on the defensive.

The "gates of Hell" conjures up a picture of a city, a city where evil reigns in direct opposition to the City of God.[27] In biblical times, the city gate was where the rulers and elders met and where important decisions were made (see, for example, Ruth 4:11). In His promise, Jesus is saying the Church will be victorious even over the very gates (or strongholds) of Hell.

Conclusion

In the book of Acts, God used a *non*-Christian to make a great observation at the inception of the Christian faith. While the Sanhedrin, the Pharisees, and all the Jewish leaders were trying to stop the apostles from spreading the Christian message, Gamaliel, a Pharisee and teacher of the law, got up and addressed his people. He warned them not to go overboard on the anti-Christian persecution in which they were busily engaged. He said,

> Men of Israel, take heed to yourselves what you intend to do regarding these men. For some time ago Theudas rose up, claiming to be somebody. A number of men, about four hundred, joined him. He was

slain, and all who obeyed him were scattered and came to nothing. After this man, Judas of Galilee rose up in the days of the census, and drew away many people after him. He also perished, and all who obeyed him were dispersed. And now I say to you, keep away from these men and let them alone; for if this plan or this work is of men, it will come to nothing; but if it is of God, you cannot overthrow it—lest you even be found to fight against God. (Acts 5:35–39)

How prophetic! Keep in mind when he said this that the Church was a small group of persecuted, bedraggled outcasts. They were hardly a threat to the powers that be. Christianity is indeed "of God" and no force has been able to squelch it, although repeated attempts have been made. What Gamaliel said is a great reminder, from an unlikely source, that indeed the gates of Hell shall not prevail!

Now let's look at Hell's vain attempt to prevail. Let's look in more detail at some of the most prominent hammers of our day that are striking away at the immutable rock of Christianity.

The Hammer of the Media

If you were of the world, the world would love its own.
Yet because you are not of the world, but I chose you
out of the world, therefore the world hates you.
—John 15:19

A fter the Duke of Wellington beat Napoleon at Waterloo, the news of this victory was carried by sail and then brought to London. Back then, there were no mass media, so a system of semaphore (visual signaling using flags) was used atop Winchester Cathedral. As the sign began to spell out the important news, the anxious onlookers read, "Wellington defeated . . ." and then fog set in. This tragic news began to spread all over London—Wellington had lost! But then, the fog lifted, and the signal was spelled out again, only the Londoners below were able to read the *whole* message: "Wellington defeated Napoleon."[1] Wow, that's quite a difference! In the media of our day, when directly anti-Christian content often fills the airwaves, it seems as if the message on some programs is: "Christ defeated . . ." The last word of that sentence, "Satan," is not there. The fog still shrouds the truth. But you and I know that Satan has already been defeated, even if that fact never seems to make it to prime time.

The hammer of the media (and I only refer to the hostile, anti-Christian aspects of the media) seems to slug away at the Christian faith. But try as they might, they cannot stop the advance of the kingdom of God. This chapter will chronicle many of those attempts, primarily as found on television.

Cal Thomas pointed out that we should *expect* the slander of the world and recognize it as a sign that we're on the right track. He said, "To a very large extent, I welcome 'Christian bashing' if it is for righteousness' sake. I think we should look for ways to live even more righteously that the 'bashing' might increase. After all, if they hated Him, they're supposed to hate us too, right?"[2] Thus, we need not lose sleep over the latest program of some Hollywood producer with some anti-Christian axe to grind.

"The Reason Beverly Hills Is So Clean"

Woody Allen once said that the reason Beverly Hills is so clean is because they turn their garbage into television programs! When it comes to anti-Christian content, there's a lot of garbage in prime time.[3] Here are some examples:

- An episode of CBS's *Picket Fences* airing just in time for Christmas revolved around a crazed Christian gynecologist trying to bring about a type of virgin birth. He artificially inseminated a virgin with his own semen. When she learned what he had done, he attempted to kill her by staging an accident that left her comatose. After he got caught, he said, "Look what I've done for Christianity. People all over reliving the possibility [of a virgin birth]. I was trying to provide a little hope."[4]

- A couple of episodes of Fox Network's *Martin* featured a pimp-turned-preacher, Leon Lonnie Love. But he "still behaves like a pimp." When asked by his date about the source of his money, he responded, "God does provide. God provides like a son of a [expletive deleted]."[5]

- In an episode of *Grace Under Fire*, the ex-mother-in-law of Grace called herself a "decent Christian woman." And yet her behavior and attitude contradicted her statement. Meanwhile, Grace, the star of the show, defended and spoke highly of homosexuality.[6] Thus, as we find on many TV programs today, the Christians are portrayed as the villains and the homosexuals as the good guys.

And on it goes in the attack on Christ in the media. Yes, Beverly Hills sure looks clean these days!

Sometimes the darkness gets so dark that it's easy to forget that the gates of Hell shall not prevail. But we must never forget the big picture. If you were a soldier in a war, and you absolutely knew for certain that your side would win, wouldn't that change how you fought? Wouldn't that bolster your confidence—no matter how bad the conflict may get? Of course it would. Even if certain battles are lost, we have no doubt as to the outcome of the war.

Meanwhile, the present is dark and foggy. Many years ago, a Methodist pastor who didn't watch much TV sat down to enjoy a relaxing evening of television with his family. He was in for a shock when he found something objectionable on just about every channel—including one scene in which one man was hitting another man on the head with a hammer (speaking of hammers). The pastor was Don Wildmon of Tupelo, Mississippi. Right then and there he decided something must be done to clean up TV. He founded and directs what is today known as the American Family Association, which monitors television programming and the sponsors who pay for this trash.

Through the years of tracking what's on TV, Wildmon has seen the repeated attack on Christ. For example, in a recent issue entitled "Network Programs Continue to Denigrate Christian Faith, Diminish Traditional Family, Promote Sexual Perversions," his *American Family Association Journal* summed up a recent TV quarter:

> The fall season, with the exception of Christmas specials, saw the continuance of network television's "politically correct" (PC) programming in almost every imaginable area—the denigration of religion, particularly the Christian faith; the advocacy of homosexuality, mercy killing, promiscuity and teen sex; and the redefining of the concept of family to diminish traditional ideas.[7]

Unfortunately, this assessment could just as well have been written for 1982 as 1992. The problem has been with us for years.

The Media's Anti-Christian Bias

To their discredit, the media are overwhelmingly hostile to the Christian faith. Together they make quite a powerful hammer, and the hammer has not yet broken against God's anvil. But it's only a matter of time.

There are a few exceptions to Christian bashing in the secular media, for example, the recent CBS TV movie and series *Christy,* or the way Mother Teresa or the Salvation Army are sometimes fairly treated. As far as the nun from Calcutta and the legions of General Booth are concerned, I think the reason they generally get good press is that people are naturally attracted to the self-sacrificial work of those who sincerely help the poor. Unfortunately, the media more often than not present such good deeds in a way that tries to divorce them from their cause, which is a love for Jesus Christ.

So, by and large, the media today are covertly and sometimes overtly hostile to religion in general and Christianity in particular. The purpose of this chapter is to explore that hostility, including the blatant censorship of things Christian. But keep in mind as you pore through this that any attack against Christ will fail. Period. Even when it seems as if Napoleon is beating Wellington, we have to remember that Christ has *already* won. The hammer of the media may smash away, but it will surely break one day on God's anvil.

To assess TV's treatment of religion, the entertainment division of the Media Research Center (a conservative organization primarily dedicated to monitoring television programming) "studied all prime time television shows . . . [1,674.5 hours' worth] . . . airing in 1993 on ABC, CBS, Fox, and NBC."[8] What they found was the continual denigration of religion, especially Christianity—with Catholics getting the worst treatment.

Writing for the Media Research Center, Thomas Johnson pointed out that first and foremost, "Hollywood ignores faith far more than it demeans it."[9] But when prime time deals with religion, it most often casts the subject in a negative light. Johnson wrote,

> On the rare occasions when prime time deals with religion, it does so unfavorably, but by a plurality, not a landslide. Overall, 42% of the portrayals of religion in the study are negative, 30% are mixed or neutral, and 28% are positive. . . . However, as professions of faith become more devout, the characters espousing such beliefs are more likely to be depicted negatively, particularly if they are Catholic [which is by far the largest denomination]. By 68 to 18%, the laity—not just casual churchgoers, but those who are shown taking their faith seriously—are depicted negatively. . . . Negative depictions of the clergy dominate, 59 to 15%.[10]

A year later, in 1995, the Media Research Center conducted another "Faith in a Box" study on the treatment of religion from network news and prime-time TV. Fortunately, they found a slight improvement in the way religion was treated in entertainment programming. Unfortunately, they found worse treatment for religion (compared to the year before) in news programming. They report: "While prime-time television's treatment of religion has improved in the past year, network news coverage actually fell further into obscurity."[11] The findings of their study are illuminating:

The number of portrayals of religion in prime time more than doubled, from 116 in 1993 to 253 in 1994, even though the number of hours of original prime-time programming increased only slightly, from 1,674.5 to 1,716.

- CBS was the only network on which a majority (55 percent) of treatments of religion were positive. Fox was next (46 percent), with NBC (38 percent) and ABC (36 percent) trailing. Last year, the highest proportion of positive portrayals was only 37 percent, on ABC.

- Overall, positive depictions outnumbered negatives almost 2 to 1 (44 percent to 23 percent), whereas in 1993, negatives outnumbered positives by a 3-to-2 ratio (42 percent to 28 percent).

- Shows singled out for their positive treatment of religion were CBS's *Touched by an Angel* and *Christy*, ABC's *Thunder Alley*, and NBC's *L.A. Law* and *Homicide: Life on the Street*. Probably the most offensive to believers was NBC's *John Larroquette Show*.[12]

The good news, then, is that entertainment television is getting slightly, ever so slightly, better when it comes to how it is dealing with Christians and the Church. The bad news is that religion continues to be marginalized and ignored in network news coverage. Commenting on the survey and this conspicuous absence of religion coverage in the news, Media Research Center Chairman Brent Bozell said,

Network news continues to operate on the false and ignorant premise that good news is no news, even if it [religion] affects the overwhelming majority of Americans in a positive way. In spite of having a full-time religion reporter at one of the networks, overall coverage of religion was down in 1994 from only meager coverage in 1993. That is shameful.[13]

When the news *did* deal with religious conservatives, they were often depicted very negatively. Bozell pointed out that "the religious right was again portrayed by the networks as a hateful, frightening force, of 'intolerance and extremism,' as NBC's Bryant Gumbel put it."[14]

Overall, despite the improvements in how religion is portrayed in entertainment television programming, Bozell said that "both prime time and the network news shows still have light years to go before they can accurately claim they reflect the everyday aspect of religion in American life, because right now it's just not there."[15]

A One-Party Media

We live in a country with a two-party political system, but as one writer pointed out, we have a one-party media. Eighty-six percent of the media elite, according to the research of Lichter and Rothman, never or rarely attend any church or synagogue.[16] They are godless people and godless people hate the godly (John 15:19)—they always have and always will. But compared to the public at large, members of the media tend to be more ungodly.

Because of the power they wield, the media could present normal, law-abiding, church-attending Christians to the American secular public as deranged, demented, and as dangerous as the Branch Davidians.[17] And the people in America would believe it! Reality for millions of Americans is what is on the six o'clock news.

The Liberal Media: The True Censors

The media are always decrying censorship, especially when Christians take exception to titillating or profane programs. Ironically, one of the most phenomenal pieces of censorship in the history of the world is going on today and some of you are not even aware of it!

For some reason, it seems, the modern media moguls have decided that Christianity is to be censored from today's television and movies, in spite of the fact that there are more people that go to church in America than ever before.

Barbara Reynolds wrote an excellent column in *USA Today* a few years ago calling religion the "greatest story ever missed."[18] She gave numerous examples of how the media often edit out the statements from newsmakers if they attribute credit to God. For example, during the time of the fall of Communism in Eastern Europe, the media underplayed the vital *spiritual* dimensions that helped bring about the anti-Communist revolutions in every one of those countries. Yet Laszlo Tokes, the Reformed pastor who "sparked the Romanian revolution," said: "Eastern Europe is not just in a political revolution but a religious renaissance";[19] his observation went essentially unreported by the mainstream press. So Reynolds goes on to ask: "What does the press have against Jesus? Is there a bias against Christianity? . . . In concluding that God isn't important, the press is trying to play God itself."[20]

Sports Versus Religion: It's No Contest

A great example of Christianity being ignored by the media can be seen in the comparison between how sports and religion are covered by the media. The statistics tell an incredible story!

Question: What would you think Americans spend more money on—sports or religion? Surely, you'd think it would be sports with all the media attention lavished on it. But not so! In 1992, Americans gave $56.7 billion to churches, ministries, and synagogues. In contrast, they spent $4 billion on the three biggest sports—major-league football, baseball, and basketball.[21]

Compare the attendance figures for sporting events with those of church. More Americans will go to church this month (for example, church attendance in 1990 was 433 million per month) than all those who will attend all the sporting events this entire year (sporting events attendance in all of 1990: 388 million)!22

Somebody said, "Though you may find seventy pages of sports per week in the average newspaper, you will do well to find one or two pages of church news there on Saturday—and most of what is printed has to be paid for by the churches!"

George W. Cornell, religion writer for the Associated Press, wrote,

> The facts don't seem to fit. They appear incompatible. As measured by attendance and money, Americans show much greater interest in religion than sports, but it receives far less attention from the news media . . . religion gets only a fraction of media notice compared to the huge volume of attention lavished on sports. . . . Sociologist Jeffrey Hadden of the University of Virginia said the media have "disseminated a pattern" that religion doesn't belong. "Others pick up that policy in what has been a trickle-down process."[23]

A Martian's Perspective

If you were a Martian visiting this planet, knowing nothing except what you saw on network television, you would assume that Christianity had become virtually extinct in America.

One who can attest to the media ignoring religion is John L. Siegenthaler, a long-lasting newspaper executive who retired from the business after forty-three years and now heads up the Freedom Forum First Amendment Center. He said that when it comes to religion, the press "is not doing the job. It's not meeting the need and demand for it. . . . Religion gets short shrift. . . . So do the readers interested in religion. Anything else, whether it's politics, sports, health care or whatever, is given primacy over the religion beat."[24] And, as we've seen, this inattention to religion in the print media applies to the television media as well.

The Privatization of Religion

John Siegenthaler's center looked at the sentiments of newsroom personnel toward religion, and found that they weren't "particularly irreligious." However, at base, they believe that religion is a very private matter. Because it's private, there is "a nervousness and hypersensitivity about invading this no man's land."[25]

The belief that religion is merely a private affair is held religiously by the ACLU, the American Civil Liberties Union— which one wag labeled the "Anti-Christian Litigation Union." A few years ago, Ira Glasser, the executive director of the ACLU, was interviewed for our Coral Ridge Ministries documentary on this left-wing organization. Mr. Glasser literally said—*with a straight face!*—that the ACLU has done more for religious freedom in this country than any other organization by keeping religion *private*.[26] There's that word again—*private*. The media view religion as *so* private that they often ignore Christianity—except to denigrate it or to blow its hypocrisies way out of proportion. The Soviet Union also tried to privatize religion—right out of society!

The eminent social commentator, Michael Novak, pointed out that television has become much more secularized than the American people. He stated,

> What seems to have happened is that the public life of the United States, particularly in the media (and, more particularly still, television), has been far more secular than the American people are. In the face of the public media, countless devout Americans feel as if they are "strangers in their own land."[27]

Christians of one stripe or another make up a sizable group in our nation; 78 percent of Americans claim to be Christians according to a recent study reported in *Time* magazine.[28] And yet this fact is clearly ignored on network television. In the vast programming of network television, including seven evenings of prime time a week, can't there be more Christians on TV? We are told by Hollywood producers that their programming merely reflects life. Balderdash! When one is hard pressed to find many *positive* Christian characters on network television—in a nation in which a huge percentage of the population is evangelical, then clearly Hollywood is not reflecting life as it is. Some polls show that at least one-third of Americans claim to have had a born-again experience involving Jesus Christ.[29] You wouldn't know it from prime-time programming.

The extent of prayer on TV nowadays is when a tragedy occurs, the wounded party cries out, "Oh, God." That is prayer on television—if that is supposed to be a prayer; usually it's just an exclamation or a bit of profanity.

Furthermore, you will never see on television anyone seeking spiritual counseling, although about half of all counseling done in America is done by clergymen. C. V. Garnett, in an article called "Some Things You Never See on Television," wrote, "It's as if TV had a 'God-Bypass.' In real life people are always wrestling with or at least considering the place of God in their lives."[30] In television such wrestling never seems to take place at all. In fact, TV people make all sorts of decisions without giving any conscious or serious thought to whether or not God may be looking on at all.

Gregg Lewis, in a very descriptive article entitled "Telegarbage," said,

> At the same time that TV emphasizes these [materialistic and glitzy] values, it ignores many values the Bible teaches. On TV, there seems to be no such thing as sin. Almost the only people who believe in God are from another time in history—like the *Waltons* or the family in *Little House on the Prairie* [or more recently *Christy*]. It's as if God and His guidelines didn't even exist today. And that's just the picture TV viewers are getting—a partial, godless picture. The more viewers watch, the more they assume that real life is the same as what they see on TV. That means that God's absence on the tube is making it harder and harder for people to believe He has anything to do with real life.[31]

Thus, the more TV you watch, the more you assume God—our Creator, who knows us better than we know ourselves—has nothing to do with everyday life. Recently, a book written by a rabbi was spotted, bearing the title *Does God Belong in the Bedroom?* No matter what the rabbi's answer was, the question *itself* reflects a very limited view of God—as if He were in some little box and only was connected to our spiritual life but had nothing to do with the rest of our lives. Does God belong in the bedroom? God is the source of all life, including life in the bedroom![32]

It is entirely possible that many religious movies and scenes that try to portray genuine religious experiences often come off corny or seem unnatural, because God is so effectively removed from most movies and TV programs. We're so used to seeing life in movies and on TV without God, that when He is a part of the picture, He seems like an intruder. Hence, in movies and on TV, religion seems to have no part of life—except for weddings, funerals, and scandals. We've been brainwashed by Hollywood for too long!

The *Wall Street Journal* several years ago carried an article by Benjamin Stein on the absence of religion in prime time:

> On prime-time network television, there is virtually no appearance of religion at all. Whenever a problem requiring moral judgment appears—which is on almost every show—the response that comes is based upon some intuitive knowledge of what is good and evil, the advice of a friend, a remembered counsel, or, more likely, the invisible hand of circumstance. . . . The good people do what is right and the bad people do what is wrong by some kind of automatic secular compass. . . . prime-time network television [has become] an island without religion in an ever-more-religious America.[33]

Meanwhile, as God and godly people are growing invisible on TV, there is, at the same time, a growing presence of gay and lesbian characters on TV. These are always presented positively. The fictional homosexual characters generally exhibit more Christian character than do the occasional Christian characters one finds on network TV. For example, on Fox's *Melrose Place*, a homosexual who's a regular on the program "often comes across as the most caring, most sensitive, and most ethical character in the series. While he goes about his noble ways, other characters continue their bed-hopping, profane, hedonistic lifestyle."[34] But the reality is that the gay lifestyle is generally very promiscuous. It's simply not true that Hollywood reflects life—maybe life as it's found in parts of L.A., but that's about it.

So, on the one hand, we find the media regularly ignoring the Church—its contributions to society, its solutions to the many problems plaguing us, its steady growth in society. On the other hand, when the media do portray Christian characters, for the most part we find them portrayed very negatively.

The False Stereotype of Christians

If Christians are portrayed at all, they are characterized as fanatics, hypocrites, extremists, ignoramuses, backwoods fundamentalists, uneducated, and bigoted. For instance, an episode of ABC's *Going to Extremes* appearing around Christmastime featured a promiscuous woman claiming that she and a bedmate were "going to celebrate the birth of Christ together"—implying that their "celebration" of Christ's birth would be illicit sex.[35] It's open season on Christianity in pop culture today! Could you imagine television programs just in time for Hanukkah denigrating Judaism? Could you imagine programs belittling Martin Luther King, Jr., aired on his birthday?

In another instance, on CBS's *Picket Fences*, two of the main characters were warring priests, one an Episcopal, the other a Catholic. They were petty and selfish. The Catholic even punched the Episcopal priest in the face. When the sheriff reminded them not to resort to violence, the Catholic priest shouted, "Where have you been? Every war in the world is based on religion. There's no greater source of violence!"[36]

That's a distortion of history, as we documented in our previous book, *What If Jesus Had Never Been Born?* In reality, far more people have been killed in this century alone by the atheistic Communists than have been killed in all previous centuries combined! The world waited until this century for the term "genocide" to be coined. As the eminent historian Paul Johnson points out, the totalitarian states of the twentieth century (all of which were atheistic and anti-Christian) have proved to be the greatest killers of all time.[37]

Another example of the network's anti-Christian bias is an episode of NBC's *Law & Order*, in which a Christian police officer mercilessly allowed a fellow officer to die because the latter was gay. The officer jeered, "Newhouse is a fairy. If he's in trouble, he can flap his wings and fly out!" The officer used the Bible as his defense: "Personally, I was taught that God didn't approve of that kind of thing [homosexuality]. It's in the Bible." The real hero of the show was the slain officer's partner, who also was homosexual and who came out of the closet to "testify to the harassment suffered by homosexuals in the department."[38]

And on and on pound the hammers of the media against the anvil of the Christian faith. Sadly, this pattern of denigrating Christianity—not to mention Christian morality—has been going on for decades. Surely, this constant Christian bashing colors the thinking of millions toward the Christian faith.

L. Brent Bozell, chairman of the Media Research Center said that "entertainment television's portrayal of religious people as objects of ridicule demonstrates how out of touch the entertainment industry is with the American public." Bozell went on to cite Lifetime's "Great American TV Poll" which found that religious faith was the "most important thing in people's lives."[39] But, in contrast with this, the networks (broadcast and cable) often denigrate religion. Of course, one could legitimately ask, If religion really is that important to us, why do we put up with all this Christian bashing in the media? Apathy? Hypocrisy? In Chapter 12, we'll explore ways we can deal with the media's onslaught against the faith.

A Telling Example of Christian Bashing in the Media

TV's anti-Christian bias was clearly seen a few years ago when the Jim Bakker and Jimmy Swaggart scandals rocked the Church. When Bakker fell in 1987 and Swaggart in 1988, the response of the media was electric. The media had a field day with religion and seemed to enjoy every minute of it. They often seemed to paint all televangelists with the same broad brush. As a minister whose services are televised, I am sometimes called a "televangelist," but I reject the term because of the numerous negative connotations that go with it.

Even on a children's cartoon show, *Tiny Toons*, the word was used as the height of derogatory labels. One character was calling another character a number of bad epithets along the lines of "you snake in the grass." The climaxing epithet was "you televangelist!" Granted, some TV ministers have sinned in terrible ways. But should this give the whole field a collective black eye?

Through the centuries there have been numerous others who have fallen on their ecclesiastical faces. But never in the history of the Church has there been so much media coverage.[40]

I think that the broad-brush approach of many in the secular media has been blatantly unfair. An attempt to identify *any* Christian who is involved in *any* sort of broadcast media with Swaggart and Bakker is malicious at best. It has been called "media McCarthyism"—guilt by association. This is the type of thing that the media lamented a few decades ago when Senator Joe McCarthy was doing it, but now they are guilty of the same thing themselves! They often insinuate that all Christian ministers, or at least those involved in the media, are equally guilty with Swaggart and Bakker.

A Double Standard

The double standard against Christians is incredible—you can find it all over TV. Contrast two of the "Eye on America" features of the *CBS Evening News*. One dealt with Muslims in a very positive light, stating that they are America's fastest-growing religion but are misunderstood by many Americans. Many positive images and interviews were shown and the point was even made that Islam is opposed to violence.[41] The other "Eye on America" dealt with the terrifying assault on freedom at the hands of fundamentalist Christians who had won a majority on the school board of a California district. These Christians—who had won fair and square in the ballot box—were portrayed as posing an ominous threat across the country!

To see anti-Christian bias in action, simply watch the news, a news magazine, or a talk show when homosexuality is the topic. Then, watch the same program when it deals with Christianity. Watch it when abortion is the issue. Rare is the day that pro-lifers—who are largely Christians, and who are among the most compassionate people in our society—are dealt with fairly, much less positively. But, of course, all of this gets back to those who are the television power brokers.

The Media Elite

Who are the people that control the media? We have a definitive profile given us by a Lichter-Rothman report on the "media elite." S. Robert Lichter is a research professor in political science at George Washington University. Stanley Rothman is a professor of government at Smith College. Linda Lichter is codirector (along with Robert Lichter) of the Center for Media and Public Affairs in Washington, D.C. They did an important survey of 104 of the "most influential television writers, producers, and executives," which found—as could be expected—that these were very liberal people.[42] Here is what they found:

- Ninety-three percent "say they seldom or never attend religious services."

- Seventy-five percent "describe themselves as left of center politically, compared to only 14 percent who place themselves to the right of center."

- Ninety-seven percent "believe that 'a woman has the right to decide for herself' whether to have an abortion."

- Eighty percent "do not regard homosexual relations as wrong."

- Only 5 percent "agree strongly that homosexuality is wrong, compared to 49 percent who disagree strongly."

- Eighty-six percent "support the rights of homosexuals to teach in public schools."

- Fifty-one percent "do not regard adultery as wrong."

- Only 17 percent "strongly agree that extramarital affairs are wrong."[43]

This survey shows so clearly why we find an anti-Christian bias in the media. These are nonreligious people projecting their own worldview on the screen.

However, when compared with earlier results, we see a slight improvement in Hollywood's values. For example, the number of media elite who believe adultery is wrong increased from only 16 percent in 1980 to 49 percent in 1992! That's a sizable increase. Nonetheless, 85 percent of the country believe it to be wrong;

hence, Hollywood is out of step with the rest of the country. Meanwhile, in other areas—particularly religious affiliation (45 percent of the Hollywood elite has no religious affiliation compared to just 4 percent of the American public) or their views on abortion (97 percent favor a woman's right to an abortion versus 59 percent of the general public)—there were no changes from 1980 to 1992. As far as homosexuality, 20 percent of the media elite believe it to be wrong. That's up from 7 percent in 1980. But it's still a far cry from mainstream America, where 76 percent believe it to be wrong. Thus, we see the media getting *slightly* more conservative.[44]

The tragedy of the media's anti-Christian programming is the sheer number of people who are constantly watching TV uncritically—those who live on a steady diet of "prime-time slime." What they think about Christians is shaped by what they're seeing night after night. It's tragic for those led astray. And it's tragic for those who produce this trash, for they will be held accountable one day to Him whom they now ridicule. Thank God for His mercy available to all—even His enemies—if they would but seek it.

Anti-Christian "Stars"

There was a time when it was acceptable for Hollywood stars to at least have a modicum of respect for people of faith, while not necessarily accepting religion's morals and values. Today it's almost chic for Hollywood stars to put down people of faith.

Here is what Roseanne, one of today's most popular TV stars, had to say about pro-lifers, who are mostly Christians:

> You know who else I can't stand is them [sic] people that are anti-abortion. [Expletive deleted] them, I hate them. . . . They're horrible, they're hideous people. They're ugly, old, geeky, hideous men. . . . They just don't want nobody [sic] to have an abortion 'cause they want you to keep spitting out kids so they can [expletive deleted] molest them.[45]

One actress, Amanda Donohoe, was in a TV role where her character spit on a crucifix. She said she enjoyed doing that: "I'm an atheist, so it was actually a joy. Spitting on Christ was a great deal of fun—especially for me, being a woman. . . . I can't embrace a male god who has persecuted female sexuality throughout the ages. And that persecution still goes on today all over the world."[46]

And then there are the stars who are "spiritual" but not "religious." Actress Rosie Perez said, "I'm spiritual. I don't believe in a lot of religions, like Catholicism or anything like that. I think it's a lot of man-made BS. I know who my God is. Me [sic] and him are friends."47

The Denigration of Christian Morality

Not only are the media grossly guilty of ignoring religion or engaging in routine character assassination against Christians, they are also notorious for denigrating Christian morality. With a steady fare of sex and violence, God's commands about adultery and murder are regularly flaunted.

The sexual immorality that is so prevalent is the stock and trade of so much of television today. Don Wildmon reports that 88 percent of sexual activity in prime-time television is between people who are not married, thus making "lust more attractive than love."48 Many of the daily talk shows seem to exalt sexual perversion. For example, one of the guests on a recent daytime talk show was a woman who claimed to have had sex with 250 men in the span of ten hours.49 Unfortunately, there are millions who have a steady diet of watching this garbage.

Much could be said about TV and violence and the disregard for God's commandment against murder. It's tragic that before an American child finishes elementary school, he or she will have seen an average of eight thousand murders and one hundred thousand acts of violence!50

Furthermore, profanity is on the rise. More and more you hear the name of God taken in vain and the name of Jesus Christ dragged through the mud. Barbara Kaye of Southern Illinois University studied two weeks of prime-time programming in 1990 and then two weeks in 1994 (on ABC, CBS, NBC, and Fox). She found that "foul language" increased by 45 percent in that period! Kaye says, "These days, language that was once banned on the airwaves is delivered without much ado."51

"But It Doesn't Affect Anybody"

Sometimes we hear apologists for the media say that the sex, violence, profanity, and anti-Christian propaganda don't affect anyone, that they don't impact behavior. My question is, If that is the case then why did advertisers pay $1.3 million just for a thirty-second spot in Super Bowl XXX? Why do advertisers pay $279,000 to run a thirty-second ad during *Roseanne*?52 If what we see on TV doesn't influence us, then what a waste of money that is! Common sense cries out that the media *do* impact our lives.

The anti-Christian bigotry found on television today, and in movies and in pop culture, is not without its toll. A 1989 Gallup poll showed that 30 percent of Americans would object to having a neighbor who is a fundamentalist, whereas only 5 percent object to a Jewish neighbor.[53]

Granted, some of our own past discretions may add to this statistic, but I think overall it reflects that a steady diet of slurs in the media have had a strong impact. Furthermore, I think Christian fundamentalists (who emphasize a literal interpretation of the Bible) get lumped in with Islamic fundamentalists, who are sometimes terrorists. But that again is wrong. To put Jerry Falwell on the same level as Ayatollah Khomeini is just not accurate; Falwell would *never* advocate violence.

So why does Hollywood continue to say that what they produce doesn't affect anyone—that they're only *reflecting society* and not in any way *accelerating the bad trends* of society? Could it be a defense mechanism on the part of Hollywood to disassociate themselves from the responsibility they bear for the deleterious effects of their programming on society?

Is the Tide Beginning to Turn?

As stated earlier, there have been some slight improvements in the treatment of religion in prime time just recently. Is the hammer of the media (their anti-Christian aspects) about to break? For example, in an article called "What's Right about Television," the Media Research Center wrote: "Those prepared to dismiss prime time television should reconsider. *TV, etc.* found much to cheer about, with several shows aggressively promoting traditional values."[54] Programs they listed as positive about faith or family values included *Touched by an Angel*, *Christy*, *Home Improvement*, *Dr. Quinn, Medicine Woman*, *The Commish*,[55] *Me & the Boys*, and the weekly *ABC Family Movie*.

Furthermore, there is some evidence that more and more people involved in the media are becoming Christians. For example, the producers of the number one show (as of this writing), *Home Improvement*, are Christians. A very entertaining show, *Home Improvement* presents a well-adjusted family that even attends church sometimes. This is a far cry from the trash that Hollywood has been putting out in recent years.

Christy

A great example that the tide may be turning, albeit slowly, is that of Ken Wales's *Christy*. A Hollywood producer, who's also a committed Christian, Ken Wales had the vision for a full-length feature film to be based on Catherine Marshall's best-selling book, *Christy*. Based on a true story, *Christy* is about a young,

Christian teacher in the Appalachian Mountains. As can happen in Hollywood, Ken tried for years to sell his idea to make *Christy*. Finally, in 1994, his vision became a reality—though in a slightly different way than anticipated. Instead of becoming a movie, it was made for television (but it was shot on 35mm film). *Christy* was produced as two made-for-TV movies and a TV series. When it was shown the first time, *Christy* finished number five out of ninety programs for the week.[56] Would that more productions like this come out of Hollywood.

The Media Research Center called *Christy* a "cause for celebration." Kerrie Mahan of the Center writes: "Not only is religion treated respectfully, but characters regularly pray and speak of their commitment to faith."[57] *Focus on the Family* spoke with Ken Wales about *Christy* and wrote about it in a recent issue of its magazine: How did *Christy* ever make it to prime time? Through the perseverance of film producer Ken Wales, who pitched *Christy* for more than fifteen years to anyone who would listen in Hollywood.[58]

Wales believed in the project so much that he "emptied his savings account and refinanced his home to buy the rights"[59] in the mid-1980s when it became available for sale. Sometimes it takes this kind of commitment to turn things around. May God raise up more of the likes of Ken Wales! It would profoundly change what's on in prime time.

Sadly, as of this writing, CBS, which has undergone some changes in management, has canceled *Christy*—which many of us view as unfair. Even *TV Guide* commented: "Actually, it's a marvel that the series was able to establish a loyal core audience at all, considering that since it debuted in April of 1994, its time period has been changed *five* times during its 18-episode run."[60] All in all, *Christy* reflected a most welcome change in prime-time fare.

Conclusion

Even if the tide *doesn't* turn, even if the Christian bashing in prime time gets worse, that still doesn't negate the timeless truth that Christ is building His Church despite the opposition from the forces of Hell. When we take a quick history lesson, as we will in Chapter 11, we can see so clearly how God has turned the tables on His enemies—or better yet, converted them.

We've seen repeatedly in this chapter how God is often openly mocked, from coast to coast and in living color. All of this reminds me of a farmer who lived in New England a few generations ago. He was a complete unbeliever and skeptic. He believed in nothing at all. He mocked his Christian friends, especially in their efforts to try to observe the Sabbath. This skeptic wrote a letter to the editor of his newspaper: "I purchased my seed on the Sabbath. I planted it on the Sabbath.

I harvested it on the Sabbath, and now it is the middle of October and I have the largest harvest in the valley. What do you think of that?"

The editor, apparently a wise and godly man, appended this one simple sentence to the letter. He said: "God does not always settle His accounts in October."

There is a great day coming when all accounts will finally be settled, when Jesus Christ will sit as Judge. I pray many of these producers, actors, writers, and directors will find Christ as their Savior and Lord before they find Him as their Judge.

The Hammer of Movies and Pop Music

Those who hate me without a cause
Are more than the hairs of my head;
They are mighty who would destroy me,
Being my enemies wrongfully;
. . . .
Those who sit in the gate speak against me,
And I am the song of the drunkards.
—Psalm 69:4, 12

In the last century there was an outstanding Hindu Brahman scholar, who was concerned over the progress that Christianity was making among his people in India, and he determined to do all in his power to combat it. After some contemplation, he decided he would study the life of Christ and discover the inconsistencies and the failures and the sins in His life. Then he would write a pamphlet outlining these sins and failures and distribute it widely. This, he felt, would put an end to the spread of Christianity in India. With this purpose in mind, he purchased a New Testament and began to carefully and assiduously peruse its pages searching for some inconsistency, for some blemish in Christ's character, for some fault in His life. He continued this study for eleven long years, and then, finally, he gave up. He could find no weak points, no sins, no stains, no blemishes in the life of Christ. It has been said that Jesus Christ has no strong points in His character—because He has no weak points. He is equally outstanding in every virtue.

Alas, this poor Brahman scholar! He gave up too soon. If only he had waited for Hollywood to come to the rescue! Hollywood has been pouring out for years all sorts of anti-Christian films. With films like Martin Scorsese's *The Last Temptation of Christ*, perhaps the largest hammer Hollywood has produced yet, the Brahman would have seen how simple it is. You can throw away the New Testament and create all the blemishes, spots, sins, and failures purely out of your own imagination. Then you put it on a giant screen (not a pamphlet) and many millions of people will see it and believe it. That's exactly what Hollywood has been doing with one of the most powerful means of communication known to man in some of their anti-Christian movies.

In the last two and a half decades, much of our pop culture—including movies and pop songs—has become a hammer that attempts to tear down Christianity by poking fun at the Church, or worse, making it appear evil. In these movies or songs, Christians have been negatively stereotyped. Christian missions have been presented in a bad light. History has been turned on its head, so that the young person who is fed a steady diet of this stuff hasn't a clue about the positive contributions of Christianity to civilization and society.[1]

In the last chapter, I focused on Christian bashing in the media, primarily television. In this chapter, I want to focus on the hammer of anti-Christian movies, and, to a lesser extent, on the hammer of anti-Christian rock songs. As powerful as these hammers are, they, too, will one day crack. Like the Brahman scholar, anyone who takes the trouble to examine the facts will see that Christianity is true and cannot be easily dismissed by lies and propaganda.

As you'll see in this chapter, there are already some positive changes underfoot in Hollywood. Already some hammers have begun to break. But we still have a long way to go.

"So What Was *The Robe*?"

Time magazine recently asked a provocative question related to movies. To me their question itself underscores how far we've come *away* from faith-honoring films. Dolly Parton, reported *Time*, had recently pitched an idea for a TV program to Hollywood. But it involved showing Christians in a positive light. She was turned down, to which she commented that she wasn't surprised, given the anti-Christian bias in Hollywood today. In commenting on this, *Time* magazine then asked, "So what was *The Robe*?"[2] I would respond: "*The Robe* was a 40-year-old movie! And they usually don't make them like that anymore!" (To those not familiar with it, *The Robe* was a very positive, Christian-oriented movie, starring Richard Burton, about the conversion of one of the Roman soldiers who crucified Christ.)

A Telling Contrast

Too often in movies today we find an antipathy against Christianity—not "religion" in general, but Christianity. Note, for example, the contrast between how Disney dealt with two movies with offensive elements. Miramax, a subsidiary of Disney, released an anti-Catholic film, *Priest*, just a few days after Easter 1995. (Originally, they were going to release it on Good Friday!) The film portrayed "a troubled gay priest, a self-satisfied heterosexual priest openly living with his housekeeper, an alcoholic priest, a spiteful bishop and a teen-age girl abused by her Catholic father—all warped by the doctrines to which they adhere."[3] Fortunately, the movie sunk without a ripple—another broken hammer falls to the earth. Nonetheless, contrast Disney's behavior with *Priest* to how they dealt with *Aladdin*. When Disney released the popular full-length cartoon, there was a song in the beginning that some Arabs (who are mostly Muslims) complained about. So Disney had the song excised from the video release of *Aladdin*, rather than offend these people. And yet here they mock the faith of millions of Catholic Christians in a full-length film without batting an eyelash!

It's amazing to me how Hollywood will show itself sensitive to all kinds of different groups—except Christians. Catholics and fundamentalists get the worst of it. For Native Americans, homosexuals, Arabs, Asian Americans—whatever the group—Hollywood often bends over backward to avoid offending them; yet in just about every Hollywood movie the name of the Christian God is taken in vain, even in good films that are devoid of other offenses. There seems to be no greater punching bag in our pop culture today than Christianity.

But the gates of Hell shall not prevail! Nothing can stop, or even slow down, the amazing growth of the Church!

Remember the Golden Era of Hollywood

Movies that directly blaspheme Christ or that show Christians as psychotic killers virtually did not exist thirty years ago in this country. Our culture was much more sympathetic to Christians or clergy during the Golden Era of Hollywood. Some of the best movies ever made were inspirational in nature. A few movies that come to mind are *It's a Wonderful Life* (the 1946 Christmas classic), the 1954 Academy Award's movie of the year, *On the Waterfront* (in which Karl Malden played a rough, but respectable, Catholic priest who helped the protagonist, Marlin Brando, to do the Christian thing in key scenes), the 1959 movie of the year, *Ben-Hur* (which clearly glorified Jesus Christ), and the 1965 movie of the year, *The Sound of Music*. Next came the 1966 movie of the year, *The Man for All Seasons*, where Sir Thomas More unwaveringly stood by his Christian convictions, despite the threat of death. But as the rebellion and counterculture of the 1960s began to rise, religion was denigrated along with other forms of authority.

A Sampling of Hollywood's Christian Bashing

Consider these major motion pictures released in the last few years:

At Play in the Fields of the Lord (1991). This $30-million escapade viciously depicted Christian missionaries in South America as exploitative and evil. Film critic Michael Medved called this "the most ambitious all-out attack Hollywood has ever launched on organized religion." The native religions of the region were treated with much greater regard than the Christian faith, which was constantly downgraded. At one point, the movie likened Jesus to "Kisu," "a local god of demonic force." One of the characters, a mercenary gone native, asked a missionary: "Jesus, Kisu, what's the difference. . . . It's all hocus-pocus anyway, isn't it Martin?"[4] There's a *big* difference. For starters, cannibalism and human sacrifice were widespread throughout South America precisely because of deities like Kisu, until the gospel of Christ came.[5]

The Handmaid's Tale (1990). With major stars, such as Robert Duvall and Faye Dunaway, this film presented a nightmare vision of what would happen if Christian fundamentalists took over the country. This work of fiction showed Christians as "considerably less lovable than Nazis."[6] Women became slaves (although in truth Christianity has elevated the status of women worldwide). Books were burned. Public executions were revived. Margaret Atwood, the writer of the novel on which the film was based, said this work of fiction was about "how religious fanatics would run the world if they got their druthers."[7]

Cape Fear (1991). This remake of a classic thriller had a dangerous maniac on the loose as a Scripture-quoting Pentecostal, played by Robert De Niro. Scripture and a big cross were tattooed on his body. He raped and terrorized people. He even bit out part of a cheek of his rape victim. Do you know anyone like this? Do you know anyone who is led to this kind of behavior because of their memorizing of Bible verses? This movie is Scorsese's revenge on Christians for protesting his 1988 film, *The Last Temptation of Christ*, according to Michael Medved.[8]

None of these were "B" movies. These were not filmed in out-of-the-way lots with a cast of unknown names, released independently to small distributors.

These are *major* motion-picture releases with big budgets. But they didn't necessarily do well in the box office, with the exception of *Cape Fear*.

I submit to you that *Cape Fear* was a success because of its ability to thrill, not because of its anti-Christian propaganda. As we'll see in a moment, the films that are one-dimensional, anti-Christian mouthpieces for the writer, director, or producer with an anti-Christian ax to grind are virtually always flops. They are broken hammers that litter the ground at the foot of God's anvil.

In addition to such films where the *central* plot is anti-Christian are the numerous films in which Christian bashing is a subplot. This can be seen in such movies as *The Quick and the Dead* (1995), in which the preacher's faith and his God were shown to be irrelevant;[9] *Alien 3* (1992) in which born-again Christians in a future world were rampant rapists and violent criminals; *Star Trek V: The Final Frontier* (1989), which presented God as an evil being and showed that all religion is man-made and will be obsolete in the future;[10] or *Johnny Mnemonic* (1995), which I think should be called *Johnny Demonic* because the evil character was a street preacher who used a crucifix to stab people to death.

Does anybody get tired of this stuff? I sure do. In fact, that's why I rarely even go to the movies. I'm much more cautious about plopping down six to eight dollars for a movie ticket without doing some research. I highly recommend Ted Baehr's *Movieguide*.[11] It gives a biblical perspective on the current movies. Armed with this kind of information, you can save many a dollar and many an evening.

The Most Watched Film in History

As bad as Hollywood's Christian bashing is, there's some great news that may have escaped you. Question: What is *the* most watched film in the history of the medium? *E. T.*? That's way up there with 296 million viewers (with viewers of the video factored in). Is it *Gone with the Wind* (with 281 million viewers)? How about *Star Wars* (with nearly 252 million total viewers)? Or *Jaws* (with 235 million viewers)?[12] No, it's none of these.

In the history of the motion picture the most watched movie (not the most commercially successful, but the one film viewed by more people than any other film) is *Jesus*, which is based on the Gospel of Luke. The most realistic film made on the life of Christ, this movie was released in the theaters in the late 1970s and has been shown by missionaries in remote parts of the globe with mobile projectors. More than 460 million people worldwide have now seen this film, making *Jesus* the most watched movie in history! It has broken another record as well: "*Jesus* has become the most widely translated film in history. It is currently available in more than 200 languages. The producers claim that it has been seen by more than 460 million people and that *'more than 32 million have indicated a decision to place their faith in Christ.'"*[13]

I praise God for those Christian missionaries and nationals projecting *Jesus* in villages, in auditoriums, in open-air settings—wherever they get the opportunity. Even with many movies today tearing down Christianity, it's fascinating to see God using the *very same medium* to draw millions to Himself! The gates of Hell shall not prevail against Christ's kingdom!

Hollywood, an Equal Opportunity Basher of Christianity

Would that more American moviegoers saw the likes of *Jesus*. Unfortunately, that is not the case.

Michael Medved—the film critic who cohosts *Sneak Previews* on PBS—is, in my opinion, the finest film critic in America today. He is an Orthodox Jew, and his movie critiques come from an overall Judeo-Christian point of view. I highly commend him and his book *Hollywood vs. America* and his video *Hollywood vs. Religion*, in which he documents one case after another of Christian bashing in the movies. He pointed out, for instance, that in the old films, during Hollywood's Golden Era, "if a character appeared on screen wearing a clerical collar it served as a sure sign that the audience was supposed to like him." Not so today! Today, virtually the opposite is the case. Medved listed a number of films that engaged in "kicking the Catholics," or "bashing the born-agains," or "jabbing the Jews" (although they only get a small fraction of the terrible treatment that Christians get). One of the lines in the inane and anti-Catholic *Nuns on the Run* (1990) summed up what would seem to be the heartfelt feeling of many Hollywood filmmakers: "It's not supposed to make sense! It's religion!"[14]

Hollywood appears to be an equal opportunity basher when it comes to Christians of different stripes. The anti-Catholic movies like to show a perverted hierarchy that is seemingly corrupt from top to bottom. This can be seen in films such as *Monsignor*, *Agnes of God*, *Heaven Help Us*, and *The Pope Must Die*.

Born-again Christians suffer equally at the hands of the Hollywood filmmakers. A recurring character seems to be the sweaty, smarmy, Bible-toting, Bible-quoting, *violent* fanatic. Frankly, I hope you've never heard of these titles that Medved describes: *Crimes of Passion* (1984); *Children of the Corn* (1984); *Poltergeist II* (1986) (I've heard of the first one, but not this sequel); *The Vision* (1987); *Light of Day* (1987); *Salvation!* (1987); *Pass the Ammo* (1988); *The Rapture* (1991);[15] *Guilty as Charged* (1992). These are all films in which the major character, the major theme, or the major plot held evangelical Christianity up to ridicule, or worse, made it appear sinister, evil, and dangerous. Not included in this list are several other films in which the anti-Christian theme was more of a subplot, for example, the remake of *The Blob* (1988), or *Footloose* (1984).

Some of today's anti-Christian films literally feature evil characters who actually kill *because* they are born-again Christians, such as *Guilty as Charged*, *The Handmaid's Tale*, or *The Rapture*. How perverted and how twisted could Hollywood get? Today, Hollywood often glamorizes the bad guy—the moral reprobate—and demonizes the good guy—the Christian. This reminds me of what Isaiah once said: "Woe to those who call evil good, and good evil" (Isa. 5:20a). Unfortunately, much of Hollywood's output violates that biblical principle.

Follow the Money?

But some will say that the bottom line for Hollywood is the bottom line. They make these movies because they make money. Right? Wrong! Medved has exposed the lie to that argument.

On the one hand, a number of studios produced small pictures that placed Christians in a favorable light, but interestingly, they were always set in either faraway locales, like Australia in *A Cry in the Dark* (1988), or long-ago eras, like *Chariots of Fire* (1981). Nevertheless, they did portray Christians positively. Every one of those films made money. On the other hand, many major releases that have been antireligious have lost a lot of money at the box office.

Medved says that the bottom line is not money but some sort of demonic power within these people that causes them to lash out against Jesus Christ and against Christians in spite of the fact that it is going to cost them tens of millions of dollars to do it. They must let out their venom. Medved observed that, "it is clear that a powerful prejudice is at work."[16] He wrote,

> If a formula is frequently successful, it's easy to understand why producers keep repeating it and reworking it in the hopes of further profit, but it's difficult to explain why the industry should continue to favor and finance the same anticlerical characterizations and messages that have failed in the past with such stunning predictability. *Taken together, the cinematic assaults on religion have lost hundreds of millions for the people who made them, but the major studios (as well as the independent production companies) persist in throwing good money after bad.*[17]

Medved estimates that the combined total of money spent on antireligious movies is up to one billion dollars.[18]

The Last Temptation of Christ is estimated to have lost ten million dollars. The crack you hear is a large sledgehammer breaking on God's anvil! This 1988 film by Martin Scorsese is the worst case of anti-Christian bigotry at the box office. It is the climax, or the nadir, of our culture's Christian bashing. It is perhaps the most blatant, vicious attack on Christ in America ever—or yet. Because of that fact and because it was released by a major studio, MCA's Universal, it reveals so much about Hollywood and its view of religion. Here the impeccable character of the only perfect human being who ever lived is viciously attacked.

Films like *The Last Temptation of Christ* are nothing else but a return to paganism. In the early centuries the pagans used their art forms to mock Christ. I clearly remember in one of my history books, seeing some Greek Christian on his knees worshiping his savior and god. It was drawn by a pagan, and it showed a man crucified on a cross and the title said so-and-so "is worshiping his god," and this man on the cross had the head of an ass—but even that is not as bad as a Jesus who is filled with the devil, as *The Last Temptation of Christ* depicts Jesus. But this film, which one critic said should have only been shown in the art theaters, was far from a commercial success.

Not Censorship, But Self-Censorship

Some have accused me and other vocal critics of censorship. Not so. I have never called for censorship, but I have said this: There is constantly, with all of us, a self-censorship that takes place. In a civilized democracy there must be constant self-censorship, or else the very fabric of society breaks down and chaos and violence result. You do not say every bad thing you think of to everybody and about everybody all of the time. That's self-censorship, and it is the foundation of decency and pluralism.

Pat Buchanan, in a column entitled "Hollywood's War on Christianity," talked about Jack Valenti, president of the Motion Picture Association. At the time of the release of *The Last Temptation of Christ*, Mr. Valenti defended the film with glowing words of patriotism, as if one were supporting the First Amendment and upholding America by going to see this film! Buchanan wrote,

> But the issue is not whether *Last Temptation can* be shown; but whether such a film *should* be shown. . . . We live in an age where the ridicule of blacks is forbidden, where anti-Semitism is punishable by political

death, but where Christian bashing is a popular indoor sport; and films mocking Jesus Christ are considered avant-garde. . . .

"Sensitivity" is supposed to have become the mark of the man of decency in modern American life, so we are told. A "sensitive man" does not repeat ethnic jokes; he does not abide insults to any minority; he monitors his rhetoric, lest he inadvertently give offense. James Watt and Earl Butz were driven from Cabinet seats for violating that taboo. Jimmy the Greek was fired by CBS for showing "insensitivity" in his postprandial musings about the natural superiority of black athletes.[19]

Don Feder—who, as I pointed out earlier, is not a Christian, but is upset at Christian bashing—said this in response to *The Last Temptation of Christ:* "Christians are the only group Hollywood can offend with impunity, the only creed it actually goes out of its way to insult. Clerics, from fundamentalist preachers to Catholic monks, are routinely represented as hypocrites, hucksters, sadists, and lechers. The tenets of Christianity are held up to ridicule."[20]

But What About "Artistic Integrity"?

The film producers said that artistic integrity demanded that they produce *The Last Temptation of Christ.* Does their artistic integrity demand that they produce a defaming film about Malcolm X? Where is their integrity then? Does their artistic integrity demand that they produce a defaming film about Muhammad? Salman Rushdie wrote a book about Muhammad; Rushdie hasn't been heard from for a long time. He was last seen going down a rabbit hole somewhere, trembling. Even if the death sentence against him is officially removed, one can't help but feel that he'll spend the rest of his life looking over his shoulder.

Lloyd Billingsley, author of the helpful book *The Seductive Image: A Christian Critique of the World of Film,* said with tongue in cheek that Hollywood abides by "the constitutional principle of separation of church and screen." Billingsley observed,

One can't imagine a Hollywood film whose entire purpose was to ridicule, say, homosexual activists, feminists, animal rights crusaders, or environmentalists. That would be blasphemy. Hollywood understands that religious people, particularly Christians, are the last group in America besides businessmen who may be defamed with impunity.[21]

Christian Morality Mocked

In addition to the direct denigration of Christianity, Christian morality is constantly violated. Sin is often celebrated rather than condemned. God's word is turned upside down in many Hollywood films. I'm not condemning everything Hollywood makes; there are some good films out there. A cynic could criticize just about everything if he wanted. Someone facetiously pointed out that even the symphony orchestra could be rated R—too much "sax and violins"! Humor aside, the hedonistic lifestyle of many in Hollywood is all too often reflected in their work. You wouldn't even know there was a God and that He has given us rules for *our* happiness, safety, and well-being. Consequently, so many films revel in gratuitous sex and violence.

God's Name Taken in Vain

A more subtle form of Christian bashing is the constant drip drip drip of profanity in the movies. The holy name of God and His Son, Jesus Christ, are *regularly* taken in vain. In fact, in most films—even family films that are overall delightful, such as *Rookie of the Year* or *Beethoven's 2nd*—you find God's name taken in vain. It's taken in vain so often that a regular moviegoer becomes virtually numb to it!

Surely a good actor could communicate his intentions without resorting to profanity. In the Golden Age of Hollywood, they did all the time. And I believe the movies were of a higher quality back then, without all the blasphemy.

In the Scriptures the name of God is tantamount to the person of God; to pray in the name of Christ is to pray in Christ, as one who by faith is connected to Him. So, to call upon the name of God is to call upon God the Almighty Himself. To take God's name in vain is to take God Himself in vain. The Bible says that God will not hold him guiltless that takes His name in vain (Ex. 20:7). Many Hollywood writers, directors, and stars will be in shock on Judgment Day when they are held accountable for all their profanity (and other immoral content as well).

The Old Testament Hebrews took this matter very, very seriously. They were so afraid of taking the divine name, at least the name "Jehovah," in vain, that they took it not at all. It was never pronounced among them, except by one person on one day, and that was by the High Priest on the great high Day of Atonement.

How far we have fallen. The name of God and the name of Christ are constantly taken in blasphemy, used as curse words in motion pictures, television, books, and magazines, until there is a veritable avalanche of blasphemy, a flood of filth, covering our land. And *millions* of Americans are numb to it. It doesn't even affect them when they hear God's holy name taken in vain. I remember being in a restaurant one time and noticing at a table some distance away a family listening to a five-year-old boy taking God's name in vain over and over again. Each time he did it, they laughed. Well, why not? It's done all the time, thanks in large measure to Hollywood and the media.

It's interesting to note that, apart from sex scenes, when an actor portrays any sin but this one, he violates God's law only theoretically. If, for example, he plays the part of a thief, he's only pretending to steal. But if he takes God's name in vain, he's directly violating God's law just by saying his lines.

There are even major motion pictures wherein characters insert curse words in between the names "Jesus" and "Christ," such as Oliver Stone's *Platoon* (1986 movie of the year). How deep-seated is Hollywood's antipathy toward Christ and Christians!

The Beginning of a Revival in Hollywood?

Despite all of the above, some of these negative trends may be beginning to change. Some of Hollywood's broken hammers litter the base of God's anvil; however, it still may take a while to see the full effects of these changes. In the opinion of Ted Baehr, president of The Christian Film and Television Commission and the publisher of the biweekly *Movieguide*, there are signs that a revival may be under way in Hollywood![22] He said the number of ministries and support groups for Christians in Hollywood has blossomed recently, from about one or two, two decades ago, to about sixteen or seventeen today! Campus Crusade has a ministry in Hollywood. Hollywood Presbyterian Church, whose former pastor Lloyd Ogilvie is now chaplain to the Senate, has a ministry in Hollywood. The Church on the Way, which is pastored by Jack Hayford, has a significant ministry in the nation's movie capital. Ted Baehr has been ministering in Hollywood for years, as has my friend Larry Poland. And they are all beginning to see results.

U.S. News & World Report wrote about this change in Hollywood in a recent issue in an article entitled, "Hollywood: Right Face." The subtitle reveals a lot about what may be fueling this change: "Under Siege, Filmmakers and TV Bosses Become More Family Friendly." The article quotes Michael Medved as saying, "It's really extraordinary how fast the change has come about." The article cites a recent survey that shows an improvement in filmmakers' views on religion. Says *U.S. News & World Report*: "In the Hollywood elite poll, 72 percent of respondents said they believe in God and almost a third said religion had become important in their life in the past decade. However, 56 percent said they had little or no faith in organized religion."[23]

Ted Baehr is also quoted in the *U.S. News & World Report* article: "I'm happy to report that 1994 was an extraordinary breakthrough for the good, the true and the beautiful in popular entertainment."[24] He told us in a recent conversation that there are now many active Christians in different branches in Hollywood, including television and animation. Baehr said that of about forty to fifty top producers of Hollywood's prime-time shows, twenty-one of them now are Christians, such as Michael Warren, coproducer of *Family Matters*.

These facts are good indicators of what could be the winds of change in Hollywood. Evangelizing Hollywood's movers and shakers has been paying off. Some more hammers against the cause of Christ fall to the ground.

For instance, Baehr said that Christian bashing in the movies has *decreased*, not increased, in the last few years. For example, he said that in 1988, the year of *The Last Temptation of Christ*, there were ninety films with negative Christian references. In 1994 there were about six to seven such films! He said that in 1985 there were two family films; in 1994 there were seventy-five family films! He said that in some recent movies, including *Corrina, Corrina* and *The Santa Clause*, unbelievers of sorts—not Christians—were the bad guys or the ones in need of change; we could add *Forrest Gump* to that list as well.

Michael Medved concurs that there is a change underfoot in Hollywood. "Religion took over the devil's playground," said Medved at a conference of the Religious Public Relations Council in the spring of 1995. He said that "Religious values are making a difference in the values expressed in movies and television."[25] But this, encouraging as it is, does not mean that Hollywood is finished with its Christian bashing. Within a couple of weeks of Medved's statements, Disney—*Disney!*—released the sacrilegious movie *Priest*.

Blasphemy in Song

Meanwhile, on another front of our pop culture, namely rock music, we see perhaps even greater blasphemy against Jesus Christ. The hammers of rock and roll (and again, I only refer to the anti-Christian aspects) slander Christ, and thus they set themselves up for a big fall. These rockers haven't yet realized the truth that Christ will one day vanquish His foes, regardless of how silly their songs or sacrilegious their lyrics.

Hollywood has paved the way, so now it's open season on Christianity in the pop culture. Anti-Christian diatribes and stereotypes are found throughout one of the most popular forms of music in recorded history, rock and roll. While country music often promotes an immoral lifestyle, it virtually never makes direct attacks on Christianity. Not so with rock.

The tragedy of rock and roll is that it is immensely popular and that much of it—the lyrics, the performers, and the videos—is directly anti-Christian. Not all, but much of it. Interestingly, talented Christian artists are using the medium, tainted as it is, in their attempt to advance the Christian message. People have been brought into the kingdom of God through their efforts.

It isn't rock music per se that I want to address here; it's the anti-Christian aspect of so much of it. The assault on Christian morality is bad enough, but to be found in much of rock are *direct* attacks on Christ and the Church. If you were to watch MTV for a few hours straight—as your children possibly do—you would likely see caricatures of Christian ministers and priests, who are irrelevant at best or menacing at worst. You would see upside-down crosses and other occult symbols. You would hear the Word of God directly mocked. You would see many church buildings broken down and in decay—implying that the Church is irrelevant today. You would see blasphemous references to the crucifixion of Christ. You might see Madonna profanely mixing sex and religion. The tragedy is that MTV has *millions* of viewers and high ratings.

Millions of young people today exist on a steady diet of this kind of fare. They are exposed to no religious doctrine, no religious values. In fact, if they have any exposure to Christianity, it's almost always distorted. And then, as a society, we suppose they are just going to pick up values on their own!

Rock and roll has had a powerful anti-Christian subtheme for decades now. Madonna, whose very *name* is of Christian derivation, seems to enjoy mocking Christianity, Catholicism in particular. She seems able to combine sex and religion simultaneously. For example, in her music video "Like a Prayer," she dances around in a sensual way with a low-cut dress while leading a church choir. She once told *Spin* magazine: "Crucifixes are sexy because there is a naked man on them."[26] It's open season on Christianity in our pop culture today!

Big Business

Rock music is big business. Successful rock musicians are among the world's wealthiest people. Last year, the Associated Press reports, the Rolling Stones' "Voodoo Lounge" tour took in $121 million.[27] The third-biggest rock tour in 1994 was the Eagles, a group who has some occult (therefore, anti-Christian) songs. One of their most popular albums, *Hotel California*, is all about the Church of Satan (although many listeners might not readily pick that up). Unlike the movies, the anti-Christian diatribes don't seem to hurt rock musicians. Ticket sales alone for major rock tours in 1994 brought in $1.4 billion.[28] This reminds me of what one owner of a franchise of nude-dancing bars once said: "The wages of sin is quite good these days, thank you." In the big picture, he's as wrong as Lucifer was.

Sympathy for the Devil

One of the classic songs from the Rolling Stones was "Sympathy for the Devil." This was one of their all-time major hits. Mick Jagger sings the line, "I was around when Jesus Christ had His moment of doubt and pain, made [expletive deleted] sure that Pilate washed his hands and sealed His fate." This song takes Lucifer's side in the age-old conflict between God and the devil!

But, Mick, do you not know? Have you not heard? That conflict has *already* been settled; God has won. He defeated Satan when Jesus hung on the cross. It's only a matter of time before the effects of that victory are felt completely. C. S. Lewis put it very well in his classic, *Mere Christianity*:

> This universe is at war . . . it is a civil war, a rebellion . . . we are living in a part of the universe occupied by the rebel.

> Enemy-occupied territory—that is what this world is. Christianity is the story of how the rightful king has landed, you might say landed in disguise, and is calling us all to take part in a great campaign of sabotage. When you go to church you are really listening-in to the secret wireless [radio] from our friends: that is why the enemy is so anxious to prevent us from going. He does it by playing on our conceit and laziness and intellectual snobbery.[29]

Mockery of Christ

Just about everything about Jesus' life is held up to mockery from some quarters of rock music. Eric Holmberg, who directs Real-to-Reel Ministries, has put together an excellent (but disturbing) video on the dark side of this genre of music entitled *Hell's Bells, the Dangers of Rock 'n Roll*. Holmberg stated, "Jesus has become the focus of more ridicule in rock music than any other personality. Virtually every facet of His life and ministry is mocked and criticized."[30] Holmberg's video is cautiously recommended for those churches who want to see what young people are being exposed to today. I say "cautiously" because it is so graphic and much of it is so depressing. (If you're not familiar with much of the hard-core rock music of today, you're in for an unpleasant shock.) Holmberg's video was helpful for this portion of the chapter.

There is probably no single event in history that gets more perverted, distorted attention from rock and rollers than the crucifixion of Christ. It is repeatedly depicted in some blasphemous way on album covers and in songs; the crown of thorns is often seen on rock album jackets in some way that ridicules Christ—sometimes in ways with sexual overtones.

Holmberg points out that the cross is the most popular jewelry of the rock stars, most of whom stand against all it means. He says: "How Satan must enjoy the irony. This type of desecration is virtually rampant in rock. With crosses the most popular jewelry choice of the stars, it seems as though the more perverted the artist, the larger, the more numerous or the more obsessive is their focus on the cross." Eric adds, "Crosses show up so often you would think that rock music was a Christian industry—until one looks at their intent, message, and lifestyle."[31]

Blasphemy from Famous and Obscure Groups

The anti-Christian bigotry is found in both popular and well-known acts and among more obscure groups. Sometimes among the lesser known groups, we find even more pronounced anti-Christian diatribes. There was a group named "Ludichrist." The name of the last album of the rock group, The Dead Kennedys (how's that for good taste?) was *Frankenchrist*—equating Jesus to a monster!

In Psalm 69, David said, writing prophetically of the Son of David, the Messiah, "I am the song of drunkards." How true that was of Jesus, who was mocked without cause; He was the song of drunkards. It is still true. Ironically, another of these anti-Christian groups, Ministry, has an album named *Psalm 69*! Mercifully, the "music," if you could call it that, is so overpowering that it is difficult for the average hearer to decipher the lyrics. The album features mocking songs, such as "Jesus Built My Hot Rod." Another of their albums refers to a practice that Christianity has managed to stop the world over—cannibalism: "A Mind Is a Terrible Thing to Taste."

A very popular group today, Nine Inch Nails, has a sacrilegious song, "Heresy," on its album *The Downward Spiral*. The whole song is a terrible railing against Jesus Christ, accusing Him of shutting His eyes to the world. Imagine that, Jesus, who left His glory in Heaven and entered our world of suffering and shame caused by our sin in order to bring us salvation, accused of "sew[ing] his eyes shut because he is afraid to see." The refrain of the song declares, "your god is dead and no one cares." Not quite.

A Vision of a False Christ

These rock and rollers have a vision of a false Christ. They see someone pasty and mild who wouldn't hurt a fly. They don't see the Christ of the Bible who will either convert His enemies or one day vanquish them. We have to see Christ as who He is—Christ the Victorious!

Once we have caught the vision of the victorious Christ, we will not allow the garbage of the world that fills the movie screens or airwaves to get us bent out of shape. For God has designed all history so that Jesus Christ will have supremacy. No power in Heaven or earth can hinder God's plan. Christ, in His resurrection, has conquered, and He sits at God the Father's right hand while His enemies are made His footstool (Pss. 2; 110:1–2). Strum away, oh ye of no faith; your songs are but the fading echoes of Satan's dying gasps. Christianity will triumph, for Christ is victorious. Your hammers will all be broken into bits.

What Famous Believers Have Said about Jesus

We have looked at what some of our modern, trashy troubadours have had to say about Jesus. In contrast to all these negative instances of mocking Christ, there is a wealth of positive statements about Him, both from believers and skeptics alike. Now let us notice what Christian luminaries throughout the ages have declared:

- Shakespeare: "Jesus Christ, my Saviour."[32]

- Blaise Pascal: "Jesus Christ is the center of all, and the goal to which all tends."[33]

- Daniel Webster, the great statesman: "If I might comprehend Jesus Christ, I could not believe on Him. He would be no greater than myself. Such is my consciousness of sin and inability that I must have a superhuman Saviour."[34]

- Phillips Brooks (composer of the Christmas carol "Oh Little Town of Bethlehem"): "Jesus Christ, the condescension of divinity and the exaltation of humanity."[35]

Skeptics Testify of His Greatness

Not only believers but even skeptics have testified to Jesus' greatness:

- Ernest Renan, the greatest of the French critics who was himself an infidel and spent most of his life attacking Christianity, in his mature years wrote: "Whatever may be the surprises of the future, Jesus will never be surpassed."[36]

- William Lecky of Dublin, the historian of rationalism, said Christ has exerted "so deep an influence that it may be truly said that the simple record of three short years of active life has done more to regenerate and soften mankind than all of the disquisitions of philosophers, and all the exhortations of moralists."[37]

- Lord Byron, profligate poet as he was, affirmed: "If ever man was God, or God man, Jesus Christ was both."[38]

- Napoleon said: "I know men, and I tell you, Jesus is not a man. Superficial minds see a resemblance between Christ and the founders of empires and the gods of other religions. That resemblance does not exist. . . . There is between Christianity and whatever other religions the distance of infinity."[39]

Conclusion

The hammers of today's pop culture, as seen in the movies or heard in the rock songs, may well continue with their assault on Christianity. It won't change Christ's status one iota. But it will continue to have a detrimental effect in the hearts and minds of many young people. It would be great if there were a true revival in Hollywood, as Ted Baehr believes, and in the music industry as well. But even if the Christian bashing were to get worse in our pop culture, that would not in any way nullify Jesus' promise that the gates of Hell shall not prevail.

Years ago, John Lennon of the immensely popular Beatles said at the height of their popularity: "Christianity will go. It will vanish and shrink. I needn't argue about that, I'm right, and I will be proved right. We're more popular than Jesus."[40] Well, at last count, the Beatles have disbanded, Lennon is dead, and Christianity is growing by leaps and bounds. Another broken hammer falls to the earth. Indeed, the gates of Hell shall not prevail!

The Hammer of Hostility in the Public Arena

*Light has come into the world, and men loved darkness
rather than light, because their deeds were evil.*
—John 3:19b

t was pure pandemonium as the crowds were going berserk. They
smashed their way into the main cathedral in town and desecrated
it, even placing a scantily clad actress, whom they entitled "Reason," atop the altar.[1] The leaders closed all the churches in town.
Next, in direct defiance of Christianity, they dropped the Gregorian
calendar and created a new system of counting the years (not based
on B.C. or A.D.), that counted "year one" with the beginning of their
movement. Furthermore, they confiscated all of the lands of the
Church and beheaded many of its leaders. Thus, the leaders of the
revolutionaries tried to dethrone Christ in their country.

Then, within a few years, one revolutionary leader after another
killed one revolutionary leader after another. Chaos reigned, and the
streets ran with blood. Only a dictator could restore order.

Do you recognize this true story? It's the French Revolution,[2] and
the cathedral was Notre Dame. While the revolutionaries rightfully
complained about the lack of justice and the Church's disregard for
the lowly and poor, they went overboard by taking the law into their
own hands and by their great hostility toward things Christian. Napoleon restored order, including the cathedral and the calendar, via

dictatorship (anarchy leads to tyranny). Thus, another hammer trying to smash against the kingdom of Christ fell broken to the ground.

In our day, it seems, there are many in the same spirit as the French revolutionaries. But they, too, will find their hammers of opposition to Christ's kingdom smashed on the anvil of God.

The hammers of the present-day attack on Christ in America may well be a far cry from the anti-Christian hammer of the French Revolution. Nonetheless, in more subtle ways, they continually try to pound away against any vestige of Christianity left in our public life, schools, and culture. Consider the following:

- *Orange County (Orlando), Florida.* A fourth-grader brought his Bible with him to school one day to read during free time. His teacher took it away and scolded him, telling him to never bring it back. As part of his punishment, he was forced to "sit in a corner facing the wall!"[3] Later, he was interrogated by the principal and detained in her office all day for this ominous violation of "church and state."

- *San Jose, California.* City officials built a statue of the Aztec god Quetzalcoatl, costing taxpayers half a million dollars. The mayor said the Aztec religion possessed "those elements that seek to elevate the human consciousness to a higher plane."[4] The irony is that the Aztec religion routinely engaged in *human sacrifice*! Here is a statue built to honor the god of human sacrifice—the worship of whom cost the lives of hundreds of thousands of human beings. Yet the same city ruled that there is no room for a manger with baby Jesus in it. Jesus, whose teachings and followers have banished human sacrifice from every corner of this world, is out. A god demanding human sacrifice is in!

- *Chicago, Illinois.* The city, over a period of four years, shut down about thirty South Side storefront churches, and it denied building permits to more than a dozen other churches by stringent zoning restrictions that effectively stopped those congregations from being able to practice their faith. This sparked a class-action lawsuit by some forty members of the clergy against the city for denying them their religious freedom.[5]

On and on pound the hammers of hostility against Christ in the public arena. These officials are not acting constitutionally.[6] And, as you can see in the Appendix, there are numerous legal resources available today to fight this anti-Christian bigotry.

A few years ago *Time* magazine reported on the absurdity of our present position: "In this nation of spiritual paradoxes, it is legal to hang a picture in a public exhibit of a crucifix submerged in urine, or to utter virtually any conceivable blasphemy in a public place; it is not legal, the federal courts have ruled, to mention God reverently in a classroom, on a football field or at a commencement ceremony as part of a public prayer."[7]

While seemingly every idea under the sun is allowed to flourish in the public arena in America, historic Christianity is now often forbidden from the marketplace of ideas. Lawsuits fly to remove any vestige of Christianity left in the public square. As of this writing, Judge Roy S. Moore, a state judge in Gadsden, Alabama, a hero in my book, is being sued by the ACLU. Why? A hand-carved copy of the Ten Commandments adorns his courtroom wall, and he continues the tradition of allowing a guest clergyman to pray at the opening of the general sessions (which takes place, at the most, once a month), a tradition that Alabama has had at least since the turn of the century. Historically, the Ten Commandments have been the basis of our laws, and it was not until recent years that the public display of them caused anybody to throw a fit.

Judge Moore refuses to be intimidated and will fight this thing all the way to the Supreme Court if necessary. His main point in not backing down is that an acknowledgment of God is not the same thing as the establishment of religion (which the First Amendment prohibits). He points out that the founders of this country didn't think so, as is evident in their writings and actions. Furthermore, he observes that even the Supreme Court building contains some carvings that show Moses and the Ten Commandments, such as the sculpture work on the outside, east wall near the roof, where Moses holding the Ten Commandments is the central figure.

Rush Limbaugh, who to my knowledge has never professed to be an evangelical Christian, has correctly perceived the attack on Christianity in America. He said recently on his television program, "There is an all-out assault now on the Christian community in this country."[8] In his best-selling book, *The Way Things Ought to Be*, Limbaugh wrote,

- Surveys show that Americans are the most religious people of any advanced nation. . . . But our intellectual and political elites are often hostile or ambivalent toward religion.

- Religious displays have been banned from public buildings during holiday seasons unless they contain enough secular images such as Frosty the Snowman to satisfy the ACLU-lulus.[9]

Secularism in the Name of Pluralism

In the name of *pluralism*, a hostile *secularism* attacks the expression of Christian ideas or beliefs in public. The philosophy of secularism has made it so that the

Constitutional ideal of freedom *of* religion has now become freedom *from* religion. As Nathan A. Forrester of the Beckett Fund for Religious Liberty put it, "The perception now is that the Constitution requires that we purge all religion from the public square."[10]

It is interesting now that a guilt trip is being laid on the moral and the religious. Bring out a Bible and they say, "Naughty, naughty!" The kind of attitude that used to be reserved for those who might come out with a dirty magazine is now being reserved for those that would read the Scriptures or say something positive about God.

How Far Does This Go?

How far has the fear of Christianity gone? During President Clinton's inauguration there were even some cultural elites and a media commentator questioning whether it was appropriate that Hillary Rodham Clinton was wearing a cross around her neck![11] At last check, Hillary was not a friend of religious conservatives.

Jesse Jackson recently likened the Christian Coalition to the Nazis. Rod Dreher of the *Washington Times* wrote, "In an interview with the *Chicago Sun-Times*, Mr. Jackson said Nazis, slave owners in the Old South and segregationists who opposed Martin Luther King were the Christian Coalition of their day." Fortunately, the credibility of such criticisms seems to lessen with the passing of each new day. Even fellow liberals disagree with Jackson about this. Abraham Foxman—executive director of the Anti-Defamation League of B'nai B'rith, whose organization came out with a report that was critical of the Coalition—said that Jackson's remarks were out of line.[12]

Tax-Funded Blasphemy

It's well known that you and I have been funding anti-Christian art for the last few years through the National Endowment for the Arts. Some of these "works of art" have been directly blasphemous against Jesus of Nazareth—such as the bust of Christ as a transvestite, the picture of Christ as a heroin junkie, the photo of the crucifix submerged in the artist's urine, or the sketches of Christ engaged in homosexual acts.[13] Now, in opposing this, I'm not advocating censorship. But I am recommending the lack of sponsorship and tax support.

Think about the implications of this *state-sponsored* blasphemy: on the one hand, the government, in all its various branches, prohibits the public expression of *pro*-Christian symbols (even if paid for privately). On the other hand, that same government sanctions *anti*-Christian expressions (and even sponsors them). Wow!

The NEA's funding of anti-Christian art has clearly put the *official* government sanction of the attack on Christ in America.

But the NEA is on shaky grounds and has an insecure future. With widespread criticism against its having funded such blasphemies, the agency has cut back on its support of such "art." Not that they have made these changes out of sensitivity to Christians whom they offend, but rather, so they can keep their government funding! In any event, the hammer of the NEA is smaller today than it was a few years ago. As a budget-conscious Congress continues to tighten the fiscal belt, I think we can look forward to less and less Christian bashing funded by the NEA.

Litigation against Churches

Churches are being sued in this country like never before. This is another hammer pounding against the kingdom. Lawsuits are understandable when a priest or minister abuses his position and engages in sex with a parishioner, or worse yet, a child. But apart from that which we bring upon ourselves, churches and ministries are today targets of an unprecedented number of lawsuits.

That's true in part because we have become a highly litigious society. This is a time of rampant, often frivolous lawsuits. It's a time when an accident is often viewed as a type of lottery ticket that the victim can try to cash in with a personal-injury suit. Here's an example of how ridiculous this can get. A jury in these United States awarded a psychic a $1-million judgment against a hospital because she supposedly lost her psychic powers in a CAT scan performed there![14]

And yet churches are sometimes being singled out as a source of "deep pockets." At a meeting under the auspices of the American Bar Association, lawyers were informed about how to sue churches. The seminar was advertised as being for "attorneys who want to be on the leading edge of an explosive new area of law." Subjects presented at the seminar included: "Expanding the Use of Tort Law against Religions," "Tort Law as an Ideological Weapon," "Tort Law as Essential Restraint on Religious Abuses," "Tort Liability for Brainwashing," and "Liability Arising out of the Employment Relationship."[15] Does anybody doubt that it's now open season on Christianity in this culture?

Fortunately, many, if not most, of these suits are won by the Christian side. The sad aspect is seeing money and time, earmarked for spreading the kingdom, being spent to fight lawsuits. Nonetheless, in our day, God has raised up many legal resources and an army of Christian litigators who are fighting this anti-Christian bigotry. Thus, many hammers are breaking all around us.

The Hammer of the ACLU

One of the biggest hammers in our day is the ACLU, the American Civil Liberties Union, which was founded in 1920. Seeing themselves as the champion of the Bill of Rights, they indefatigably attempt to destroy any vestige of religion left in the public square. A very large hammer indeed. They see any public religious expression as a major assault on the First Amendment. Their favorite Christmas carol would seem to be "Away *with* the Manger"! They are very active during "the holiday season" to make sure there are no manger scenes on public property or any other "sneaky remnants of religion."[16] The ACLU reminds me of the Grinch trying to steal Christmas; but just as Dr. Seuss's character failed in that pursuit, so will they.

The ACLU will sometimes go to *absurd* lengths to separate any vestige of the Church from the state. Here's a little-known example from the late 1970s, for which they've never apologized;[17] it reveals the type of activities they'll engage in to achieve their ends. At that time Congressman Henry Hyde (R-Ill.) had sponsored legislation ("the Hyde Amendment"), which prohibited federal funding for abortion. The ACLU tried to derail this legislation by declaring that it violated the separation of church and state. They provided evidence in court that there was a link between Congressman Henry Hyde's religion (Catholicism) and his views against abortion. They argued that since Hyde was a practicing Catholic, he was utilizing "the fist of government to smash the wall of separation between church and state by imposing a peculiarly religious view of when a human life begins."[18] That argument alone is frightening. If such tactics had been applied against the black churches in the 1950s and 1960s, there never would have been a Civil Rights movement! Our history is replete with examples of Christianity molding and shaping social policy—the abolition movement, the end of duels, prohibition, and so on.

Meanwhile, to gather the "dirt" on Hyde, the ACLU hired a private eye to trail him to church for a special service, at which he read aloud from the Scriptures. What's more, the ACLU had his mail analyzed to find any references to religion; if a constituent wrote Hyde and said "God bless you" in the letter, then even this was viewed as incriminating evidence and was subsequently entered in their lawsuit! They were intent on proving the link between his religion and his public policy.

Fortunately, the court ruled on Hyde's behalf and threw this "evidence" out. But isn't the whole incident frightening? To what lengths will this group *violate* civil liberties in the name of upholding civil liberties?

Hyde himself said,

The anger I felt when they tried to disenfranchise me because of my religion has stayed with me. These are dangerous people who make dangerous arguments. Some powerful members of the cultural elites in our country are so paralyzed by the fear that theistic notions might reassert themselves in the official activities of government that they will go to Gestapo lengths to inhibit such expression.[19]

Indeed, how far are we to take the ACLU's version of the separation of church and state? Until one's religious beliefs have been so privatized that they can only be found in his brain? If we go that far, then what's the difference between us and the former Soviet Union?

The ACLU has been a longtime advocate of the strict separation—or even segregation—of church from state, of the separation of God from our public life. We can see this clearly from an incident after, as well as during, the Scopes "Monkey Trial" of 1925, which the ACLU initiated. In the court, their attorney, Clarence Darrow, used the opportunity to belittle biblical fundamentalism as personified in William Jennings Bryan. Interestingly, the key "scientific" evidence used at the trial to prove evolution was soon after found to be false;[20] but the damage to biblical creationism had been done, thanks in large part to the satirical correspondent, H. L. Mencken. And here's the rub: a few years after the trial, Darrow returned to Dayton, Tennessee, the sight of the trial, for a short visit. He saw a church being constructed and quipped, "I guess I didn't do much good here after all."[21] There it is—an off-the-cuff admission of their true feelings toward Christianity. But what can we expect from the ACLU when its very founder said in 1935 (during the height of Stalinism), "Communism is the goal"?[22]

To this day their antireligious hostility continues. Dr. William Donohue, the head of the Catholic League and the author of *The Politics of the American Civil Liberties Union* and *Twilight of Liberty: The Legacy of the ACLU* has been following the activities of this left-wing legal group for two decades now. Donohue asserts: "The ACLU sees religion as something to be guarded against, at least in terms of its public manifestations. That is why it takes a position that effectively marginalizes the public role of religion in society."[23]

In their "Workplan 1994: Defending the Abiding Values of American Democracy," the ACLU outlined their agenda for the year. They wrote, "The force and duration of right-wing fundamentalist Christian activism has succeeded in confusing the American people about the separation of church and state."[24]

The ACLU even addressed the issue of Christian bashing, although, not surprisingly, they've got it all wrong: "By cynically twisting basic American beliefs about fairness and tolerance to suit their own political needs—'it's the Christians who are discriminated against'—right-wing leaders set the stage for a new wave of divisiveness and social conflict."[25] Let me get this straight. Christianity is under attack in our culture from just about every corner, thanks in large part to the ACLU, and by our speaking out against this anti-Christian bigotry, Christians are "divisive" and are causing "social conflict." Who is "twisting" what?

Despite the ACLU's success to date, their power is more perceived than actual. John Whitehead, founder and director of the Rutherford Institute, which has butted heads with the liberal legal group on many occasions, said,

> My opinion of the ACLU is that a lot of their so-called power is a myth, that they're in large part a creation of the national media and that's where a lot of their power comes from. . . . the ACLU can write a letter. . . . they don't have to file a lawsuit. . . . they work a lot on intimidation through the press, through letters. Less though, in my opinion, through cases.[26]

Thus, their bark is worse than their bite.

For so many decades the ACLU stood virtually unopposed as they did their dirty work against religious freedom in this country. It is not so anymore. From the American Center for Law and Justice to the Liberty Counsel, from the Alliance Defense Fund to the Rutherford Institute, there are more attorneys today fighting *for* religious liberty than ever before. The ACLU may still try to impose their anti-Christian agenda on this nation, but not without a *serious* fight on their hands. Furthermore, as we'll see in Chapter 13, when Christians fight back for religious freedom, we win more than we lose. In its anti-Christian goals, the hammer of the ACLU *will* fail, just as everything that sets itself against God will fail. The gates of Hell shall not prevail!

The Hammer of "People for the American Way"

Another liberal group hammering away at conservative Christianity is People for the American Way (PAW). They are actively engaged in lobbying against conservative Christian positions. They are making grassroots efforts in various parts of the country to oppose a Christian or family-friendly agenda. People for the American Way could be more aptly titled "People for Norman Lear's Way"—in reference to the founder. Norman Lear is the television producer who gave us *All in the Family*, *Maude*, and *Soap*. Some have observed that *All in the Family* was a watershed. Before it, just about every family portrayed on television was like the Cleaver household in *Leave It to Beaver*; after *All in the Family*, just about every family portrayed was dysfunctional!

I remember years ago seeing a letter whereby Norman Lear was raising five million dollars for a campaign of ads directed against religious conservatives. Lear's group began showing TV spots that essentially tried to silence Christians in matters of public concern in our nation. To me this would be ludicrous if it were not indeed dangerous, because certainly Christianity is not foreign to the American way of life. At least I think that John Witherspoon, the Presbyterian clergyman who signed the Declaration of Independence, would have found it quite strange to hear that ministers were not to have anything to do with the political life of America.[27]

There is, however, a religion that *is* dangerous to the American way of life. I refer to the religion of secular humanism. (The Supreme Court even labeled it as such in 1961's *Torcasso v. Watkins*.) The secular humanists cannot stand the idea that it is indeed righteousness that exalts a nation and that God's laws have a place in the public policy of our country. One of the most interesting outcries that I have read was by a commentator who said in a magazine that not since Genghis Khan turned westward has there been such a trembling in the land—the Christians were coming! Why, that is a fearful thought indeed, at least to the so-called People for the American Way, whose way seems to be the way of atheism, secularism, and ungodliness.

Founded in 1982, with its headquarters in Washington, D.C., People for the American Way has offices in New York, California, Colorado, Florida, and even North Carolina. Karl Day of the Family Research Council in Washington, D.C., says this about People for the American Way: "Funded primarily by Hollywood, the Playboy Foundation and other liberal sources, PAW's announced purpose at the outset was to counter the religious right."[28] The media, however, put a different spin on PAW. For example, the Associated Press said it was "created to fight to preserve the separation between church and state"; however, they did at least *accurately* label PAW as "a liberal advocacy group."[29]

The PAW exists almost exclusively as a thorn in Christianity's side. But numerically, the PAW's significance pales in comparison to that of evangelicals today. They claim a membership of 300,000,[30] yet the Christian Coalition, a conservative political organization younger than PAW by at least five years, has a membership of 1.7 million[31]—five times the number of PAW! Furthermore, the Coalition has an active network of 100,000 churches through which they can communicate to *millions* of Christians. During the critical 1994 elections, the Christian Coalition distributed fifty-seven million pieces of nonpartisan voter guides, which told where the candidates stood on the issues.[32]

I think it's really only the secular media that give PAW such credibility. One day, perhaps soon, I anticipate the hammer of PAW to join the other broken ones at the foot of the anvil of God. As was said so long ago,

> *There is no wisdom, no insight, no plan*
> *that can succeed against the LORD.*
> (Prov. 21:30 NIV)

Defamation by the Anti-Defamation League

In the summer of 1994, Christians were dismayed to hear of a new book that was receiving national attention. It was a report put out by the Anti-Defamation League of B'nai B'rith: *The Religious Right: The Assault on Tolerance & Pluralism in America.*[33] The book asserts that "the religious right brings to cultural disagreements a rhetoric of fear, suspicion, even hatred."[34]

When this report came out, I looked up the eight or so references to my name in the index; they didn't have one single thing there that I had said. It was all guilt by association, which is something they would no doubt deplore. It was media McCarthyism. I was guilty, according to the ADL, because I had endorsed or had some sort of relationship to someone else, who in turn endorsed someone else, who in turn reportedly said something anti-Semitic. Yet by putting me in the book so often, I was painted as some sort of anti-Semite. Here's the Anti-Defamation League engaging in defamation themselves, defamation of the Christian right.

Even many Jewish Americans agree with the assessment that the report engaged in defamation. Several of them advertised on the op-ed pages of *The New York Times* to decry the ADL report. The headline of their ad asked "Should Jews fear the 'Christian Right'?" Some of those who signed it included Elliott Abrams, Mona Charen, Midge Decter, Suzanne Fields, Bruce Herschensohn, Irving Kristol, our friend Michael Medved, and Dennis Prager. They wrote, "It ill behooves an organization dedicated to fighting against defamation to engage in defamation of its own. The separation of church and state is not the same thing as the elimination of religious values and concepts from political discourse."[35]

Mona Charen, the syndicated columnist, who is one of those who signed the ad, wrote an excellent column about the ADL report. She said, "Anti-Christian bias is the one prejudice that is still permitted in America. Does saying so make me anti-Jewish?" She also wrote: "The Anti-Defamation League has committed defamation. There is the crude but undeniable fact that the ADL is in the anti-Semitism business. The more it finds, the greater its prominence, and the easier it is to raise money. It is playing upon ancient fears and worries of American Jews—and is doing so dishonestly, with quotes taken out of context and flagrantly false accusations. It rails at imaginary enemies and betrays true friends."[36]

Charen touched on another bothersome aspect of the ADL report; it depended on shoddy research.[37] With tongue in cheek, *National Review* gave an example of just how shoddy:

> In its nearly-200-page tome the ADL stretches for *anything* to cast the Religious Right in a bad light. Thus, to demonstrate Paul Weyrich's "grim apocalypticism" (wow!), it quotes Robert Novak saying, "Paul's the only person so tough that he gets hate mail from Mother Teresa." Somehow it fails to mention that Mr. Novak made his comment *at a roast.*[38]

The ADL has it all wrong. The anti-Semites of this country are not born-again Christians. The typical anti-Semites are the semiliterate kids who are going to the public schools, who have no clue about God or Christianity. To them the Jews are a ready target. It's not born-again Christians or children of fundamentalists who are out spray painting swastikas on synagogues. It's not unlike the battle between Catholics and Protestants in Northern Ireland. I've talked to some Protestant preachers about that conflict. They said such people never darken the doors of their churches. These aren't Protestant Christians. They may have been baptized as such as babies, but that's about all. Furthermore, I remember the Gallup poll from a few years ago that revealed that for the most part fundamentalist and evangelical Christians are not anti-Semitic. Next to the Jews, they are the most pro-Israel group in America. But somehow these truths get lost as the hammers of secularism try, unsuccessfully, to squash the spread of Christianity in America.

The Schools: The Chief Battle Zone

Have you heard the joke about the teacher who discovered a number of students kneeling in a corner of the playground during recess? She rushed over and said, "Students! Students! What are you doing?" They answered, "We're sorry, we were just shooting craps." She replied, "Phew! I was afraid you were praying!" While that may be humorous, it underscores a tragic truth.

There have been many, many indirect consequences of the Supreme Court's 1962–63 decisions to ban school prayer. And the fallout has literally amounted to expelling God *in toto* from our entire school system and, beyond that, from the public square—the public life of America. God has been thrown out, and the metal detectors have been put in.

The public school is the chief battleground of the present attack on Christ in the public arena.[39] It seems like these days just about *any* idea is allowed to be presented in the public schools—except the *G* word, *God*. Columnist Cal Thomas said, "I think the philosophy in our public schools, and many other institutions today, is that a dose of God is more hazardous to your health than a dose of herpes or drugs."[40] Consider the following:

- *Tulsa, Oklahoma.* A student in the fourth grade attempted to pray before a math test. He was marched to the principal's office and forced to write one hundred times, "I will not pray in class."[41] Johnny may not be able to read or write, say some educators, but at least we're ridding his mind of religious superstitions!

- *Coral Springs, Florida.* One of the members of my congregation told me about a five-year-old neighbor who had just attended the first day of kindergarten, where the teacher had told the class "no one can know for sure whether Jesus ever really lived." Whether or not the teacher actually said this, we don't know. What we do know is that the five-year-old said that the teacher said this. Interestingly, the historicity of Jesus Christ is well documented; we can reconstruct the highlights of the life of Christ through *non-Christian* writers of the first century.[42] After this incident my church member thought to herself, *His first day in public school . . . and all of that in one morning! Imagine what they can accomplish in twelve years!*

- *Bloomingdale, Michigan.* A painting of Jesus had been hanging in the public high school since 1962, when the doors first opened. One agnostic student claimed he received "psychological damage" by seeing the portrait. The ACLU sued on his behalf. The court agreed, even though one concurring judge in the case said it regrettably creates "a class of 'eggshell' plaintiffs"— plaintiffs who are fragile and get offended too easily. The painting came down.[43] Just another day in an increasingly secularized America.

- *Foster City, California.* A former member of my church settled into a new home in a new state and enrolled her seven-year-old in their local public school. She and other parents of the second-grade class were all encouraged to come in and share with the class how they would celebrate the holidays.

Several parents came in and explained Hanukkah and the Menorah. So my former congregation member asked to briefly share something related to Christmas, the birth of Jesus. She was told by the teacher, "That's not allowed. That's religious."[44]

And on it goes with the hammers of public school officials against religious expression in our day. When you hear about these stories, it's hard to believe they're true—they seem so absurd. Lynn Buzzard, the founding director of the Christian Legal Society, says that with so many of these cases in which the Christian children are being discriminated against, one begins to think, "Well, they're extreme in the sense of [being] ludicrous and ridiculous, but they're not uncommon."[45]

While there are earnest Christians on *both* sides of the school prayer issue, the problem is much deeper than school prayer. The problem is that schools have been turned into virtual "religion-free" zones. Schoolchildren receive a skewed picture of the world. The public schools today are often not neutral toward religion; they are hostile to it.

But despite all these situations, the law is on the side of the Christian students to express their opinions, even on matters of religion. The Supreme Court has upheld the right of students to have Bible clubs after school hours, *Mergens v. Westside High School* (1990), if secular clubs are allowed on the same campus.

Even President Clinton, not known for his conservative views, has spoken out against our schools having been turned into religion-free zones. His administration, to its credit, recently drew up guidelines on religion in schools. Education Secretary Richard Riley sent guidelines on "religion in school" to school superintendents across the nation to help clarify all this. The gist of the guidelines, as *USA Today* put it, was that "students may express personal religious views, but schools may not endorse religious activity or doctrine."[46]

Insights from a Founding Father

Interestingly, Founding Father Benjamin Rush from Pennsylvania, a surgeon in the American Revolution, predicted the link between removing the Bible from the schools and the rise of crime in the schools. Dr. Rush was a member of the Continental Congress. He signed the Declaration of Independence and helped draft the Constitution. In the 1830s, in a tract entitled "The Bible in Schools," he bemoaned the growing trend in the schools of demoting the Bible as the chief textbook. Rush wrote that in light of the Bible's diminishing role as a textbook, "I lament that we waste so much time and money in punishing crimes, and take so little pains to prevent them."[47] In short, Benjamin Rush was saying that teaching the Bible minimizes crime. That was circa 1830! Imagine if Dr. Rush were to visit today's public schools—with their special police officers on duty! I just heard this week about one of these police officers assigned to a local high school, who had the ignoble task of putting out the fire in the hair of one student that another student had lit! Benjamin Rush must be doing proverbial somersaults in his grave.

I remember seeing a political cartoon that made a strong point. It shows two big fat soldiers with "ACLU" written across their helmets. They are in a high school and they are looking with a flashlight into a young student's locker and reading the contents: "Handgun, cocaine, condoms . . . but no Bible. This one's clean." Now there the real tragedy comes through.

History Distorted

Another result of the fallout from the Supreme Court's decisions to ban prayer and Bible reading from our public schools is that even the *history books* have been rewritten; God has been erased. Even People for the American Way, with whom we would disagree on just about everything, has come out stating that religion had received short shrift in our history textbooks. In a 1986 report entitled *Looking at History* they said,

> Religion is simply not treated as a significant element in American life—it is not portrayed as an integrated part of the American value system or as something that is important to individual Americans. The two themes which have been in tension since the earliest colonial times—religious intolerance and religious idealism—are not recognized as essential to an understanding of the American character. When religion is mentioned, it is just that—mentioned. In particular, most books give the impression that Americans suddenly became a secular people after the Civil War. It is common for books to do a fairly good job of covering religion in the Colonial period and even the early 19th Century, but fall off sharply post-1865, particularly in modern times.[48]

You know something's wrong when even your opponents agree it's wrong!

"Children Are the Prize"

Why are the public schools such a major battle zone between the forces of light and the forces of darkness today? Dr. James Dobson of *Focus on the Family* has pointed out repeatedly that we're engaged in "a civil war of values" in our culture, and the prize is our children. He wrote,

> Children are the prize to the winners of the second great civil war. Those who control what young people are taught and what they experience—what they see, hear, think, and believe—will determine the future course for the nation. Given that influence, the predominant value system of an entire culture can be overhauled in one generation, or certainly in two, by those with unlimited access to children.[49]

A Lesson from the Nazi Era

During the Nazi regime Hitler recognized how important it was to control the schools. As William Shirer, author of *The Rise and Fall of the Third Reich*, points out, "The German schools, from first grade through the universities, were quickly Nazified."[50] Hitler showed how important it was to control the schools in a speech on November 6, 1933: "When an opponent declares, 'I will not come over to your side.' I calmly say, 'Your child belongs to us already. . . . What are you? You will pass on. Your descendants, however, now stand in the new camp. In a short time they will know nothing else but this new community.'"[51]

Hitler later declared on May 1, 1937: "This new Reich will give its youth to no one, but will itself take youth and give to youth its own education and its own upbringing."[52] Thus we can learn an important lesson from the Nazi era: Those who control the classroom will control the future. Providentially, his anti-Christian "thousand-year reich" only lasted twelve—another sign that the gates of Hell shall not prevail.

Anti-Christian Atheist Center in Disarray

As everyone knows, the notorious atheist, Madalyn Murray O'Hair was the driving force behind one of those key Supreme Court decisions that ousted prayer from the schools, a decision which, subsequently, has caused so much damage. But everyone might not be aware of the current status of O'Hair's anti-Christian empire. It is crumbling, at least according to a recent article in the *Miami Herald*. The newspaper reports that her atheist center in Austin, Texas, is essentially vacant. Furthermore, at the time of this report, Ms. O'Hair was missing. Also missing were her son, Jon Murray, who has been actively following in his mother's footsteps, and her granddaughter, Robin Murray O'Hair. Speculations as to her whereabouts ranged from the possibility that she and her son and granddaughter were out visiting Civil War cities for recreation to the possibility that she was dead and her body was frozen for some future cryogenics experiment! Even if she shows up soon, she will be reigning over a fallen empire.

Funding for the atheist's work has dwindled in recent months. Many staff members allegedly have been laid off, and one of their former employees allegedly burglarized them. According to this article, the entire American Atheist Center is in disarray.[53] It would seem that another hammer just fell in the dust.

God at Work

Meanwhile, in the nation's public schools, there are encouraging signs that God is at work. Around the beginning of each school year, thousands (if not millions) of Christian students gather together on a designated day at their public school flagpoles for a morning prayer before classes. The event is called "See You at the Pole." Dr. James Dobson has recently publicized that Moms in Touch, support groups of mothers who are helping, praying for, and supporting the public school teachers, are growing in popularity across the nation.

The Bible is even making a comeback of sorts in public schools. A few years ago, Elizabeth Ridenour of North Carolina discovered that the Supreme Court decision that forbade *mandatory* Bible reading in the schools also allowed for *voluntary* Bible curriculum in the public schools. So she designed a Bible curriculum, based on acceptable Supreme Court guidelines, and founded the National Council on Bible Curriculum in the Public Schools. Her Bible curriculum is now being taught in more than 120 high schools in North Carolina alone! And it has been adopted in seven states and is spreading.[54] Although the group Americans United for Separation of Church and State doesn't like it, students are getting to learn about the basis for our culture—the Bible. Another hammer is beginning to show signs of stress fractures.

Colleges and Universities

Although my focus here is primarily on what's going on in the elementary and secondary schools, I find that Christian bashing is alive and well on college and university campuses also. In fact, it's ever more direct and overt because Christianity is not "politically correct." Never has been. Never will be.

I read recently a letter from a man from Campus Crusade for Christ who heads up a campus ministry. He tells of religion courses at a state university in the Bible Belt, wherein a professor teaches such rubbish as "Jesus was a homosexual," "Jesus had sex with Mary Magdalene," "Both Jesus and Moses were legends," and "Jesus had a twin brother."[55] The professor likens the resurrection of Jesus Christ to the sightings of Elvis. One student remarked that this course should be relabeled, "Christianity Hating 101."[56] Unfortunately, there are many other instances, not so extreme perhaps, where Christianity is denigrated in the college classroom, and often you and I fund this through our tax dollars in the state schools.

Ironically, many of our nation's leading colleges and universities were started by Christians for Christian purposes. This includes Harvard, Yale, Columbia, Dartmouth, William and Mary, Brown, Princeton, New York University, and Northwestern University. When you think of how anti-Christian Harvard University is, it's easy to forget that the oldest college in the U.S., named after the *Reverend* John Harvard, was founded to train ministers of the gospel.[57]

While homosexuality is openly practiced and encouraged by the faculties and administrations, openly Christian professors and students are more and more coming under fire in the hallowed halls of many of our universities. A few years ago at Harvard, a small Christian group came under fire for the politically incorrect crime of distributing a magazine that explained the Christian way out of homosexuality.[58]

But Harvard's not a totally lost cause. I heard recently the astounding fact that the largest group on the Harvard campus is Campus Crusade! Furthermore, one of the most popular courses is a class on Jesus, which handles the subject respectfully.

Meanwhile, on many Christian college campuses, revival seems to be sweeping the land. It has even spread to some Christian groups at Yale, Dartmouth, and Columbia! At Wheaton, Gordon, Taylor, Trinity, Biola, and other Christian colleges, thousands of students have begun to confess their sins and express a deep yearning for God. In fact, the revival (or renewal, as some call it) has now affected fifty campuses! One of the pastors to students at Howard Payne University in Brownwood, Texas, where the revival began, said, "I believe the best is yet to come. . . . There is no sign of letup."[59] I pray that revival will be the wave of the future that shatters the hammer of the stifling, anti-Christian "thought police" otherwise known as political correctness.

Most Americans Favor Religious Liberty

Americans, by and large, are much more in favor of more religion and religious freedom than our political and cultural elite are. For example, a *Time*/CNN poll found that 78 percent of Americans favor "voluntary Bible classes" and the same number supports "voluntary Christian fellowship groups." Seventy-eight percent also favor "allowing children to say prayers in public schools." Even more, 89 percent, support "allowing children to spend a moment in silent meditation in public schools." Fifty-five percent said there's "too little" religious influence in American life. Sixty-seven percent said they favor "displaying symbols like a Nativity scene or a Menorah on government property."[60]

That poll just cited came from a *Time* magazine cover story on our church-state conflict from a few years ago. The title was "One Nation under God," the subtitle, "Has the Separation of Church and State Gone Too Far?" They concluded the article:

> For God to be kept out of the classroom or out of America's public debate by nervous school administrators or overcautious politicians serves no one's interest. That restriction prevents people from drawing on this country's rich and diverse religious heritage for guidance by placing a whole realm of theological reasoning out of bounds. The price of that sort of quarantine, at a time of moral dislocation, is—and has been—far too high. The courts need to find a better balance between separation and accommodation—and Americans need to respect the new religious freedom they would gain as a result.[61]

Amen.

Conclusion

Although Don Feder, the witty columnist, is not a Christian (he's Jewish), he is often an outspoken critic of anti-Christian bigotry. Why? Because he knows if society tolerates this, the Jews will likely be the next victims. A few years ago, Feder wrote an excellent book of interesting observations from his perspective, entitled *A Jewish Conservative Looks at Pagan America*. He sums up what's going on in our schools, which well sums up the hammers of hostility against things Christian in the public arena:

> It has reached the point where public school students can experience anything—things the average sailor on shore leave doesn't encounter—except God. Sex education, suicide studies, life-boat ethics, condom distribution, abortion pleading, which, when taken together, constitute the propagation of the humanist creed—all are essential aspects of the public school experience in the 1990s. It's only prayers,

Bibles, and references to a supreme being [sic] which offend the sensibilities of secularist puritans. . . .

We may fail to teach our students the rudiments of literature, science, and history. Twenty percent of high-school graduates may be functional illiterates, or semi-literate. We may be unable to maintain even a semblance of order in our urban schools, which increasingly resemble happy hour in Beirut. But, hallelujah, we sure know how to protect kids from God.[62]

To that I will add: Hallelujah, we know who wins in the end. Hallelujah, we know what will happen eventually to all the hammers that oppose the spread of Christianity. Hallelujah, the gates of Hell shall not prevail!

The Hammer of Oppression: Distortion of the First Amendment

Where the Spirit of the Lord is, there is liberty.
—2 Corinthians 3:17

Ken Roberts, a dedicated grade-school teacher in the Denver area, would never have thought there would be a problem with him *silently* reading books on religion during silent reading time. As his students did their reading, he would read books about Native-American religion, Hindu religion, and he sometimes read the Bible. And for that last one, and only that last one, he was censured. He also had a collection of some two hundred books available to the children to read during this silent period. Of these two hundred, two were Christian books—therefore, they were removed by the principal.[1] Ken fought this case in court on behalf of other teachers, but unfortunately he lost.

As we saw repeatedly in the last chapter, in a day when all sorts of books and ideas, including religious ones, are allowed to flourish in the public arena, only Christian ones are set apart for censorship. Why? Why all the perils to religious freedom in the schools and in the public arena? The answer in large part can be found in a misunderstanding of the separation of church and state. This misunderstanding has become a powerful hammer pounding away at the public expression of Christianity in our time.

The Separation of God and State

Today in America we not only separate the institution of the Church from the institution of the state, but we separate God from the state. If the latter were appropriate, then it's time to take a bulldozer to some of our national monuments in Washington, D.C., because almost all of them quote Scripture or say something about God. If it were true that God should be separated from the state, then it's time to take a jackhammer to Abraham Lincoln's speeches engraved in bold letters in the Lincoln Memorial. Why? Some of his sentences are quotes from Scripture! For example, his second inaugural address is carved there, containing such sentences as: "Woe unto the world because of offences! for it must needs be that offences come; but woe to that man by whom the offence cometh" (Matt. 18:7 KJV) and "The judgments of the LORD are true and righteous altogether" (Ps. 19:9 KJV). Lincoln was clearly a student of the Bible; he said that it is the source by which we know right from wrong.[2] If God is to be separate from the state, then why does our money say, "In God We Trust"? Why do we have military and congressional chaplains? Why is the president sworn in with his hand on the Bible? We've been duped in the last few decades as to what the First Amendment is all about.

The World's Great Bastion of Freedom?

Despite all this, America has been and perhaps still is the world's greatest bastion of freedom and liberty. Of all the freedoms we most enjoy, that which was most important to our founders and remains so for us, is the freedom of religion! In fact, in the Bill of Rights in the First Amendment, before the Founding Fathers guaranteed the right of a free press or the freedom to peaceably assemble or the freedom to petition the government or even the freedom of speech, they guaranteed the freedom of religion!

The creation of religious liberty by the Founding Fathers of this country was a unique act in the history of the world. On that day, for the first time in the history of this planet, religious freedom became a reality. There had been religious *toleration* before, but it had never risen to the level of religious freedom.

What was the source of this freedom? Christianity. John Quincy Adams, our sixth president, said, "The highest glory of the American Revolution was this: it connected in one indissoluble bond, the principles of civil government with the principles of Christianity."[3]

Suppose we took that statement and compared it with a statement of the opposite sentiment: "The highest glory of the American Revolution was that it forever separated the principles of civil government from the principles of Christianity." You could ask a thousand Americans today which of these two statements is closer to the truth. And unfortunately, most of them would get it wrong.

In 1830 a young Frenchman came to these shores to see the American experiment in practice. Alexis de Tocqueville was a very astute observer who wrote the classic work *Democracy in America*. He stated,

> There is no country in the whole world in which the Christian religion retains a greater influence over the souls of men than in America and there can be no greater proof of its utility, and of its conformity to human nature, than that its influence is most powerfully felt over the most enlightened and free nation on earth.[4]

Many of the great political thinkers of our country's past—whether Christian or otherwise—saw the important link between Christianity and liberty. All of these statements culminate with a climactic pronouncement from the Supreme Court in 1892. After spending some ten years poring through thousands of documents from our history, they wrote this in the classic *Trinity* decision:

> This is a religious people. This is historically true. From the discovery of this continent to the present hour, there is a single voice making this affirmation . . . these are not individual sayings, declarations of private persons: they are organic utterances; they speak the voice of the entire people . . . these and many other matters which might be noticed, add a volume of unofficial declarations to the mass of organic utterances that this is a Christian nation.[5]

Note it well. The United States Supreme Court has declared, "this is a Christian nation."

This view has been upheld more recently as well. Larry Witham of the *Washington Times* pointed out,

In 1931 the U.S. Supreme Court noted that the United States is a Christian nation. In a mid-Atlantic summit with British Prime Minister Winston Churchill in the darkest hours of World War II, President Roosevelt—who had described the United States as "the lasting concord between men and nations, founded on the principles of Christianity"—asked the crew of an American warship to join him in a rousing chorus of the hymn "Onward Christian Soldiers."

In 1947, writing to Pope Pius XII, President Truman said flatly, "This is a Christian nation."

Nobody argued with any of them.[6]

And, I might add, nobody sued them either!

Gary DeMar, president of American Vision and author of the excellent book *America: The Untold Story*, asserts that in our age of political correctness, these kinds of statements would be heavily challenged if they were made today. "Churchill, Roosevelt, and Truman would get an argument today in the highly charged atmosphere of Political Correctness that is sweeping across our nation."[7]

We should remember that the Christian nation established here allowed more religious freedom for more people of more diverse viewpoints than had ever been known before. Only in America could people worship any kind of God or no God at all. Only in America could they proclaim their views from the housetop, and today they can voice them over radio and television. It is a land where the teachings of Christ prevail.

If the secularists and atheists succeed in replacing our nation's Christian foundation with a godless one, I assure you that the religious liberty that made this nation great will become a thing of the past. We've seen repeatedly that when atheists take over a country, not only does religious liberty go but so do other basic freedoms. Ask the Russians, the Albanians, or the Chinese. But because Christianity is the Truth, the Christian is not afraid to allow other voices to be heard. All we desire is for the chance to be heard in the marketplace of ideas. As Jay Sekulow puts it, all we ask for is "a level playing field."[8]

The Great Deception

But instead of our voice being heard, a Great Deception has taken place in this country. The First Amendment—written to guarantee religious freedom—is now used to take it away! Hitler used to say there was something called "the Big Lie."

If you tell it often enough and loudly enough, finally, everybody will come to believe it, regardless of how absurd it is.[9]

And there is no doubt that the proponents of this deception have been enormously successful and have convinced the majority of the American people that the Constitution of the United States declares that there is something called a "wall of separation" between church and state. This great deception has been used to destroy much of the religious freedom and liberty this country has enjoyed since its inception.

The attack on Christ in America in the public arena stems from a misreading of the religion clause of the First Amendment: "Congress shall make no law respecting an establishment of religion or prohibiting the free exercise thereof." You'll note there's no mention of the separation of church and state.

Although the First Amendment has historically given Americans unprecedented religious freedom, today the amendment's interpretation has been so twisted that it has become a hammer of oppression. Traditionally, it has always been understood that the Establishment Clause of the First Amendment meant that in America there would be no national church like they had and have in England. The framers wanted a separation of the function of the Church from the function of the national government. But they did not want a separation of God or Christianity from the state, which we find in our country today.

The Bill of Rights

You will recall that the Constitution would not be ratified by the states until some key provisions for freedom were guaranteed—first among them being freedom of religion. Thus Congress established the Bill of Rights, the first ten amendments of the Constitution. Only when these were set in stone did the states all agree to join the union. The Bill of Rights was written for one purpose: *to restrain the power of the Federal government and to protect the freedoms of the people.* That is why people like George Washington and Patrick Henry demanded a Bill of Rights so that this new leviathan that was being created would not consume the people's rights.[10] Therefore, Congress was further restrained not to limit the people's free speech, not to limit the freedom of the press, not to prohibit them from assembling peacefully, and so forth.

The Origin of "the Separation of Church and State"

Where, then, did we get this idea of a "wall of separation between church and state"? It comes not from the First Amendment nor any part of the Constitution nor any other part of the Bill of Rights. Rather, it comes from a *private letter* written in 1802 by Thomas Jefferson (who was not a member of the Constitutional Convention; he was in France when it was being written) to the Danbury Baptists in Connecticut. He said there should be a "wall of separation between church and state." A wall of separation works both ways (unlike the founders' intent, which was to prohibit government from restricting religion in any way and not vice versa). A wall prohibits and restrains those on one side of the wall as much as those on the other side. Instead of the restriction that the framers originally intended for the First Amendment, Jefferson's concept has gradually gained preeminence in the past few decades, so that, in practice, the amendment became a wall.

Furthermore, in the last several decades, the First Amendment has been turned around in the opposite direction! The phrase "separation of church and state" has come to mean what religion, and specifically what the Christian Church, shall or shall not do. This is 180 degrees from the First Amendment! The tool for liberation has now become a hammer of oppression. As Constitutional attorney and author Lynn Buzzard puts it, the First Amendment has now been turned into a "search and destroy mission against any sneaky vestiges of religion left around."[11] Thus, the First Amendment has been turned into a hammer, smashing away at the Christian faith. But even if the secularists were to succeed in making Christianity illegal in America, and I don't believe they will, they could never stop the Christian faith from spreading, for it is divinely ordained. As the great Jewish leader Gamaliel said of the Christian faith, "If it is of God, you cannot overthrow it—lest you even be found to fight against God" (Acts 5:39).

Nonetheless, it is tragic that the average American—even the average Christian American—does not know what the First Amendment really says or what it has meant historically. If you were to ask the average person on the street: "What does the Constitution say about religion or the Church?" they would tell you that it says there should be a separation between church and state. If you asked them what the First Amendment says, the vast majority would probably reply that it says there should be a separation between the Church and the state.

That is *not* what it says and that is *not* what it means; but it is, instead, a dangerous distortion of the First Amendment. The First Amendment was designed to limit Congress, not the Church. It says nothing about what the Church may do or what preachers may do or what religious people may do. It says nothing that would prohibit a little child from saying grace at school during lunchtime or the Salvation Army proclaiming "God bless you" on a placard on a city bus, or schoolchildren being able to say "Merry Christmas" as opposed to "Happy Winter

Solstice." The First Amendment only limits what the *Congress* may do. A wall, on the other hand, limits people on both sides of the wall.

If that were not bad enough, the media have promulgated this total reversal of the First Amendment, thus perpetrating the great lie. The media would lead you to believe that the First Amendment was not written to protect the rights of the people to worship and practice their religion, but, rather, the First Amendment was written to protect the government from the influence of religion. In other words, the modern secularist is saying that the Constitution gives freedom *from* religion, not freedom *of* religion! This, too, is a 180-degree turnabout from what the First Amendment says. And again, the vast majority of the people in America don't even realize it.

The secularist—with his insistence that Christians should not get involved in politics, that representatives of the Church should have nothing to do with the affairs of the state—seems to buy into an assumption. The assumption is that only the ungodly shall rule and that people who have relationships with God or people who are "religious" are not qualified to rule. No wonder the ACLU would stoop to hiring a spy to tail Congressman Hyde to church!

I recently read in a newspaper that Christians were not qualified to sit on the Supreme Court because they were biased! The secularist is essentially saying that those in authority should seek the advice and counsel only of ungodly and irreligious people. Now isn't this ridiculous?

Indeed, the First Amendment has now been stood on its head. Let's take the example of ten-year-old Raymond Raines of St. Louis, Missouri. This brave little Christian was saying his grace in the school cafeteria, and on three occasions he was whisked off, in full view of everyone, to the principal's office. Why? For praying in school. Three times he was publicly humiliated; one of these times, the principal himself was reported to have "physically removed" him. The Rutherford Institute states that the fourth grader "was further disciplined with detention in the school cafeteria for lengthy periods of time, segregated from other students and ridiculed for his religious beliefs and practices."[12]

Some might say, "Well, that's plausible. Maybe the boy was violating this 'separation between church and state.'" But the First Amendment addresses what *Congress* can and can't do. That boy isn't Congress. The First Amendment doesn't say anything at all about students in a lunchroom. It talks about what *Congress* can't do, not what *Christians* can't do. The First Amendment was not written to keep religious people from influencing government or practicing their religion; it was written to keep the government from interfering with religious people practicing their religion!

Even the ACLU claims to have problems with children being prohibited from praying like this! Of course, they've helped create the climate that our schools are a virtual religion-free zone. But the ACLU states in a recent publication, "Individual students always have a right to pray, for example, to say grace before eating in the school cafeteria. But no one is challenging that, certainly not the ACLU."[13] Perhaps not, but they seem to be challenging just about everything else! It reminds me of an overzealous medieval knight stopping a peasant that he suspects of treason. He then chops off the poor man's limbs in search of evidence. And when the man's arms and legs are severed and no proof has been found, the knight says, "OK, you're clean. You can go now." The ACLU works tirelessly to remove even a *hint* of prayer in school, and then when a nervous administrator overreacts to grace being said in the cafeteria, the ACLU claims to take the side of the child!

The shackles have been taken off the leviathan—the Federal Government— and have been put onto the religious people of America—the very opposite of what the Founding Fathers intended.

The Founders' Intent

So what then *did* the Founders intend with the "establishment clause" of the First Amendment ("Congress shall make no law respecting an establishment of religion")? The clause was only intended to stop the formation of a *national* church, that's all.

At the time of the American Revolution, nine of the thirteen colonies had *state* churches. The Anglican Church was the established church in Virginia, in the "lower counties" of New York in Maryland, in South Carolina, in North Carolina "nominally," and in Georgia. In Massachusetts, Connecticut, and New Hampshire, the Congregational Church was the established state church. By the time of the Constitutional Convention in 1787, that number had whittled down to only five states with a state church. By that time, "only Georgia, South Carolina, Connecticut, Massachusetts, and New Hampshire had retained their religious establishments."[14] These state churches only became viewed to be unconstitutional after a while. The last state church in these United States was that of Massachusetts, which ceased as late as 1833. Thus, while the Constitution clearly prohibits the creation of a national church, it did not even prohibit a state church (not that I would advocate that today). Thus, we see that the First Amendment was never intended by its adopters to unleash the nonsense taking place today.

A terrific book on this subject is by constitutional scholar Robert Cord, a professor of political science at Northeastern University. The book is *Separation of Church and State: Historical Fact and Current Fiction*, and in it Cord tells of James Madison's first draft of the religion clause of the First Amendment:

> Madison's original wording of the Establishment of Religion Clause also supports my thesis concerning the separation of Church and State: "The Civil rights of none shall be abridged on account of religious belief of worship, *nor shall any national religion be established*, nor shall the full and equal rights of Conscience be in any manner, or on any pretext, infringed."[15]

Thus, we see from the chief architect of the Constitution himself that the establishment clause means no national religion shall be established.

Because of the variety of Christian denominations in America, the Founding Fathers wisely built safeguards so that no one sect would be able to lord it over the others. Madison said as such. On June 12, 1788, he said this to the Virginia Convention:

> Fortunately for this Commonwealth, a majority of the people are decidedly against any exclusive establishment—I believe it to be so in other states. There is not a shadow of right in the general government to intermeddle with religion. . . . The United States abound in such a variety of sects, that it is a strong security against religious persecution, and it is sufficient to authorize a conclusion, that no one sect will ever be able to outnumber or depress the rest.[16]

Did you hear that, EEOC? Are you listening, ACLU? Are you taking notes, Department of Education? The father of the constitution declared, "*There is not a shadow of right in the general government to intermeddle with religion.*" Are you beginning to see how things have been twisted around today? The First Amendment has been turned on its head.

The Founders of this country never intended the First Amendment to be a hammer, chipping away at our religious freedoms. They never intended that the First Amendment would be invoked to prevent our children from saying grace before their meals at school!

After examining the evidence, Professor Cord concludes there were three purposes to the First Amendment, according to those who drafted and adopted it. The first we've already discussed—no national church was to be established. He enumerates the other two aims:

Second, it was designed to safeguard the right of freedom of conscience in religious beliefs against invasion solely by the national Government. Third, it was so constructed in order to allow the States, unimpeded, to deal with religious establishments and aid to religious institutions as they saw fit. There appears to be no historical evidence that the First Amendment was intended to preclude Federal governmental aid to religion when it was provided on a nondiscriminatory basis. Nor does there appear to be any historical evidence that the First Amendment was intended to provide an *absolute separation or independence* of religion and the national state. The actions of the early Congresses and Presidents, in fact, suggest quite the opposite.[17]

For example, James Madison, who framed the Constitution, served on the "Committee that recommended the Congressional Chaplain system."[18] So the First Amendment as understood by the Founders of this country is a far cry from the way the First Amendment has been interpreted in the last several decades. Thus, the First Amendment was never intended to expunge any reference to God in public. And yet it's been so misinterpreted and misapplied that religious expression in public seems amiss today.

And yet even today there are still vestiges of references to God that can be found in government. If anyone has any doubts about this, put down this book, pull out a dollar and look at the words "In God We Trust." Our national motto was not imposed on us from some alien nation; it reflects the truth that, at an earlier time, our nation's leaders wanted to acknowledge their dependence on the Almighty.

Take a walk around our nation's capital. Popular radio talk-show host and best-selling author, Rush Limbaugh, wrote, "America was founded as a Judeo-Christian country. Those of you who have been to Washington, D.C., and have toured the monuments, such as the Lincoln and Jefferson memorials, know the inscriptions have been carved in stone. You cannot read one without finding the word *God* in it somewhere."[19]

Furthermore, our Founding Fathers never intended to hinder in any way the affairs of the Church. The father of our country, George Washington, made that point in a letter he wrote on May 10, 1789, to the United Baptist Churches in Virginia. He penned: "If I could have entertained the slightest apprehension, that the Constitution framed in the Convention, where I had the honor to preside, might possibly endanger the religious rights of any ecclesiastical Society, certainly I would never have placed my signature to it."[20]

The Founders' Attitude toward Church and State

Let's delve further into the intent of the First Amendment by the Founders of this country by judging their actions at about the time they adopted the amendment. The things they did show that either they utterly disregarded the very law they enacted or that our present-day interpretation of the amendment is way off base.

For example, the first Congress of the United States, the very day after they approved the First Amendment, passed an act establishing chaplains. They established chaplains for the Army and the Navy, and they established chaplains for the Senate and the House. Now, if there is a high and impregnable wall between church and state, establishing chaplains would be unconstitutional. The ACLU and their ilk believe chaplains to be unconstitutional, and efforts have been made to try to have them abolished. Fortunately, they have been unsuccessful so far.

My coauthor Jerry Newcombe interviewed the ACLU's executive director, Ira Glasser, for our hard-hitting documentary exposing the radicalness of that organization. Jerry asked Mr. Glasser about the Founders' act of establishing chaplains. The response was illuminating. Glasser said, "The fact that the rights that they established were violated after they were written is true about any right [they passed]."[21] So, in other words, what the Founders intended they just weren't able to hold to themselves. Or looked at differently, we in the twentieth century know better what this law means than those who actually passed it!

That same first Congress also passed, at about the same time, the Northwest Ordinance, which is a very important document in our history. It's one of the principal documents in the history of the founding of America, along with the Articles of Confederation, the Declaration of Independence, and the Constitution. It gave the laws for the establishment of the Northwest Territory. In the Northwest Ordinance, Congress says something very significant—especially significant when you think that the Congress later said that no state seeking admission to the Union should have anything in its Constitution that would be antagonistic to the language of the Northwest Ordinance; they state: "Religion, morality and knowledge being essential to good government and the happiness of mankind, schools and the means of education shall forever be encouraged."[22] Notice that schools were to be established to teach *religion*, morality and knowledge!

This accurately reflects what the Founders thought of the First Amendment—totally the opposite of today's anti-Christian bigots who are using the First Amendment to suppress religion.

Another illustration of the Founders' attitude toward church and state is that they repeatedly called for national days of fasting, prayer, and thanksgiving. There were no less than sixteen such days called during the Revolutionary War alone. Even those misunderstood (and sometimes misrepresented) heroes of the modern "separationists," Jefferson and Madison, proclaimed national days of fasting and prayer. How could they all engage in these unconstitutional acts—unless they weren't unconstitutional?

Misinterpretation of the First Amendment

In light of all these things, where did we go astray? How have things become so twisted around? Much of the change began with a 1947 Supreme Court decision, a decision that was to have far-reaching implications long after the particulars were well known.

The turning point in American jurisprudence in church-state matters was the 1947 *Everson v. Board of Education* decision. Justice Hugo Black applied for the first time the "separation of church and state" concept to the First Amendment.[23] *Time* magazine pointed out: "That ruling marked a sharp separationist turn in court thinking. It unleashed a torrent of litigation that continues to flood courtrooms [forty-nine] years later. And in a succession of cases, the court drew the line ever more strictly."[24]

Over time, this interpretation came to gain wide circulation, so much so that, again, the average person today most likely thinks that the Constitution even *teaches* the separation of church and state. This misinterpretation of the First Amendment has effectively turned the First Amendment against religion, instead of protecting religion as it was designed to do.

As the effect of the *Everson* decision began to do its dirty work, it achieved its zenith under the Warren Court. In 1962 and 1963 came the infamous school prayer decisions, *Engel v. Vitale*, *Abbington v. Schempp*, and *Murray v. Curlett*. The Court could not tolerate any acknowledgment of God by the state or the state agencies (in this case the teachers). The fallout of these decisions has been horrendous. As we've already seen, principals and administrators have taken these and other High Court decisions to ridiculous lengths.

In the first prayer decision, June 17, 1962, *Engel v. Vitale*, the Supreme Court ruled this innocuous prayer unconstitutional: "Almighty God, we acknowledge our dependence upon Thee, and we beg Thy blessing upon us, our parents, our teachers and our country."[25] At that time, only one Supreme Court justice dissented (Byron White, new to the court, didn't vote). "I think this decision is wrong,"[26] said the lone dissenter, Justice Potter Stewart. At that time, *Newsweek* wrote of Stewart:

> He could not see, he said, how "an official religion" is established by letting those who want to say a prayer to say it. Citing several examples of U.S. institutions that invoke prayer (including the Supreme Court itself, which opens with the words, "God save the United States and this honorable Court"), the Ohio jurist summed up his attitude with a line from a ten-year-old Court decision [*Zorach v. Clauson*]: "We are a religious people whose institutions presuppose a Supreme Being."[27]

The only way that the modern secularist can come to the conclusion that the Founders of this country intended a purely secular state, where the state is "neutral" (translate "hostile") to religion is by *selective history*. They base their decisions on a few selected passages from our history and ignore a mountain of evidence to the contrary.

Parallels with the Former Soviet Union

In modern America we seem to be moving irresistibly toward the church-state view that the Soviets used to have. They prided themselves on the fact that they believed in the separation of church and state. They believed that the Church was free to do anything that the government was not engaged in, but their government was engaged in almost everything! Therefore, they held, the Church was free to stay within its four walls, to pray, and sing hymns; but if it did anything else, it was in big trouble. Also, ministers were not free to preach on the Millennium (since the Communists had *already* ushered in the Millennium!) and many other subjects. Thus the church-state view of the Soviets muzzled the freedom of the Church.

Something similar is happening in America, and, unfortunately, many churches, pastors, and Christians are accepting it and even defending it. Why? Because we're afraid. We're afraid of the flack; we're afraid of the controversy generated when we speak out on the issues of our day—such as to reject special rights for homosexuals, to oppose abortion, infanticide and euthanasia, or to condemn pornography, which victimizes women and children. We've run and we've hidden under our beds. We've forgotten the words of Scripture: "Fear not."

Article 52 of the Constitution of the former Soviet Union stated: "Freedom of conscience, that is the right to profess any religion or not to profess any religion, to perform religious rites or to conduct atheist propaganda shall be guaranteed for all citizens of the USSR." You will notice that Christians were free on paper to perform religious rites and atheists were free to propagandize atheism. But should a Christian in fact have tried to propagandize Christianity, he would have ended up in prison or Siberia. The Soviet system continually inculcated atheism in children, from the earliest ages, and even if a parent endeavored to indoctrinate a child in belief in God, he was subject to a prison sentence. The Soviet Constitution continued by saying, "The church in the USSR shall be separated from the state and the school from the church." It is amazing that in this country we're moving in that direction—even after the Russians have abandoned such a disastrous way!

A Theocracy, Then?

Meanwhile, many people who attack Christianity in this country accuse the religious right of trying to establish a theocracy here. That's not true. Despite the claims of our critics, we are *not* advocating a theocracy in America; we are only advocating a level playing field, so that Christianity is allowed a voice in the marketplace of ideas.

In the history of biblical religion, there has only been one theocracy and that was in the state of Israel in the Old Testament. God alone ruled, for there was no legislature in Israel. The Sanhedrin was not a legislature or parliament; it was simply a supreme court. There was only one lawgiver in Zion—God. He was the one who gave them all of their laws. Most Christians have always believed that that system of law ended with the destruction of Israel. Therefore, we as Christians do not by *any* means advocate the establishment of a theocracy. I would not agree with any push to reinstitute the Old Testament civil and legal system as replacing our whole governmental legislation. That is not what we favor. But the Old Testament laws *do* give us guidance as to the kinds of laws that civil government should form. And I do believe that the laws of every nation should be in harmony—not with the civil laws of the Old Testament—but at least with the moral laws of the Ten Commandments.

Jesus lived under the theocracy, but His death and the subsequent dispersal of Israel brought an end to it. By His Spirit working through the early Church, I think it is very clear that He did not mean to spread that system into the whole world. Even at the first Council at Jerusalem, they said, in effect, "we had a system of laws that we ourselves could not bear and now we should not try and impose this on the Gentile world" (Acts 15). I believe the Church has been acting in accordance with Christ as He revealed His will through His Spirit to the early

Church. So, therefore, I would say Jesus is not in favor of trying to restore theocracy to the whole civilized world.

Somebody asked me if I was out to Christianize America. And I said, "No, of course not. I'm out to Christianize the *whole world*." What else does the Great Commission mean but that? We are to proclaim the gospel to all people and pray that they will respond positively to the invitation to receive Christ and the gift of eternal life. And if they do, they will become Christians, and that will result in a greater "Christianization" of any country where they live. It's amazing that that is seen as somehow *un*-American or alien or foreign, whereas 99.8 percent of the people in this country as late as 1776 (one hundred fifty-plus years after the Pilgrims landed here) professed themselves to be Christians—99.8 percent![28] "Christianizing" this country is only an effort to return to where the country started; it is not an attempt to introduce something foreign, alien, or strange.

Conclusion

Ultimately, there are two views of church-state relations. Both are very different in their starting and concluding points. The historical view—that the function of the Church is separate from the state, but in no way is God divorced from government—served this country well for our first one hundred seventy years and gave us a uniquely free America. The more recent view of the First Amendment—that God is totally divorced from government, that the church is to have no bearing on the state, and that the state should have the ability to regulate the Church—has led to the secularization of America. It has turned the First Amendment into a hammer that pounds away at the Church and any public expression of Christianity. This view of the strict separation of church and state is not only not historical, it has led to measurable and serious damage to our country.[29]

But all that said, I must underscore that even if we were to continue down the same path of a strict separation of church and state and even if Christianity were to become *illegal* in America (which seems unlikely), Christianity will continue. As we'll see in Chapter 11, the Christian faith has survived the most unbelievable persecution. Try as they might, the very forces of Hell itself will not prevail against Christ's Church, even if the First Amendment continues to be perverted as it has been for the last four decades.

Before he was chief justice of the Supreme Court, William Rehnquist wrote a dissenting opinion on a school prayer case (*Wallace v. Jaffre*, wherein the High Court overturned Alabama's moment-of-silence law as unconstitutional). Here is what Rehnquist wrote in his brilliant dissent:

The true meaning of the Establishment Clause can only be seen in its history. . . . The Framers intended the Establishment Clause to prohibit the designation of any church as a "national" one. The Clause was also designed to stop the Federal Government from asserting a preference for one religious denomination or sect over others. . . . George Washington himself, at the request of the very Congress which passed the Bill of Rights, proclaimed a day of "public thanksgiving and prayer, to be observed by acknowledging with grateful hearts the many and signal favors of Almighty God." *History must judge whether it was the Father of his Country in 1789, or a majority of the Court today, which has strayed from the meaning of the Establishment Clause.*[30]

The Hammer of Unbelief within the Church

The solid foundation of God stands, having this seal: "The Lord knows those who are His," and, "Let everyone who names the name of Christ depart from iniquity."
—2 Timothy 2:19

More than ten years ago, *60 Minutes* and *Reader's Digest* revealed to the public a shocking truth: Tithes being given in mainline churches were going to rebel forces in Africa who were killing Christian missionaries! The World Council of Churches was the conduit for the funds.[1] This is a classic example of what I call the most grievous attack on Christ—that which comes from *within* the professing Church. Because of their outwardly Christian trappings, these hammers of unbelief within the Church are perhaps more difficult to detect. But they, too, will break one day. Signs of their weakening are already evident.

The Attack on Christ from within the Church

We know that *throughout* history believers have been persecuted—sometimes even by those in clerical garb![2] The true conflict is between God and Satan. But today, when Christianity is under siege from all directions, what is perhaps most disconcerting is the attack on Christ from *within* the Church. In this chapter we will examine some of these hammers of unbelief within the Church.

Liberal Seminaries

Tragically, many of the nation's seminaries are so liberal they have abandoned historic Christianity or key elements of the faith. They don't believe in the Bible, the deity of Christ, His atoning work on the cross, or His bodily resurrection. They are blind guides shipwrecking the faith of many a young person wishing to serve God—only to come away from seminary as virtual nonbelievers. Carl Rogers, for example, reportedly went to seminary to serve Christ. There he abandoned historic Christianity; he went on to become the father of a branch of psychology that has turned many away from true faith.

When I set off to divinity school so many years ago, I knew nothing about seminaries. I found myself in one where about half the professors were orthodox, and the other half, neoorthodox. That's another way of saying that about half them believed the Bible and the other half didn't. And I heard the Bible attacked by these unbelievers in ways that were incredibly traumatic to a young theologian-to-be. My faith was shaken during that first year because I had a number of unbelievers for professors. Providentially, those who *were* believers helped me keep my head above water. In order to spare others from a similar experience, I eventually founded Knox Theological Seminary, so that the Bible would be taught as the inerrant word of God that it is.

My friend R. C. Sproul, the author, speaker, and head of Ligonier Ministries in Orlando, recalls one day when he was in seminary. One of his unbelieving professors asked in class, "How can you possibly believe in the atonement of Christ in this day and age?" Sproul thought to himself, *How can you possibly deny the atonement of Christ and be teaching in this Christian school?*[3]

On the day after Easter 1994, the Jewish syndicated columnist Don Feder wrote about Harvard Divinity School. He pointed out how far this school is from its Puritan roots:

> Instead of singing hymns, they're sitting in the lotus position, chanting "omm" at America's oldest school of theology. The Nave's [student newsletter] calendar reminds students that March 20 is Spring Ohigon, "a special time to listen to the Buddha and meditate on the perfection of enlightenment.". . . There's no mention of Palm Sunday or Passover, reflecting their insignificance at an institution where all is venerated, save Western religion.[4]

Feder has a friend studying there who told him that at Harvard Divinity School, "all religions are equal except Christianity, which is very bad, and Judaism, which loses points *where it intersects with Christianity.*[5] Feder refers to it as a "poison-ivy" school![6] This is, of course, not at all in keeping with the intentions of the Reverend John Harvard, who donated heavily to help found the school.

Indeed, a lot of these seminaries are theologically poisoning young people with their unbelief. While there are some excellent seminaries out there today, others are theologically disastrous. Young people considering the ministry today should be exceedingly careful before they go to seminary. Make sure it is biblically sound. Alumni of Christian universities should monitor their alma maters before blindly giving them their money. There is an attack on Christ from within many formerly Christian schools.

The good news is that seminaries that believe the Bible is the Word of God are on the rise, whereas many of the unbelieving seminaries are closing their doors. Another smashed hammer falls to the ground. Furthermore, the quality of evangelical scholarship is growing. We're no longer on the outside looking in.

Bible "Scholars"

Meanwhile, there are numerous Bible "scholars" who undermine the Scriptures. A recent example was the so-called Jesus Seminar, where more than seventy scholars voted anonymously whether they thought Jesus said the various quotes attributed to Him in the Gospels. They ended up concluding that He only said 18 percent of that which He said! For instance, these scholars voted that Jesus never said, "I am the way, the truth, and the life. No one comes to the Father except through Me" (John 14:6). Out of the Lord's Prayer, the only thing the group agreed He said was "Our Father."[7] The scholars wrote a book entitled *The Five Gospels,* so named because they treat the largely apocryphal Gospel of Thomas on the same level (if not higher) than the four Gospels.[8]

Furthermore, a spate of relatively recent books have come out against the historical Christ:

- *Rescuing the Bible from Fundamentalism* by Episcopal Bishop John Shelby Spong. I'll bet you didn't realize the Bible needed to be rescued from fundamentalists, did you? After twenty centuries, Christendom has discovered that the Bible needs to be liberated from those who take it for what it claims to be—the revealed Word of God! One wag pointed out that somebody needs to rescue the Episcopal Church from Spong! This man has generated a few books now that essentially deny key tenets of the historic Christian faith. Unfortunately, the bishop is not alone.

- *Jesus the Man* presents Jesus as a divorced father of three who later remarries a woman bishop. The book was written by Dr. Barbara Thiering, a woman professor in the department of divinity of Sydney University. When it came out, the book was reportedly selling "like hotcakes" in Australia and in America.[9] Even if that sales report is true for that particular volume (and I must add that I've never come across a copy), there's no doubt that in the religious book market, the evangelical volumes (that promote faith, not denigrate it) sell the best, even though they're often hard to find in secular bookstores.

* *Jesus: A Revolutionary Biography* is an iconoclastic book written by Dr. John Dominic Crossan, a scholar and professor at DePaul University, a major Catholic university in Chicago. He views the Gospel writers as engaging in what one journalist labeled "retrospective mythmaking."[10] The book denies such essential Christian doctrines as the virgin birth and Christ's resurrection; instead, the book states that it's likely that the body of the Lord was eaten by dogs!

These are not obscure books with a tiny audience. These are widely publicized books sold (in small quantities) by major publishers. The tragedy is that if you go to your average secular bookstore and you make your way to the *back* where the religion section normally is (it's to the "back of the bus" for Christians today), you will generally find as many books *against* Christianity as you will find books *for* it! In fact, you'll often find more con than pro. *Christianity Today* even had a cover story on some of these new books about our Lord, appropriately entitled, "The New, Unimproved Jesus."[11] In one sense the antibiblical scholarship is not new; on the other hand, it does seem to be gaining momentum, except insofar as adherents are concerned. The more a denomination moves toward embracing these antibiblical notions, the more it loses membership.

Waning Denominations

Mainline denominations and liberal seminaries are vanishing because of a lack of interest and relevance. Note that in 1965 there were 3.4 million Episcopalians in the U.S.[12] By 1994, that number was down to 2.4 million.[13] Note that during the same time, the U.S. population grew from 194.5 million in 1965[14] to 262 million in 1994.[15] Not all Episcopalians are liberal, of course, but that the denomination continues to allow John Shelby Spong to serve as a bishop speaks volumes about its lack of biblical standards.

In 1958 the Presbyterian Church (Presbyterian Church in the U.S. combined with the United Presbyterian Church in the U.S.A.) had 4 million members. Today the membership of the Presbyterian Church (U.S.A.) (the two merged in the 1970s) is 2.7 million.[16] Again, not all Presbyterians in the U.S.A. branch are unbelieving, but many are. And in some areas, the denomination has veered greatly from its biblical roots. I have never been a part of the Presbyterian Church, U.S.A. It's too liberal for me. Instead, I am a minister with the Presbyterian Church in America, a Bible-based, Christ-centered body.

Simultaneous with the waning of the liberal denominations, the evangelical groups have been growing significantly. A study conducted in 1990 found that of the "500 fastest-growing Protestant congregations" in this country, the vast majority—89 percent—were evangelical![17] Thus, we see the breaking of some of the hammers of unbelief in the Church.

Open Season on Christ

Unfortunately, when one hammer breaks, it seems like another one arises to take its place. There are things being said about Jesus Himself that would never have been said before. One Bible scholar of the Jesus Seminar had the audacity to call Jesus "a party animal"[18]—a very disrespectful way to label Him. The head of the Jesus Seminar, Dr. Robert Funk, said that Christ was "no goody two shoes."[19] What's more, The Atlanta Journal reports that: "Jesus probably was a homeless drifting sage who ate and drank freely, was not celibate and challenged the religious customs of his day, according to the head of the Jesus Seminar."[20] Not celibate? Doesn't it seem like it's open season on Christians—and even *Christ*—these days? The character of the only perfect human being to ever live is being dragged through the mud by those with the respectability of a degree behind their names.

I should point out that I've earned a Masters of Divinity (cum laude) at Columbia Theological Seminary (where former Senate Chaplain Peter Marshall went), a Masters of Theology (summa cum laude) at Chicago Graduate School of Theology, and a Ph.D. at New York University, and *nowhere* is there evidence that Jesus was not celibate or that He was "a party animal"! Nowadays, some theological circles seem to play a game of "can you top this?"

So how are we to come to grips with this kind of scholarship? I remember what my seminary professor, Dr. William Childs Robinson, said. (He was one of the *orthodox* ones.) He said you have to remember that you *choose* your scholars. There are scholars that say everything! *To whom you choose to listen determines the outcome.*

While there are liberal Bible scholars who deny some or many tenets of the faith, there are just as many—if not more—scholars who hold to a much more conservative position. For instance, there is a much larger group of biblical scholars—than those seventy-eight or so of the Jesus Seminar—who believe Jesus said *everything* that is recorded of Him in the four Gospels. But that's never going to make *Time*, or *Newsweek*, or any other magazine. They seem to only print that which is contrary to the Bible. However, I must quickly add that lately the tide seems to be turning. Lately, the explosive growth of conservative Christianity has often been grabbing the attention of many of these news magazines.

A Deeper Look at the Jesus Seminar

Let's delve further into the Jesus Seminar. The critical point to understand is that there was no *new* evidence in the Scripture that drove the scholars at the seminar to their conclusions; it was rather their own liberal approach that led them even to undertake the project in the first place. The Jesus Seminar is best understood as worn-out, liberal theologians who have turned to a publicist instead of the truth—the Jesus of Scripture. Dr. James Montgomery Boice of Tenth Presbyterian Church in Philadelphia points out the Jesus Seminar is "really an example of liberal ministers and professors coming out of the closet. All they're really doing is in *public* what they do in a more private way in the classroom and in their own studies." Dr. Boice points out the obvious: "Imagine a group of scholars, now, two thousand years from the time that Jesus lived and whose words were written down by eyewitnesses, a group of scholars *two thousand years later* voting in a meeting on what Jesus really said and what He didn't. That is laughable."[21]

"It just seems like the more preposterous you can be," observes R. C. Sproul, "the more radical you can be, the easier it is to get a degree or to get a hearing in certain academic circles."[22]

"Liberal" and "unbelieving" are synonymous when it comes to theology. So the Jesus Seminar is essentially unbelieving scholars sharing their unbelief. When they ask a question like, "Did Jesus make this statement or not?" and then vote on that anonymously, as the scholars at the Jesus Seminar did, what they're voting on is simply their own prejudices. There is nothing in the historic record, nothing in the biblical manuscripts, that supports what they say. And while manuscripts may differ in places when it comes to spelling or words, they are in complete agreement in *every* point of theology.

So, if there are any things in question, they are all listed in the critical apparatus. But the people of the Jesus Seminar weren't dealing with the *manuscript* evidence, they were dealing with, frankly, their own feelings, and with extrabiblical writings (primarily, the Gospel of Thomas, which the early Church decidedly rejected as Gnostic heresy).

Material in the Gospels where manuscripts differ in spelling or in words concerns maybe 1 or 2 percent of the text; the New Testament documents are very reliable. Instead, what the Jesus Seminar has done is to get rid of 82 percent of the text! Textually, they stand on quicksand.

An important new book rebuts the Jesus Seminar from an evangelical perspective: *Jesus under Fire: Modern Scholarship Reinvents the Historical Jesus*, edited by Michael J. Wilkins and J. P. Moreland.[23] Among those who have written essays for this book is Dr. Gary Habermas, author and coauthor of numerous books on the historicity of Jesus Christ. In the chapter entitled "Where Do We Start Studying Jesus?" Denver Seminary professor Craig Blomberg has this to say about the group:

> The Jesus Seminar and its friends do not reflect any consensus of scholars except for those on the "radical fringe" of the field. Its methodology is seriously flawed and its conclusions unnecessarily skeptical. . . . The conservative nature of oral tradition in ancient Judaism, particularly among disciples who revered their rabbis' words, makes it highly likely that Jesus' teaching would have been carefully preserved, even given a certain flexibility in the specific wording with which it was reported . . . there is a huge volume of scholarship to support the picture of Christ that Matthew, Mark, Luke, and John portray.[24]

The "Gay" Church

It's disheartening to witness the rise of the so-called "Christian" gay movement. In addition to choosing their unnatural lifestyle, some homosexuals now want to retain the blessings of the Church. The fact is, they fool themselves into believing that God somehow accepts them just as they are—in their *unrepentant* sin.

Homosexuals form churches in an attempt to find justification and acceptance from God while they continue to practice their sin. Their effort is vain and futile. No practicing homosexual will enter the kingdom of Heaven (1 Cor. 6:9). (Nor will any practicing fornicator, idolater, adulterer, thief, or drunkard.) Even some homosexuals can see through the lies. Luke Sissyfag, the gay who twice has interrupted President Clinton on national television, told this to *Rutherford* magazine recently: "The gay Christian movement is hysterical. Christians know it's bogus. I know it's bogus. Who are they fooling? Nobody."[25] "Gay churches" remind me of the ancient pagan temples, which deified adultery and made pious prostitution the act of the day. They changed the truth of God into a lie.

The attitude of the Christian to homosexuals should be the same attitude as God's—He loves homosexuals.[26] We are not to hate them, but to love them, as God loves them. That does not mean that you love or condone their acts; you accept *them*, not their *deeds*. Sadly, some Christians have missed this point and have marched around with signs saying, "God hates fags" or the like. All they do is drive homosexuals farther away from Christianity and provide fodder to the gay movement to further harass true Christians.

A recent homosexual publication blasphemed Christ, which is not uncommon; only this one went further than most. Robert Knight wrote the following in *The Kansas Christian*:

> *The Advocate* front cover of December 13, 1994, asks, "Is God Gay?" and depicts Jesus Christ in garish colors as a homosexual, complete with sexual devices around his neck and obscene body-part imagery around and on Him.
>
> Inside the magazine is an even more obscene portrayal: a full-color, full page picture that includes realistic renderings of male and female genitalia. It accompanies a disingenuous article about the merits of the homosexual-oriented Metropolitan Community Church.[27]

Much of the antipathy toward Christianity and Christians comes from the homosexual community. Of course, the media is clearly pro-gay, so many of the threats and violence against Christians don't get reported. But homosexuals in San Francisco have allegedly set on fire the home of Presbyterian minister Chuck McIlhenny to try to kill him and his family. Chuck became an object of their wrath more than a decade ago by firing his organist when he learned he was gay.[28] One hundred unruly homosexual protesters disrupted the evening service of Hamilton Square Baptist Church in San Francisco, assaulting women, children, and the handicapped. They destroyed much of the property and tore down the Christian flag, replacing it with the homosexual one. They even banged on the doors and cried out, "We want your children!"[29] In New York City gay protesters have disrupted the mass at St. Patrick's Cathedral more than once, desecrating the Communion host (the "elements" in Protestant terminology), and profanely insulting the worshipers. The services of Calvary Chapel in Costa Mesa were marred by homosexual protesters, and I refuse to print here what one of them did in public in front of members of the congregation. Many in the pro-family movement, including myself, have received death threats from the gays. And, again, thanks to a media hostile to Christians, virtually all of this goes unreported!

Some people who speak out for special rights for homosexuals claim to be Christians, and they claim that "homophobia" against them is akin to the racial bigotry directed against blacks for hundreds of years in this country. Mel White, a former writer and film producer for "the religious right," declared himself gay and incurable a few years ago; he has also "declared war on the religious right." White encourages his readers to build "networks with our friends and allies. . . . with the ACLU, with People for the American Way, with NOW. . . . "[30] You can tell which side one is on by his allies. As we've seen, some of those organizations are the most involved in the attack on Christ in America!

But despite all of this, there are some good things happening on this front that we don't normally hear about. Today there are *thousands* of homosexuals who are coming to Christ and getting out of their sinful lifestyle. Some homosexuals literally get their first exposure to any form of "Christianity" through homosexual churches; they then go on to true faith in Christ! Richard Culbertson, one such individual, now helps other homosexuals to change their sexual orientation through Christianity. He says that he hears over and over from the people he helps that they didn't realize this was changeable. They thought they were born this way and that there was nothing they could do about it. But they are finding forgiveness for their sins and the strength through Christ to change their orientation. Richard heads up the Worthy Creations ministry here in South Florida, and he's been seeing the ministry growing and expanding. Worthy Creations is just one group, one of the many under the umbrella of Exodus, International. Exodus is also growing. In fact, just recently they have begun to expand in a major way in South America.[31]

Furthermore, Christian ministry to AIDS patients is becoming better organized and more active. Most notable is the work of the Christian AIDS Services Alliance (CASA). They have a network of referrals of Christian agencies across the nation ready to help AIDS patients regardless of their religious affiliation. Thus, AIDS patients are receiving physical, medical, and spiritual help in the name of Christ like never before.[32]

The Far Left

Another hammer trying to pound away at orthodox Christianity is the liberal position taken by many in the mainline denominations: Strong elements of the so-called "pro-choice"[33] movement can be found within the professing Church. So can humanistic judges, politicians, and school administrators who participate in the attack on Christ in America, under the misguided interpretation of the separation of church and state. There are even "Christian" ministers who are members of the humanistic People for the American Way or of the American Civil Liberties Union. Of course, we're talking about liberal ministers; nonetheless, they receive their pay from the person in the pew who gives at offering time.

Then there's the "sold-out-to-the-world-spirit" crowd—the group within the professing Church that embraces every fad that comes down the pike, even when it may be diametrically opposed to Christ. During news broadcasts about the latest attack on Christ, there is often featured some clergyman found to be a spokesman on the *anti*-Christian side. When the film *The Last Temptation of Christ* came out, the National Council of Churches spoke out *in favor* of it.

In recent years, some mainstream denominations have come out with committee reports on human sexuality to be considered by the church-governing body. Some of these reports read virtually like tracts written in the heyday of the "Sexual Revolution"—*promoting* sexual sin under the umbrella of misnomers like "justice love." They condone just about every sexual perversion under the sun in the name of Christianity. You wouldn't know there had been a downside to the revolution and that more than fifty million Americans are suffering with a sexually transmitted disease. While such viral infections can be controlled, they can't be cured, and they often recur.[34] Of course, there's what the Bible teaches about human sexuality. But to many leaders of these denominations, the Scriptures would appear to be obsolete. The Bible has been thrown out and *Playboy* brought in!

The Far Right

Those who don white sheets and terrorize blacks, Jews, or Catholics are also part of the attack on Christ in America. Fortunately, their numbers have been significantly dwindling in recent years.[35] Another hammer bites the dust. Is Jesus pleased with the KKK? Of course not! Is Jesus pleased with the Aryan Nation cult that claims to be Christian? Of course not! He said to His followers, "Love your neighbor as yourself" (Mark 12:31) and even, "Love your enemies" (Matt. 5:44).

As for those who blame Christianity for the Ku Klux Klan (such unwarranted criticisms are heard from time to time), I think it's similar to questioning the honesty of Abraham Lincoln because a savings and loan association bearing his name was involved in a financial scandal! Some of the KKK claim to be Christians and fighting for Christianity, but any resemblance between their twisted, hateful worldview and the gospel of the Prince of Peace is purely coincidental. In short, the fiery cross bears no resemblance to the cross of Christ!

To be sure, there have been people deceived into thinking they were doing God's will by joining the Ku Klux Klan—even when that meant blowing up and torching some forty-four black *churches* (as the Klan did in the summer of 1964 alone)[36] or killing black children in Sunday School.

Tommy Tarrants, Jr., from Mobile, Alabama, was a zealot for the Klan. In fact, he was viewed by one FBI agent trailing him as a "mad-dog killer." Tarrants and his colleagues were part of a violent branch of the Klan that thought that the Jews and the Communists teamed up to "destroy white Christian society"[37] by forcing integration. But even this man, blinded as he was by racism, bigotry, and hate, found the truth in a life-changing encounter with Jesus Christ, who shatters the hammers of racism.

After Tarrants was nearly killed in a shoot-out with the police and the FBI, from which he survived only through supernatural intervention, he was sent to jail. While reading the Bible in prison, God removed the scales from his eyes and he became a Christian. He said,

> I got on my knees in that cell and just gave my life completely to Christ and asked him to come in—I didn't even know that he wanted it—but I said, "Lord, I've ruined my life, but if you want it, I'll just give it to you completely. Here it is." And something changed inside of me when I did that, I could even feel it. Something happened and I became different.[38]

Today Tommy Tarrants is a *totally* changed man. The former terrorist for the Klan is now the pastor of an interracial church! Tommy even cowrote a book with his black brother in Christ, John Perkins, entitled *He's My Brother*. In that book Tarrants writes: "If we love God and want to love others and bring them into His Kingdom, we will want to rid ourselves of our lack of concern and racial prejudice, and engage the world, black and white, with the reconciling love of Jesus Christ."[39]

Tommy Tarrants's story exemplifies what is the greatest strategy we have to end the attack on Christ in America: leading His enemies to Christ! Throughout history and even in our own time, there have been many enemies of the cross who embraced the Faith. William J. Murray, the son of Madalyn Murray O'Hair, is a contemporary example. It's as if a hammer against the Lord is converted into a tool set apart for the purposes of the Lord. They are living illustrations that the gates of Hell shall not prevail.

Sophia

In November of 1993, in Minneapolis, about 2,200 people gathered for a church-sponsored "Re-imagining" conference. They were mostly women, with a handful of men. Almost all of the attendees worked for a church.

This "Re-imagining" conference was dedicated to reimagining what God is like. It dedicated itself to rethinking Jesus, the community, and the Church. When a young member of our church heard just the *title* of the conference, he blurted out: "It's all right there in the Bible; you don't have to 'reimagine' anything!"

The conference praised "Sophia, our Maker," (*sophia* is the Greek word for wisdom) while God the Father was met with derision. The atonement of Christ was denigrated by some of the speakers. For example, Delores Williams of Union Seminary said, "Jesus came for life and. . . . atonement has to do so much with death. . . . I don't think we need folks hanging on crosses and blood dripping and weird stuff." Speaker Aruna Gnanadason of the World Council of Churches said, "In a global context where violence and the use of force have become the norm, the violence that the cross symbolizes and the patriarchal image of an almighty, invincible father god needs to be challenged and reconstructed."[40]

This conference was funded by mainline churches. New Age ideas, lesbianism, and even goddess worship were promoted, while historic Christianity was ridiculed. Virtually all the funds for this conference came from church funds. Picture the believer in the pew donating money for the work of the kingdom, only to have it pay for such things! The conference climaxed with an "erotic" milk and honey celebration (as opposed to the Lord's Supper) to Sophia.[41] Part of the liturgy of that celebration included this prayer: "Sophia, Creator God, let your milk and honey flow. . . . Our sweet Sophia, we are women in your image. With nectar between our thighs, we invite a lover, we birth a child; with our warm body fluids, we remind the world of its pleasure and sensations."[42]

It is the most heretical report I have ever seen of any conference. Considering their degree of theological error, the "Sophists" make Mormons, Jehovah's Witnesses, and Christian Scientists look like Orthodox Christians by comparison. In all of Church history, I have never read of anything that was as heretical and blasphemous as that conference was. When someone would mention the Trinity, they would laugh. When someone would mention God the Father, they would boo. It was blasphemous to the worst degree, and it just shows you the depths to which some of the liberal denominations have plummeted. They even held a similar conference, on a smaller scale, about a year later. Furthermore, there is even a new "Sophia caucus" within the Presbyterian Church (U.S.A.).[43]

Fortunately, the National Council of Churches, a consortium of liberal churches (including some of those involved in the Re-imagining conference) is nothing like it was thirty-five or forty years ago. They were once powerful, but now they have come close to going bankrupt. They have laid off all sorts of personnel. The same is true for many of the liberal denominations. (I heard one report that more Americans attend Calvary Chapels, part of the evangelical movement, than attend Episcopal Churches, one of the mainline denominations.) The liberal mainline denominations are all dying, and the NCC, as their cooperative agency, is going down with them. Many of the remains of these hammers lie broken at the foot of God's anvil.

These Sophia-worshiping activities remind me of an incident the week before the well-publicized 1995 World Conference on Women sponsored by the United Nations in Beijing, which promoted a radical, antifamily agenda. Many women, delegates from around the world, attended workshops in China the week before the conference. The largest group was a coalition of feminists who stood squarely against the Bible and the Vatican on the issue of human sexuality (not to mention other areas). They claimed the Bible "teaches complete sexual freedom"— including fornication. As believers in free speech (except for the kind they don't like), they shouted down the opposition that tried to counter this lie. Next, they gathered together for prayer to Mother Earth. They held hands in a circle and a delegate from Brazil said the prayer: "Thanks to Mother Earth, for you give life. Thanks for water. People from my community decided no more Crucifixion. We believe in life. We celebrate life, not the Crucifixion. We are power." Then many of them, including Bella Abzug, the former Congresswoman from New York, held their hands in the air and chanted "I am power, I am power, I am power."[44] Whether these women were a part of the Re-imagining group or not, they are certainly one in spirit with this movement.

It's interesting to note that all of these women, and for that matter, all the anti-Christian people the world over, will one day acknowledge that *Jesus Christ*— not Mother Earth or any other false god—is Lord. They will one day bow the knee and with their tongue confess that Jesus is Lord to the glory of God the Father (Phil. 2:9–11). One day Hitler will bow the knee before Jesus Christ. So will Marx, Lenin, Stalin, Mao, and Castro. One day Martin Scorsese, Oliver Stone, Madonna, and Roseanne will bow their knees and profess with their mouths that He is Lord. For most of these people it may well be too late (after their death, with no hope of salvation). Everyone the world over, including every trendy, unbelieving clergy person, will make this admission that He is Lord. Keep that in mind the next time you hear some blasphemer spout off against Christianity.

What *Is* the Church?

We've seen in this chapter hammers of unbelief from within the Church attempting to strike at orthodox Christianity. These forces are not as prominent as they might seem, but the hostile media often exaggerate the influence or credibility of these anti-Christian church leaders. Nonetheless, how are we to understand how they can be within the Church and yet be enemies of Christ?

I think it helpful to back up for a moment and define the Church. The Church is the body of believers, in whom Christ dwells (1 Cor. 12:12–27; Rom. 8:10–11). They are those redeemed by the blood of Jesus Christ (Rev. 1:5). But there is a much wider definition of the Church. The professing Church consists of nearly two billion people who *claim* to be believers in Jesus Christ. Within the "visible Church" is the "invisible Church." The invisible Church is a smaller group; it consists of those who *truly* have been redeemed by the blood of Christ. God, and only God, knows all those who belong in the invisible Church.

This distinction between the visible and invisible Church is creatively shown by C. S. Lewis in his book *The Screwtape Letters*, a series of imaginary letters from an uncle demon, Screwtape, to his nephew demon, Wormwood. In one of these, the older devil observed,

> One of the great allies at present is the Church itself. Do not misunderstand me. I do not mean the Church as we see her spread out through all time and space and rooted in eternity, terrible as an army with banners. That, I confess, is a spectacle which makes our boldest tempters uneasy. But fortunately it is quite invisible to these humans.[45]

We can't know (this side of Paradise) all those who truly believe; that's why we are to work out our own salvation with fear and trembling (Phil. 2:12). Paul says in 2 Timothy 2:19, "The solid foundation of God stands, having this seal: 'The Lord knows those who are His,' and, 'Let everyone who names the name of Christ depart from iniquity.'" So we don't know who's truly saved, but God does. We also know that we *can* have assurance of our own salvation. First John 5:13 says, "These things I have written . . . that you may *know* that you have eternal life" (emphasis mine). If we are truly Christians, we will strive in our hearts to obey God's Word and bear fruit for His glory. What a far cry from a group like the "gay church," which pretends as if God made them that way and that He accepts them in their *continuing* sin. Not that homosexuality is a worse sin than others; but as Christians we are not to *continue* in our sin. That doesn't mean we don't ever fall. It does mean we don't *stay* down.

So, although the professing Church consists of almost two billion people, only God knows exactly who are really His.[46] Thus, we have within the nominal Church many nonbelievers who are spreading their nonbelief. This is reminiscent of Christ's parable of the wheat and the tares:

> The kingdom of heaven is like a man who sowed good seed in his field; but while men slept, his enemy came and sowed tares among the wheat and went his way. But when the grain had sprouted and produced a crop, then the tares also appeared. So the servants of the owner came and said to him, "Sir, did you not sow good seed in your field? How then does it have tares?" He said to them, "An enemy has done this." The servants said to him, "Do you want us then to go and gather them up?" But he said, "No, lest while you gather up the tares you also uproot the wheat with them. Let both grow together until the harvest, and at the time of harvest I will say to the reapers, 'First gather together the tares and bind them in bundles to burn them, but gather the wheat into my barn.'". . ." He who sows the good seed is the Son of Man. The field is the world, the good seeds are the sons of the kingdom, but the tares are the sons of the wicked one. The enemy who sowed them is the devil, the harvest is the end of the age." (Matt. 13:24–30, 37–39)

And as the world contains the wheat and the tares, so, too, the visible Church contains those who are truly Christians and those who are not.

Meanwhile, as we saw in the first chapter, we are currently witnessing an amazing growth of the true Church around the world. In our nation, the evangelical Church is growing so fast that it has eclipsed (and will continue to eclipse) the mainline denominations, many of which are liberal and unbelieving. Given the present trends, by the middle of the twenty-first century, there will be two great religious forces in America, and by far the largest will be evangelical Christianity. The other will be Roman Catholicism—maybe a third or a half the size of evangelicalism.

Conclusion

I close with the words of a former nonbeliever, Napoleon, who in his last days turned to the Scriptures to find the meaning of life. In all of his fame, he only discovered who Jesus was at the last. He said to General Bertrand, who was an atheist:

> I know men; and I tell you that Jesus Christ was not a man. Superficial minds see a resemblance between Christ and the founders of empires, and the gods of other religions. That resemblance does not exist. We can say to the authors of every other religion, "You are neither gods, nor the agents of the Deity." What do these gods, so boastful, know more than other mortals; these legislators, Greek or Roman; this Numa; this Lycurgus; these priests of India or of Memphis; this Confucius; this Mohammed?—absolutely nothing. They have made a perfect chaos of mortals. There is not one among them all who has said any thing new in reference to our future destiny, to the soul, to the essence of God, to the creation. Enter the sanctuaries of paganism: you there find perfect chaos, a thousand contradictions, war between the gods, the immobility of sculpture, the division and the rending of unity, the parceling out of the divine attributes mutilated or denied in their essence. It is not so with Christ. Everything in Him astonishes me. His spirit overawes me, and His will confounds me. Between Him and whoever else in the world there is no possible term of comparison. He is truly a being by Himself. Bertrand, if you do not perceive that Jesus Christ is God, very well: then I did wrong to make you a general.[47]

The Gates of Hell Shall Not Prevail

The Attack on Christ Put into Perspective

*There is no wisdom, no insight, no plan
that can succeed against the LORD.*
—Proverbs 21:30 NIV

Thomas Paine was the only directly anti-Christian man of the founding era of which I'm aware. Paine is best known for his commendable book *Common Sense*, which helped ignite the American Revolution. But he later wrote an anti-Christian book, *Age of Reason*, to try and debunk Christianity. He sent a copy of the manuscript to some of the Founding Fathers. They all regarded it with disdain and displeasure.[1] Ben Franklin received a copy and wrote a very telling reply. It's even more telling when we remember that Franklin was among the least religious of the Founding Fathers.[2] Franklin's response to Paine fits the main theme of this book, that the gates of Hell shall not triumph over Christianity:

> I have read your manuscript with some attention. . . . the consequence of printing this piece will be a great deal of odium drawn upon yourself, mischief to you, and no benefit to others. *He that spits into the wind, spits in his own face. But were you to succeed, do you imagine any good would be done by it?* . . . Think about how great a portion of mankind consists of weak and ignorant men and women, and of inexperienced, inconsiderate youth of both sexes, who have need of the motives of religion to restrain them from vice, to support their virtue, and retain

them in the practice of it till it becomes habitual, which is the great point for its security. *And perhaps you are indebted to her originally, that is, to your religious education, for the habits of virtue upon which you now justly value yourself.*[3]

Franklin took a utilitarian approach to Christianity. If Christianity were to be undermined, then there would go morality. That is precisely what has happened to our society in the last few decades. But the main reason I quote from Franklin is the idea that Paine was just hurting *himself* by railing against God: "He that spits into the wind, spits in his own face." That's what Christian bashing is! Those who oppose God and His Christ are in for a rude awakening. Even if they may succeed for a season, even if they tragically find they can grab many souls with them on their way to Hell, they will find He is invincible and His purposes cannot fail. As the Bible says, "There is no wisdom, no insight, no plan that can succeed against the LORD" (Prov. 21:30 NIV).

The Attempt to Replace Christ

A few years ago a news article reported that a disgruntled employee of the Encyclopaedia Britannica Corporation, who was slated to be laid off, attempted to sabotage the database of the company. He chose to do this by substituting every occasion of the use of the name "Jesus Christ" with the word "Allah," the god of the Muslims. Fortunately, the defense mechanisms in the computer caught him and prevented the change.[4]

But I think that is at least *symbolic* of the age in which we live, indeed, the state of fallen man from the very beginning. Ever since man said, "We will not have this man to reign over us" (Luke 19:14), people have been trying to replace Jesus Christ with a god of some other sort. That includes the pagan gods of ancient Rome enforced by pagan Caesars, who endeavored to totally obliterate the Church, decimate its members, destroy its Scriptures, only to eventually find that a Christian Caesar had been placed upon the throne and pagan Roman religion disappeared into the shadows of antiquity.

The attack on Christ we see in our culture today may seem new, but it's as old as the catacombs. In fact, it's older than that. The current conflict is much easier to take when we put it into historical perspective.

In this chapter I want to give a historical outlook on the attacks against the Church. I will show how, in the long run, those who attack Christ and His Church are without a doubt on the *wrong* side of history.

The Odds Against Christianity

In a review of the book *The Oxford Illustrated History of Christianity*, Ron Grossman wrote,

> Except for the documentary evidence, the story of Christianity would read like a fairy tale. Consider the odds against the church. . . . A betting-man witness might have wagered that the early Christians would follow their Jewish cousins into centuries of obscurity as wanderers in other peoples' lands.[5]

Even when Jesus was born, there was an attempt to kill Him. King Herod saw the newborn King of the Jews as a threat to his throne, so he had his soldiers kill the male babies of Bethlehem who would have been born around the same time as Jesus. Of course, an angel had warned Joseph to take his family and flee to Egypt, which they did. Here was the first direct attack against Christ in recorded history.[6] The devil attempted to snuff out Christianity before it even existed!

Years later, after Christ's public ministry and His crucifixion, a small band of followers bemoaned their Master's death. They had staked *everything* they had that this was the Messiah. Three days later He appeared to them as risen from the dead. And they went and turned the world upside down!

The Jewish establishment was against Jesus' disciples. But, as seen in Acts, their efforts to stamp out the Church failed. In fact, their persecution of the early Church actually caused it to spread to many communities! The harder they tried, the farther it spread. God's purposes cannot fail! We read in Acts 8:1: "At that time a great persecution arose against the church which was at Jerusalem; and they were all scattered throughout the regions of Judea and Samaria, except the apostles." Thus, in another irony of God, what the Jewish leaders meant to stamp out *grew* because of their persecution.

Meanwhile, one of the Jewish leaders, Saul, was an active participant in the persecution against Christians. He was an accomplice to the killing of Christianity's first martyr, Stephen (Acts 7:58). He was so zealous in his molestation of the early Church that he struck fear in the Christian community. But in the mercies of God, he was transformed. His conversion occurred while he was actually on his way to further persecution of the Church. Jesus appeared to him on the Damascus road and asked him, "Saul, Saul, why are you persecuting Me?" The Lord's question throws an interesting light on the subject of this book. When people persecute Christianity, they are persecuting Jesus Himself! Think about that in light of today's Christian bashing: the filmmakers, authors, singers, attorneys, judges, school principals, and government officials that are persecuting Christianity are persecuting *Jesus Himself*!

Saul was converted that day and became the apostle Paul, the greatest Christian ever to live. He even wrote many epistles that have become a crucial part of the New Testament—Romans, 1 and 2 Corinthians, Galatians, Ephesians, Philippians, Colossians, 1 and 2 Thessalonians, 1 and 2 Timothy, Titus, and Philemon. What an irony of God that He took a great persecutor of the Church and turned him into a great lion for the very faith he tried to stamp out. As Paul says of the churches in Judea, "They were hearing only, 'He who formerly persecuted us now preaches the faith which he once tried to destroy.' And they glorified God in me" (Gal. 1:23–24). The gates of Hell shall not prevail!

Roman Persecution

The greatest force in the world at that time, Rome, also tried to snuff out the light of the Christians. In fact, ancient Rome was arguably the strongest state in the history of the world. Yet with all its fury directed against the fledgling Church, it was utterly unable to stop Christianity.

For the first three hundred years of the Christian era, a titanic struggle was under way. From Nero to Diocletian, ten huge waves of persecution swept over the Roman Empire, and every vile and vicious torture that the depraved mind of man could conceive of was tried against Christians. They were covered with pitch, ignited, and placed on poles to light Nero's gardens. They were sewn in sacks with vipers. They were fed to lions and given over to bulls. They were boiled in oil. They were placed on red-hot iron beds. They were crucified upside down. Yet they steadfastly refused to deny Him who was their life and their all. Nothing could be done to stop Christianity.

A classic book written in the sixteenth century, *Foxe's Book of Martyrs*, shows in page after page how horrible the persecution against Christianity was in ancient Rome:

> Whatsoever the cruelness of man's invention could devise for the punishment of man's body, was practiced against the Christians—plates of iron laid unto them burning hot, deep dungeons, racks, strangling in prisons, the teeth of wild beasts, gridirons, gibbets and gallows, tossing upon the horns of bulls. . . .
>
> They were exposed to all the barbarities in which the mad populace with shouts demanded, and above all to the hot iron chair, in which

their bodies were roasted and emitted a disgusting smell. These after remaining alive a long time, expired at length.[7]

But horrible as all these things were, they couldn't stop the Church. Foxe sums up: "And yet, notwithstanding all these continual persecutions and horrible punishments, the Church daily increased, deeply rooted in the doctrine of the apostles and of men apostolical, and watered plenteously with the blood of the saints."[8]

Tertullian, (c.160–c. 220) one of the early Church Fathers, said to the heathen: "All your ingenious cruelties can accomplish nothing; they are only a lure to this sect. Our number increases the more you destroy us. The blood of the Christians is their seed."[9]

Indeed, the more Christians were tortured and killed, the more their numbers grew. Everywhere they fell, others rose in their places; and they died only to conquer. Even the usually wise leader, Marcus Aurelius, participated in the effort to stamp out Christianity.

The attitude of these early Christians showed that many of them cared more about the next life than this one. Alan F. Johnson tells the story of what happened when the great Chrysostom was brought before one of the pagan rulers and commanded to recant. Chrysostom's response shows that no matter what happened to him, as a Christian he couldn't lose. Johnson writes, "When Chrysostom was brought before the Roman Emperor, the emperor threatened him with banishment if he remained a Christian. Chrysostom replied,

'Thou canst not banish me for this world is my father's house.' 'But I will slay thee,' said the Emperor. 'Nay, thou canst not,' said the noble champion of the faith, 'for my life is hid with Christ in God.' 'I will take away thy treasures.' 'Nay, but thou canst not for my treasure is in Heaven and my heart is there.' 'But I will drive thee away from man and thou shalt have no friend left.' 'Nay, thou canst not, for I have a friend in Heaven from whom thou canst not separate me. *I defy thee*; for there is nothing that thou canst do to hurt me.'"[10]

Thus, the Christian need not fear persecution.

The great Church historian, Philip Schaff of Yale, who lived in the nineteenth century and the first part of the twentieth, has written a multivolume set on the history of Christianity. He reminds us that the early Christians were charged by pagans as being incendiaries (Nero blamed the Christians for the great fire of

Rome in A.D. 64), atheists (because they rejected the pantheon of Greco-Roman gods), incestuous (because they called each other, even their spouses, "brother" and "sister" and greeted one another with a "holy kiss"). They were accused of cannibalism (because they "ate the body," and "drank the blood," of Christ at the Eucharist) and called seditionists (because they refused to call Caesar "Lord"). Still other pagans charged Christians with being grossly immoral (because they celebrated love feasts called "agapes").[11]

The apostle Peter exhorted the persecuted Christians at Rome to respond to such charges with courage, reverence to God, reasonableness and respect toward men, and impeccable moral conduct that would give the lie to such false accusations:

> And who is he who will harm you if you become followers of what is good? But even if you should suffer for righteousness' sake, you are blessed. "And do not be afraid of their threats, nor be troubled." But sanctify the Lord God in your hearts, and always be ready to give a defense to everyone who asks you a reason for the hope that is in you, with meekness and fear; having a good conscience, that when they defame you as evildoers, those who revile your good conduct in Christ may be ashamed. For it is better, if it is the will of God, to suffer for doing good than for doing evil. (1 Peter 3:13–17)

Even natural disasters were blamed on the Christians. In North Africa, an anti-Christian proverb gained currency: "If God does not send rain, lay it to the Christians."[12] So Christians would be blamed for droughts, floods, and other natural disasters. The pagans would cry: "Away with the atheists! To the lions with the Christians!"[13]

Philip Schaff points out that the *divine* nature of the Christian faith is made evident in the fact that it survived such intense persecution:

> No other religion could have stood for so long a period the combined opposition of Jewish bigotry, Greek philosophy, and Roman policy and power; no other could have triumphed at last over so many foes by purely moral and spiritual force, without calling any carnal weapons to its aid.[14]

Other forces are arraying themselves against Christianity again, and again they will utterly fail.

The persecution effort reached its pinnacle in A.D. 303 under Diocletian. So many tens of thousands of Christians died that Diocletian had a coin struck bearing these words: "Diocletian, the Emperor who destroyed the Christian name."

Ten years later, in 313, a Christian Caesar named Constantine sat on the throne of Rome. Constantine issued the Edict of Toleration and the waves of persecution were over, and Christianity continued to spread throughout the Roman Empire. For the first time in history, it was no longer illegal for one to be a Christian. Believers in Christ no longer heard the constant reproach, "You have no right to exist."[15] Christianity was no longer a "*religio illicita*, an illegal religion.[16]

Another irony of God is that the tomb of Diocletian became the cornerstone of a Christian church! That church exists today and can be found in war-torn Yugoslavia.

One of the most eminent historians of the twentieth century, Will Durant, wrote a multivolume history of the world. He said of the conflict between Rome and Christianity that there was "no greater drama in human record" than that three-century fight. He sums it all up in a sentence: "Caesar and Christ had met in the arena, and Christ had won."[17]

The Attack on Christ in the Middle Ages

After the Church gained ascendancy, by default, as the Western half of the Roman Empire began to crumble, it brought unprecedented good things to humanity—the spread of hospitals, orphanages, and untold works of mercy, the creation of the university (to reconcile Greek philosophy with Christian theology), and beautiful works of art and music to glorify Jesus Christ. Many of the world's languages were first set to writing by Christians who translated Scripture and Christian liturgy into these hitherto unwritten tongues. Christianity also civilized barbarians (including our ancestors) the world over. In short, when the Church dominated much of Western society, beginning about A.D. 476,[18] it accomplished many noble and noteworthy things—which we spell out and document in *What If Jesus Had Never Been Born?*

But there was a downside. Human nature, being what it is, made it only a matter of time before corruption marred the testimony of the visible body of Christ on earth. Power tends to corrupt, and absolute power corrupts absolutely.

When people are unregenerate—that is, if their hearts are not changed by Christ—they are prone to do all sorts of ungodly and inhumane things. It doesn't matter whether they're atheistic Communists or clerics in the church. And in the case of unregenerate church leaders, their evil actions have brought the blame of history upon Christianity. That has been seen repeatedly in Church history, especially from the dawn of the Middle Ages to the present.

When the Church became the most important institution in society, it was easier for the devil to infiltrate it. During the Middle Ages everyone in Europe, except the Jews in their ghettos and the Moors in Spain (who were Muslims), were "Christians" whether they truly believed in Jesus Christ or not.

In Church history, sometimes Christians were persecuted by the official Church. This was true of the Roman Catholic Church persecuting the Waldensians, the Hussites, the Lutherans, and the Calvinists. This was true of the Church of England persecuting the Pilgrims and Puritans. Even the otherwise-godly Puritans sometimes persecuted the Quakers (on a much smaller level). The Anabaptists were persecuted by Roman Catholics and Reformed Christians alike.

Thus we see in Church history that some believers were persecuted and even martyred by the official Church. During the time of the Inquisition (which began in the thirteenth century), one humble friar pointed out that if St. Peter and St. Paul were accused of heresy and stood trial before the Inquisition, there would be "no open defense for them"![19]

The Spanish Inquisition in particular was a monstrous epic of brutality and barbarity. It was diabolical in its nature. Was it Christians persecuting non-Christians? It was the very opposite. I am quite convinced that the members of the Inquisition Party were not Christians. Their faith was so perverted that it bore little resemblance to that which had been given by Christ. In many cases the victims of the Inquisition could be considered evangelical Protestant Christians who had come to embrace the historic gospel of Christ and who had rejected the papal superstitions of that time.

The authorities at the time of the Inquisition *banned* the Bible. The powers who sanctioned and participated in the Inquisition were the same powers who forbade their people to read Scripture! They also forbade Scripture to be translated into the vernacular. They burned at the stake people who believed in, translated, or taught the Scriptures, contemptuously tossing each one's Bible into the fire to be burned with the martyr. But Christ gained the victory against those elements of the Church that opposed His work on earth.

As bad as the martyrdom of Christians was during the late Middle Ages and during the Post-Reformation Wars of Religion, it was very little compared to what happened to Christians in *our* century—at the hands of one of history's strongest anti-Christian forces.

Millions of Martyrs in the Twentieth Century

The attack on Christ in this century is such that more Christians have been killed for their faith in this century than ever before, amazing as that might seem, and it's still going on today. This information comes from Dr. David Barrett, formerly of the Southern Baptist Foreign Mission Board, who is one of the foremost authorities on the state of Christianity in the world today.

Dr. Barrett says that from the beginning of the Church to the present, there have been some forty million Christian martyrs. They specifically were killed because of their refusal to deny the faith. *Most* of these killings took place during this century. More martyrs have been killed in the last nine decades than in the previous nineteen centuries combined![20] Millions of them were killed by one of the Church's most formidable enemies ever—the Communists! Because the Communists provide a textbook case of how the gates of Hell shall not prevail, I want to focus on them and the threat they posed to Christianity.

The Communists

The Communists have shed more Christian blood than any other enemy, including ancient Rome and Islam. But just as Christ will vanquish all His foes, He has begun to get the victory over Communism, and one day that victory will be complete!

Marx declared that religion was the opiate of the people. His disciple Lenin, and Stalin after him, systematically tried to destroy the Church in the Soviet Union. Marx, Lenin, and Stalin vehemently hated Christ and Christianity. Marx said his purpose was to dethrone God and destroy capitalism. More than 120 million human beings have been killed in the futile attempt to set up his unworkable social and economic system!

I predicted during the 1970s and 1980s, before Communism fell in the Soviet Union, that Marx and Lenin—like pagan Romanism, like Nazism, like fascism—would one day be swept into the dustbin of history and would be remembered only as a sad page in the history of the world. We do not gloat over the fall of any enemy of the cross, but we do rejoice that Jesus Christ is ever gaining the victory, and He will reign forever, Lord of lords and King of kings.

The ultimate reason for Communism's hatred of religion is that Communism itself is a religion—it demands the worship and adoration and total dedication and service of its people. During the heyday of the Soviet Union, some astute observers pointed out that Communism had all the trappings of an organized religion: its messiahs and saints—Marx and Engels and Lenin, its sacred scriptures—*The Communist Manifesto*, *Das Kapital*, and the writings of other recent Communist leaders. It had an elect nation—the Soviet Union—through which the world was to be blessed. Communists believed in a predestination—dialectical materialism. They had their temporary millennium—the socialist state—which was to last until the final state, pure Communism.

There was a state of bondage—life under capitalism—out of which people needed to be delivered. They had their own redemption, brought about by the sacrifices made by devoted Communists. They had their own conversion—conversion to the Communist Party. They had their own songs, such as "If Lenin Walks with Me," "I Am Happy with Lenin," or "Lenin Lives in My Heart"—obvious takeoffs from Christianity, Communism's greatest foe.

They had their own sacred tomb: the tomb of Lenin, where, in a hermetically sealed glass-covered coffin, Lenin's body was viewed by the visiting hordes that were orchestrated to pass by there every day to show the importance of the man. Malcolm Muggeridge once visited the tomb and literally saw a woman cross herself upon the sight of Lenin's corpse![21]

Communism finds its greatest adversary in Jesus Christ. Lenin ordered 70,000 churches to be destroyed. He wrote in his famous essay, "Socialism and Religion": "We must combat religion—this is the ABC of all materialism and consequently Marxism."[22] Aleksandr Solzhenitsyn, the great intellectual, said in his book *The Mortal Danger*: "It is no accident that the Soviet Union has made no effort more concentrated and ferocious in sixty years than its attempt to eradicate Christianity, and yet they have proved incapable of destroying it."[23] In 1925, the Soviets founded the League of Militant Godless (LMG) to eradicate all religion; by 1941 it disbanded in failure.[24] Despite all the crushing, brutal attacks; despite the fact that Stalin boasted of having killed some ten million Ukrainian Christians, they could not eradicate Christianity.

In China, Mao Tse-tung killed virtually every Christian that he could identify. Still the Church there continues, and even thrives, with millions of adherents today, proving once more that the blood of martyrs is the seed of the Church.[25]

When the North Korean Communists came into South Korea, they sprayed congregations with gasoline and turned flamethrowers on them on Sunday mornings. Closer to home, the Marxist Sandinistas of Nicaragua burned forty-nine churches of the Miskito Indians. In one place they took thirty-seven of the Miskito Indians, threw them into a pit, and shoveled dirt in on top of them, burying them alive. A former Sandinista officer testified to the U.S. Congress who the Sandinista's main foe was: "From the beginning their main enemy was religion—the Church."[26]

In 1983, when the United States successfully invaded Grenada, our military was able to obtain many documents left undestroyed by the defeated Communist government. Included were some strategies outlining how they should deal with the churches of the country. These strategies included subverting them from within and getting them to align with "liberation theology," which is more Marxist than Christian.[27] Marxism and Christianity do not mix.

Wherever the Communists have gone, they have taught and practiced a doctrine of hatred and violence. They have killed, tortured, mutilated, and raped in the name of the Communist faith. They have attacked old men, women, and children. They have killed ruthlessly to attain their ends. They have emptied hospitals and forced the inhabitants on death marches. This happened in Cambodia in the mid-1970s, and in just a few years the Communists decimated the population of that country by at least one-fifth!

Armando Valladares—the famous Cuban patriot who spent twenty-two years in one of Fidel Castro's gulags in Cuba and author of *Against All Hope*—said of the Communist occupation: "Every night there were firing squads." Note that this was only four years after the takeover. Valladares reflected on those he saw who were killed, many of whom were Christians:

> I thought about all of those men who marched to the firing squads with a smile on their lips; I thought about the integrity of those martyrs who had died shouting, "*Viva Cuba Libre!* Viva Christ the King! Down with Communism!" And I was ashamed to feel so frightened. . . . My heart rose up to God, and I fervently prayed for Him to help me stand up to this brutality, and do what I had to do. I felt that God heard my prayer.[28]

Another writer states, the "cries of the executed patriots—'Long live Christ the King' and 'Down with Communism'—became such a potent and stirring symbol that by 1963 the men condemned to death were gagged before being carried down to be shot."[29] Who is the opponent of the Communists? Who is it that the Communists have been fighting against all these decades? Christ the King. As of this writing, Christ the King has not yet gotten the victory over Cuba, but He will. Perhaps any day now!

Interestingly, for the decades when the Communist threat loomed over the whole world, we were told we only had two options—Red or dead. But I have maintained that the real solution was a third option, neither Red nor dead, but rather that the whole world be *alive and free*. This hasn't fully happened yet, but we have made great progress in the last few years. The map of freedom as it is drawn today shows a world far more free than it was two or three decades ago. Alive and free is the solution that I believe the Bible is talking about when King Jesus triumphs in the world.

A few years ago, when the Iron Curtain crumbled in Eastern Europe, *National Review* magazine featured a cover showing the map of Eastern Europe with a large cross emerging from the ground, as the Communist nations crumbled.[30] This was an apt symbol of what happened in those nations. Christ the King had regained the victory from those who would "dethrone God."

In Poland, for nearly a decade, Catholics in great numbers bravely and openly defied the military dictatorship that was a puppet government of the Soviet Union. Perhaps the most poignant aspect of the struggle was the brutal torture and martyrdom of Father Jerzy Popieluszko, whose eyes and tongue were cut out by the Communist rulers.[31] With help from the Pope and the U.S. government, the Poles ultimately succeeded; Solidarity won over the Kremlin.

In Romania, the 1989 revolution that brought down the fall of the tyrannical Ceausescu began when a brave Reformed pastor, Laszlo Tokes, took a bold stand in his town of Timisoara. Officials tried to force him to leave his church, but he refused to go. Crowds came to the pastor's support, and many were killed in a massacre. Emanating from Timisoara's epicenter came an earthquake of revolt that led to the overthrow of the nation's dictator.[32]

Interestingly, in the providence of God, I may have had a small hand in that situation. In the mid-1980s, I had been asked by a woman missionary, working behind the Iron Curtain, to write a letter to Nicolae Ceausescu. She wanted me to tell him to stop harassing two pastors in Romania—a father and son (who was a youth minister). Frankly, I felt such a letter would be in vain. Why would a Communist dictator hundreds of miles away listen to an American preacher? But I wrote it anyway, and I mentioned that the eyes of the world would be on the situation. After the tyrant's fall, I received a note from the missionary thanking me for that letter—a letter I had forgotten all about. She said that after my correspondence, "although the harassments did not stop against the Tokes family, they had diminished. The important part is that their lives were spared."[33] The name of the youth minister was Laszlo Tokes—the very man who had been instrumental in the fall of Communism in Romania!

In the former East Germany, thousands of Lutherans took to the streets to protest the continued religious oppression there, helping to bring about the tearing down of the Berlin Wall. As the Communist nations fell, many were hungering for the gospel—a hunger that continues to this day. Jesus Christ will ever get the victory over His foes.

As stated above, Mao Tse-tung tried to utterly liquidate the Church in China. During the Great Proletarian Cultural Revolution in China (from 1966–76), the Red Guards engaged in what Dr. David Barrett calls "history's most systematic attempt ever, by a single nation, to eradicate and destroy Christianity and religion; in this it fails." Every church building was destroyed, as was every copy of Scripture they could get their hands on. By the time this bloodbath was over, twenty-two million had been killed[34]—many of them Christians.

Today the Church in China, largely underground, thrives even though many Christians are routinely beaten and imprisoned for their faith. David Bryant reports that there are about seventy million Christians there.[35] Furthermore, David Barrett estimates that by the turn of the century there should be about 130 million![36] Meanwhile, Mao is unknown among many young Chinese people today! The Associated Press reports that: "Elementary school children in China know more about a Hong Kong pop singer than about the late Chinese Communist leader Mao Tse-tung." Astoundingly, 82 out of 123 students surveyed hadn't even *heard* of Mao Tse-tung![37] As another dictator, Napoleon, said a century and a half earlier: "I search in vain in history to find the similar to Jesus Christ, or anything which can approach the gospel. . . . nations pass away, thrones crumble, but the Church remains."[38]

The persecution against Christianity in Vietnam and Cambodia has been intense. For example, in Cambodia, just before the fall of Phnom Penh to the Maoist Khmer Rouge guerillas, six hundred Christians huddled in a church building to pray together. They agreed that should any survive the Communist onslaught and return to that city, they would write their names on the back wall of that church. Only three names made it to the wall. Andrew Wark writes that "the guerillas clearly marked Christianity as an entity to be terminated."[39] For now, Christianity is not strong in Cambodia.

Meanwhile, "the church in post-war Vietnam is thriving."[40] Writing on the state of Christianity in Vietnam, William McGurn observed recently in the *National Review*, "I . . . suspect that for all its trials the Cross will remain in Vietnam long after the hammer and sickle have become a footnote."[41] That's a good summary of what will happen to all enemies of the gospel: the Cross will remain long after Christ's enemies have become a footnote.

Triumph in the Former Soviet Union

In the last few years in the former Soviet Union, amazing developments have unfolded as the Communist Party has been declared illegal, the KGB has been disbanded, and the state's official resistance to the gospel has given way to genuine religious liberty. Today there is more religious freedom in the public schools of the former Soviet Union than there is in the public schools of America! Christianity is often being taught in their schools. After seventy years of brutal atheism, there is a great spiritual hunger in Russia. Religion—and, unfortunately, that includes cults and superstitious beliefs that are not Christian—is filling that vacuum.

At our Sunday evening service a few years ago, a missionary to Russia told of a most interesting event that took place a year before the disunion of the Soviet Union. He was the first to have gained the approval of the Department of Education of the Soviet Union to distribute Bibles to one Soviet high school in Moscow. On the appointed day and hour he appeared with the edition of the Bible which was being given away. It was simply entitled *The Book*. (In case you don't know, the word *Bible* means, "book," and this was called *The Book*.)

The principal, a man of medium height, stocky shoulders, square jaw, short-cropped hair, steel-gray eyes, and the look of a KGB colonel greeted him politely. When the missionary handed him *The Book*, he said, "Thank you for this book on religion. I have been thinking about possibly teaching a course on religions next year, and I'm sure this would prove to be helpful."

The missionary said, "Excuse me, sir. There seems to be some misunderstanding. This is not a book on religion. This is a Bible."

The man's eyes opened wide in amazement, and he said, "A Bible, a Bible!" He clasped it to his breast and said, "A Bible! We were once a great Christian nation, but we turned our backs upon God and we have destroyed ourselves!" When I heard that, I could not help but reflect upon the times in which we are living in America. I cannot help but feel that in large measure, we in America have turned our backs on God. We, who were once a great Christian nation, are in the process of destroying ourselves. Our abortion, divorce, and crime rates testify to this. But here, as well as there, Christ will gain the victory!

When the Soviet Union fell apart in 1991, you may have remembered the powerful picture of the people toppling the statue of the founder of the KGB, Felix Dzerzhinsky, outside the former KGB headquarters. The pedestal of that statue remains, but what is now on top of that stand is the cross of Jesus Christ![42] Here again is a powerful symbol of Christ vanquishing yet another foe. Here is another irony of God; He will ever get the victory.

Christ's victory over Communism is not yet fully complete. But we have moved much closer to it in the last few years than could be imagined a decade ago, and Christ's victory over this enemy will one day be total. All foes of the Son of God will one day be vanquished—either by voluntary repentance or by His ultimate triumph.

Note that we are not advocating that the Church take up the sword to force Christ's kingdom on earth. This type of thing has been tried in the past, resulting in such debacles as the Crusades, the Inquisition, and the witch-hunts. These are blotches on the Church's record in history because they contradict the Spirit of Christ, who told us to love our enemy, our brother, and our neighbor.

The excellent Jewish writer, Don Feder, who has been a guest on my television program on numerous occasions, has this to say about the triumph of religion over Communism in the former Soviet Union:

> Communism's inability to eradicate man's spiritual instinct must rank among the great failures of history. During the nineteenth century, high noon of rationalism, the demise of religion was considered inevitable. As enlightenment spread and reactionary, church-dominated governments fell, mankind would shrug off this ancient superstition, it was confidently predicted.
>
> But even with atheism enshrined as the official policy of a state that exerted pervasive influence over the lives of its subjects, faith survived. Consider the resources mobilized in this total warfare: mass propaganda, educational brainwashing, laws which forced organized religion into the catacombs, punishment for believers ranging from loss of employment to gulags. Yet with all of the weapons at its disposal, atheism was routed.[43]

Christ is building his Church, and the gates of Hell shall never prevail against it!

All of Christ's Enemies Will Be Vanquished

Despite the most vicious attacks from rulers and skeptics alike, Christianity survives and even thrives. Through these last two thousand years, Jesus Christ has been continually gaining the victory, a victory that began at the time of His death and resurrection and continues on through the ages.

In A.D. 363, Julian the Apostate, the emperor of Rome who tried to relight the fires on the altars of pagan gods and to overthrow the newly established Christian faith, was marching against the Persians. In his army were numbers of Christians. One of these men was being sorely derided and persecuted by some of the heathen soldiers. They mocked him, beat him, threw him to the ground, and said,

"Now tell us, where is your Carpenter now?" He responded, "He is busy constructing a coffin for your emperor." A few months later, a mortal wound in his side, Julian the Apostate took his hands, grasped a handful of his own blood, flung it against the sky, and said, "Thou hast conquered, O Galilean!"[44] The Carpenter of Galilee is busy constructing coffins for all the ungodly kings and kingdoms of this earth.

Adolf Hitler said that Christianity would be uprooted, "root and branch," and that he would destroy it all. Hitler declared his antipathy to the faith: "The heaviest blow that ever struck humanity was the coming of Christianity. Bolshevism is Christianity's illegitimate child. Both are inventions of the Jew."[45] Himmler, the ruthless head of the Gestapo, said, "We shall not rest until we have rooted out Christianity."[46] William Shirer, a journalist who covered the Nazi regime and wrote *The Rise and Fall of the Third Reich*, said: "The Nazi regime intended eventually to destroy Christianity in Germany, if it could, and substitute the old paganism of the early Germanic gods and the new paganism of the Nazi extremists."[47] So in the German churches the Bible at the altar was replaced with *Mein Kampf*, and the crosses atop steeples were replaced by swastikas.[48] Hitler himself said that he and the Nazi Party were fighting against "the God of the deserts, that crazed, stupid, vengeful Asiatic despot with his powers to make laws! . . . That poison with which both Jews and Christians have spoiled and soiled the free, wonderful instincts of man and lowered them to the level of doglike fright."[49] Jesus Christ built Hitler's coffin.[50]

Mussolini also set himself up against the Lord, and Christ constructed another coffin for him. Our Carpenter is yet making a coffin for Communism, and it, too, is being swept into the dust heap of history. Christ, the conquering hero, shall continue to ride forth conquering and to conquer. Marx, Lenin, Stalin, Khrushchev, Brezhnev, Mao, and Castro, and all who follow them shall see Christ the Conqueror.

Not only has Christ achieved a victory over the forces of evil, but He has also achieved a glorious victory over death, the last enemy to be overcome, the chief evil of mankind. Jesus Christ has conquered death!

Jesus Is Not a Doormat

Sometimes we get the impression of Jesus as "meek and mild," as a doormat who lets everyone walk all over Him. Those who denigrate Jesus Christ seem to be oblivious to the fact that He is coming in judgment. Listen to what the book of Revelation says about Him:

Now I saw heaven opened, and behold, a white horse. And He who sat on him was called Faithful and True, and in righteousness He judges and makes war. His eyes were like a flame of fire, and on His head were many crowns. He had a name written that no one knew except Himself. He was clothed with a robe dipped in blood, and His name is called the Word of God. And the armies in heaven, clothed in fine linen, white and clean, followed Him on white horses. Now out of His mouth goes a sharp sword, that with it He should strike the nations. And He Himself will rule them with a rod of iron. He Himself treads the winepress of the fierceness and wrath of Almighty God. And He has on His robe and on His thigh a name written: KING OF KINGS AND LORD OF LORDS. (Rev. 19:11–16)

This is far different from the ethereal portrayals of a pale, powerless Jesus who loves everybody but doesn't hate sin. This is the conquering Son of God, who sovereignly rules the world from behind the scenes and who will one day overtly rule the world. In the great conflict between God and the devil, there is absolutely no doubt about the outcome.

Conclusion

Christ's kingdom is like no other in history. A historical analogy will help illustrate this. By the time Alexander the Great was thirty-one years old, he had conquered Macedonia and Greece; he had sealed off the ports of the Mediterranean; he had taken the great stronghold of Tyre; he had conquered the Persian Empire; he had entered Babylon. There, at the height of his career, at the age of thirty-three, after a drunken bout, he died. He had built a world empire, but it was as a fragile vase. As soon as Alexander died, that vase fell to the floor and shattered—and the Alexandrian empire disintegrated.

Yet Jesus Christ, just a short while before He went to the cross, said: "I will build my church; and the gates of hell shall not prevail against it" (Matt. 16:18b KJV). Christ was killed also at the age of thirty-three, but He rose again. Peter and James and John and Paul have all died, yet the Church lives.

The Church will go on until Christ comes back again to drop the curtain on the history of mankind. The Church of Christ is eternal. All of the animosity and hostility of unbelievers throughout the ages have been and will be incapable of bringing it down. Indeed, the gates of Hell shall not prevail over Christ's Church!

Light in a Dark World

I will set nothing wicked before my eyes.
—Psalm 101:3

During the 1970s and '80s, Alice Cooper was one of the prominent rock stars in the pop culture, sympathetic toward the devil and, therefore, negative toward Jesus Christ. Alice Cooper was the adopted stage name of Vincent Furnier; the reason he chose a woman's name was that he claimed to be "a reincarnated seventeenth-century witch." His albums contained many satanic symbols, including the upside-down cross, a direct mockery of the cross of Christ. But recently, he has undergone a change of heart. He has become a Christian. Although still under contract to Epic, *World* magazine reports: "his heart is no longer in the image."[1]

Alice Cooper used to dress up like a reptilian demon; he looked like he was peering out from just inside the gates of Hell. His bloody stage act used to promote rebellion, death, and gore. It included a pretend decapitation complete with a bloodied head. His songs included "Time to Kill," "Dead Babies," and "Welcome to My Nightmare." Today, Vince Furnier is a new man in Jesus Christ. He has even played golf with R. C. Sproul! In the lyrics from his latest album, *The Last Temptation*, he says of the devil that "it's over." Satan has no power and is lost, "and I'm found and I'm heaven bound."[2] What a contrast this is from what he used to sing, dressed in demonic garb!

Witnessing to those involved in music, television, and the movies is perhaps the greatest way to combat the media onslaught against Christianity. We can see them transformed, like Alice Cooper, from a destructive force to a positive force by our winsome witness for Christ. We can't necessarily beat them, but we can try to get them to join us. When they do, sometimes they become the boldest evangelists. The apostle Paul was probably the greatest Christian in history; he was also filled with anti-Christian bigotry prior to his conversion.

In addition to evangelism, what else can we do about the media's unfair treatment of Christianity? The purpose of this chapter is to explore how we can fight back in love against the attack on Christ in music, TV, and film.

Christians' Responsibilities

To deal with the anti-Christian programming, we as Christians first need to make sure that our *own* TV-viewing and radio-listening habits are in conformity with the will of God. This would seem to be obvious; why even state it? The reality is *Christians* are part of the problem! We support many of the same TV programs, movies, and musicians that denigrate our faith (directly or indirectly).

It's hypocrisy for Christians to condemn the trash on TV, and then watch the very filth we condemn! Yet there are many professing Christians who actually watch, for entertainment value, some of the most offensive programs on the air. It's almost as if they put the lordship of Christ on hold for a short time while they watch an anti-Christian program. But David said so long ago, "I will set nothing wicked before my eyes" (Ps. 101:3). That needs to be our motto when we're choosing our entertainment.

Interestingly, movies and TV can have a desensitizing effect. Years ago, my coauthor Jerry Newcombe was working as a talk-show host and as operations manager for a Christian radio station. One night he turned on reruns of the sitcom *WKRP in Cincinnati*. He was so offended by some of the lewd remarks, he turned it off before it was over. But a few weeks later, he caught another episode, and it wasn't so bad; in fact, he found it entertaining. Then he started watching it on many weeknights because he found some of the characters and situations similar to the radio station he managed. But after a few months of watching it, they repeated the first episode he had seen—the one he had turned off because it was so dirty. And he thought, *This isn't so bad. I must have been too uptight or something when I saw this before.* But then he recognized that *he* had changed and not the program! This realization led to repentance and the decision to stop watching that show.

Multiply this story (not necessarily with the positive ending) by millions of professing Christians, and you can put your finger on part of the problem: Christians are watching (and thus supporting) many of the objectionable programs on TV. Without doing prior research (for instance, by getting *Movieguide*), Christians are buying tickets for many of the films that denigrate Christianity. Believe it or not, Christian teens are reportedly watching just about as many of the R-rated films as non-Christian teens, according to Dr. Ted Baehr, president of The Christian Film and Television Commission.[3] A recent poll by George Barna showed that "Christian young adults are more likely than others to have watched *MTV* in the past week"! For example, Barna found that 42 percent of Christian "baby busters" (the generation that followed the "baby boomers") watch MTV versus only 33 percent of non-Christian baby busters.[4] That's not good! Clearly we're not going to be a part of the *solution* if we're part of the *problem*!

What we feed on spiritually—what we put into our souls—will determine our spiritual growth. As this anonymous couplet puts it:

> *Two natures beat within my breast.*
> *The one is foul, the other is blest.*
> *The one I love, the other I hate.*
> *The one I feed will dominate.*[5]

So all of us need to ask ourselves what we're feeding on when it comes to the programming and films we choose to view. The radio stations we listen to say a lot about ourselves.

In Psalm 1, David said,

> *Blessed is the man*
> *Who walks not in the counsel of the ungodly,*
> *Nor stands in the path of sinners,*
> *Nor sits in the seat of the scornful. (v. 1)*

This verse applies to what media sources we choose to tune in to—are they mere outputs of the scornful, of unrepentant sinners, of the ungodly? One who feeds regularly on a steady diet of unwholesome TV viewing, radio listening, and moviegoing is harming his soul and his walk as a Christian.

Since as a man "thinks in his heart, so is he" (Prov. 23:7), and since we *are* what we think about all day long, we need to carefully choose *what* we think about! Paul tells us to think about that which is noble, pure, and lovely (Phil. 4:8). By that biblical principle, much of the media's fare would be unacceptable to the obedient Christian. A good rule of thumb is to act as if Jesus were right there with you when you choose what you watch on TV or listen to on the radio. After all, He is! If Christians en masse would choose to not view, and thus not support, the bad programming from the media, that alone would be a *huge* first step in solving this problem.

Did you ever think about the fact that every time you plop money down to buy a movie ticket or rent a video, you are voting? You cast a ballot. You say to the movie producers, "Yes, Hollywood, make more movies like this!" There are no exit polls at the cinema, determining what the viewer felt *after* the movie. All they care about is your vote—your ticket purchase—*before* you saw it. When it seems like so many in Hollywood have a personal vendetta against Christianity, how can we so cavalierly choose to watch (and thus support) films that denigrate so much of what we hold near and dear?

I'm amazed at the blind spot so many Christians have in this area. It's almost as if their view of personal holiness doesn't include entertainment. They may be godly by various criteria, but when it comes to what movies or TV programs they watch, seemingly anything goes. Someone gave me a poem that puts it so well:

A Tragic Choice!

On the table side by side; The Holy Bible and the TV Guide,
One is well worn but cherished with pride,
*   (Not the Bible, but the TV Guide).*

One is used daily to help folks decide,
*   No! It isn't the Bible; it's the TV Guide.*

As pages are turned, what shall they see?
*   Oh, what does it matter, turn on the TV.*

So they open the book in which they confide
*   (No, not the Bible, it's the TV Guide).*

The Word of God is seldom read,
*   Maybe a verse e'er they fall into bed.*

Exhausted and sleepy and tired as can be,
*   Not from reading the Bible, but watching TV.*

So, then back to the table, side by side,
*   Is the Holy Bible and the TV Guide.*

No time for prayer, no time for the Word;
*   The plan of salvation is seldom heard.*

Forgiveness of sin so full and free
*   Is found in the BIBLE, not on TV!!*

—Anonymous

The Time Factor

Groucho Marx once said this about the instructive value of TV: "I find TV very educating. Every time somebody turns on the set I go into the other room and read a book."[6]

Not only are there the moral issues involved, but I'm convinced that excessive TV viewing is a big waste of time. Not surprisingly, a study showed that many CEOs of Fortune 500 companies spend precious little time watching TV. In fact, 81 percent of them watch less than one hour of television per day.[7] That's significantly lower than the national average.

Years ago, a pastor of a small church in rural Pennsylvania decided to convert the two hours a night he spent watching TV into prayer time. As he began to labor in prayer, God gave him a vision to reach out to some New York City gang members who had been involved in a brutal, senseless murder. The pastor was David Wilkerson, who is now pastor of Times Square Church in Manhattan, a vital assembly in the heart of Manhattan. God used his simple obedience to bring some hardened gang members to Himself, including Nicky Cruz, a notorious young hoodlum, whom I mentioned in Chapter 3. David Wilkerson started a ministry, Teen Challenge, which eventually went nationwide; and he wrote about the story in his classic book *The Cross and the Switchblade*. It's an incredible story, and it all began when he converted TV time into prayer time.[8] Imagine what would happen if more and more Christians took that challenge seriously. We could see a revival sweep the land!

So the first step in fighting the media onslaught against Christianity begins with a commitment to submit our viewing and listening habits to the lordship of Christ. If the millions of professing Christians in this country refused to watch or to listen to anti-Christian programs, they could have a great effect on future programming.

Will you make that commitment right now? Will you submit all your entertainment choices to the Lord—the films you support and expose yourself to, the CDs you purchase, the videos you rent, the TV programs you watch, the radio programming you listen to, the novels, magazines, and newspapers you read? I urge you to stop right now and commit this (or recommit this) to the Lord. Let this Scripture be your guide: "I will set nothing wicked before my eyes." As Job said: "I made a covenant with my eyes not to look lustfully at a girl" (Job 31:1 NIV). Will you go the extra mile and research *before* you spend? When you choose your entertainment, will you act as if the Lord were right there in the room with you? After all, He *is*!

Protests and Boycotts

What else can we do about the war against Christ and Christianity? We cannot do what many would do. We cannot resort to violence, as if life were just one long Clint Eastwood movie. To the Christian, violence is not a viable option. Romans 12:18 declares, "If it is possible, as much as depends on you, live peaceably with all men." The Lord Himself commanded, "Bless those who curse you, do good to those who hate you, and pray for those who spitefully use you and persecute you" (Matt. 5:44).

When *The Last Temptation of Christ* was about to be released, more than 25,000 Christians gathered around the Black Tower (the name given to the main building) at Universal City, California, and I'm told from an insider that the people inside were terrified. They said, "There were just so many of them . . . they were everywhere. The crowd seemed to go on for miles." They just knew that at any moment they were going to break down the doors and come storming in and trash the building. But the throng did nothing but pray, sing hymns, speak—not a window was broken. The protesters were asking the studio to show some restraint and not air *The Last Temptation of Christ*. Their nonviolence is to be commended.

When we hear, see, or read something blatantly anti-Christian, it behooves us to voice our disapproval. I think we should call the stations, write the newspapers, and tell them that we are grieved by this kind of material. We should expose it for what it is and say something like, "You, of course, realize that this is nothing other than anti-Christian bigotry, and I'm surprised that an enlightened paper, as yours is—a paper that repeatedly claims to oppose bigotry and discrimination—continues to allow this kind of religious discrimination and bigotry to be exercised."

I have been told that if a station airs a television program in which something is said negatively about homosexuals, the station won't just get a few letters, it will have four or five leading homosexuals visiting the station for the next day or two to express their protest. In contrast, Christians are not always so quick to write an effective letter or to voice a protest. When was the last time *you* called a station and protested about the way Christians are portrayed on television? We need to call the stations and write the networks.

Boycotts are another strategy for fighting back. Boycotts can come back and slap you in the face if they're not effective. If you're going to do a boycott, you better do it right, because a boycott in which only a handful of people participate will never be felt, and the organization you're boycotting will never listen to you again.

If Christians are going to boycott something, we all ought to agree to boycott the same thing at the same time. Otherwise, we scatter our shots so much that we lose effectiveness.

A Case Study of an Effective Protest

I think an effective way to respond to anti-Christian programming is to contact the *advertiser* directly to complain of the program they support.[9] In 1992 Dr. Richard Neill, a dentist from the Dallas area, brought his daughter to the doctor's office. The television was on in the waiting room, and it was the *Phil Donahue Show*; the guest was a prostitute who claimed to have had sex with 2,500 men. Neill was shocked at this program and that six children sat glued to the set watching this!

He did some research and he found that this program was *often* sleazy; this particular show was not atypical for Donahue. Furthermore, he found that nearly half a million children watch *Donahue* each day! Dr. Neill ordered six months of transcripts from the program, and he wrote up a three-page report that set forth his case against the show. He then sent these to many of the program's advertisers. At first, his complaints fell on deaf ears. But Neill found that advertisers and "board chairmen have families too, and once their eyes are opened to this kind of harmful material, they will usually react."[10] Soon advertisers began to pull off their support of the program. So much so that Donahue even aired two episodes from Fort Worth and tried to get Dr. Neill to appear on the program, but he wouldn't. The two shows attacked "Neill's integrity, ethics, motives, and even his Christian beliefs."[11]

But the patient dentist persisted until enough advertisers pulled support from the program that the local ABC affiliate dropped the *Phil Donahue Show*! In a professional, intelligent, courteous, and Christian manner, Dr. Neill was able to accomplish something that very few Christians have. But Neill says, "God doesn't call us to be successful every time, just to be obedient."[12] As of this writing, *Donahue* has now been "unplugged," after almost thiry years (USA Today, 18 January 1996).

The Need for Solidarity

As we deal with a media that's hostile to the Christian faith, let me also point out the need for solidarity among Christians of different stripes. This does not mean I'm brushing off real denominational differences; it does mean, however, we can be cobelligerents with those of other denominations against anti-Christian bigotry. Unfortunately, too often Christians excuse themselves from getting involved in fighting anti-Christian bigotry in the media because it wasn't *their* group or *their* denomination under attack. Protestants could easily say, "So what if they denigrate the Pope? I'm not a Catholic." But when they demean any group of Christians, they demean you and me too. As Ben Franklin said, in a different context, we must all hang together or most assuredly we'll all hang separately!

A Christian Anti-Defamation League?

The time for letting the Christian bashing go on essentially *un*challenged has come to an end. We can learn from the Jews on this. The Anti-Defamation League is a part of B'nai B'rith (Hebrew for "sons of the covenant"), which was established in New York City in 1843. They founded the Anti-Defamation League in 1913 to combat anti-Semitism. They have managed to stem much of the tide of anti-Semitism. Jews comprise only 1.9 percent of Americans; they once had 3 percent. Attorney Sigmund Livingston founded the ADL and wrote a book, *Must Men Hate?* in which he said, "The beginning of the solution to the problem must be publicity."[13]

There is a great need for a Christian anti-defamation league. To some degree, there is such an organization emerging on the horizon, the Catholic League, which we'll examine next.

I have had it on my heart for about a decade—and have even expressed the thought—that a Christian anti-defamation league would be helpful. In some ways, what Don Wildmon is doing through the American Family Association[14] and what Brent Bozell is doing through the Media Research Center[15] provide the first step to an anti-defamation League for Christians: they gather accurate examples of Christian bashing. They identify anti-Christian bigotry in the media and inform hundreds of thousands of Christians to whom they can address letters of complaint, or in the case of positive programming, their thanks. Don Wildmon has paved the way in some critical battles, including the one against anti-Christian "art" sponsored by our tax dollars via the National Endowment for the Arts. At the time Wildmon began alerting the Christian community about the NEA's activities, most Christians were clueless as to what their money was funding.

The Catholic League

There is a Catholic anti-defamation league in the New York Diocese of John Cardinal O'Connor. While their headquarters are in New York City, they have offices in Boston and Milwaukee, and their work fights anti-Christian bigotry around the country. It is a lay organization, run by a Catholic layman and funded by the donations of laypeople, including non-Catholics. While I would not see eye to eye on their theology, for example, how a person receives salvation in Jesus Christ, their work is now effectively addressing and often turning the tables on anti-Christian bigotry of all stripes.

Since mid-1993, Dr. William Donohue has headed up the Catholic League, which was originally founded in 1973 by Father Virgil Blum of Milwaukee. Donohue, formerly of academia, has breathed new life into the organization; he has seen its size multiply ten times in less than two years! Dr. Donohue has written two important books about what is perhaps America's biggest threat to liberty: the American Civil Liberties Union; the books are entitled *The Politics of the ACLU* and *Twilight of Liberty*. Interestingly, Donohue knows more about the ACLU than perhaps even the ACLU knows about themselves! He was one of the leading guests on our groundbreaking, hard-hitting documentary on the ACLU.[16]

The Catholic League uses the media effectively. They aggressively put the spotlight on the culprits of anti-Christian bigotry. They'll send out faxes to five hundred key media sources to raise awareness of the offense.

One day Donohue learned of a series of anti-Christian ads that were found plastered on the sides of buses in New York City. The ads showed Madonna (the rock singer) on one side; on the other were Madonna (the mother of Jesus) and Child. Underneath these very different Madonnas were the words: "The difference between you and your parents: VH1" (Video Hits 1, a cable network akin to MTV). Donohue complained about this and managed to get a campaign going against it. He raised people's awareness about the ads and about why Christian people were offended by them. Orthodox Jews were among those complaining; they recognized that when society allows open hostility against Christians, it can easily lead to hostility against Jews. Their participation in the campaign was what Donohue calls a matter of "smart politics and goodwill."[17] Within twenty-four hours of their complaints the ads were pulled! The Catholic League, under Donohue's direction, is beginning to have a positive impact in this fight.

During Christmas 1994 an upscale clothing store in New York City had a mock nativity scene in the window that had been made by an avant-garde artist. Donohue learned about it and went to see it for himself. It was pure blasphemy against Christ. He went and told the manager about this, and he gave the manager four hours to remove it, lest Donohue inform the media. The manager said that he wouldn't remove it because he wouldn't interfere with an artist's freedom to create. Then Donohue went on a popular New York City radio show and told the listeners about the blasphemy, and he asked those who cared to call up the store. The phone lines were tied up so badly, the clothing store had to install a new line just to get business done! After that radio show, one TV camera crew after another came to his office to interview Donohue about this. The heat got so bad, the store pulled the blasphemous crèche and even spent $100,000 for full-page newspaper ads to provide what Donohue describes as a "lame apology" for the sacrilege.

The Catholic League picks their fights carefully, so that they can make the strongest impact possible. Donohue said they don't go after every instance of Christian bashing of which they're made aware. "If *Saturday Night Live* has some banter at our expense, we're not so thin-skinned that we can't take it."[18] Instead, they effectively appeal to the culture at large to expose the cases of blatant anti-Christian bigotry for what it is. They appeal to people's sense of fairness. Most non-Christians have a modicum of fairness, and they can see when the line of what's fair has been crossed. Donohue appeals to that fairness to stop the expressions of brazen anti-Christian, anti-Catholic sentiment.

The Catholic League is a strong friend to the cause of Christ in these dark days. Their work benefits all of Christianity, not just Catholicism. When Jesus Christ is being blasphemed, the Catholic League will respond. News of Christ and Christian bashing should be forwarded to them.[19]

Dr. William Donohue is on the right track. Until we fight back, in love, they will continue to slander and libel the sacred tenets of our faith in prime time, at the box office, and in popular music.

While We Slept

The unbelievers and liberals were smart. They took over a culture that was predominantly Christian. How? While we slept, or while we engaged in our theological squabbles, the unbelievers took over the bastions of power, including the media. (I should point out, however, that some stalwart souls—like christian attorney William Bentley Ball or elements of the Catholic Church, in their opposition to abortion, for instance—were doing their best to stem the secular onslaught.)

Genesis 1:28 tells us to have dominion over all things (except other people). This is my Father's world, and all glory from this world should come to Him. We exist to bring glory to God. The catechism says the chief end of man is to glorify God.

Imagine if everybody in this world were a Christian. Imagine how different our libraries would be; they would be filled with books that bring glory to God in a million different ways. Our television would bring glory to God. That doesn't mean we'd have worship services all day long, but every program of every kind, every motion picture, every newspaper would seek to bring honor to the Creator. In 1850 almost every newspaper in America was owned and operated by Christians. Editorials were filled with Scriptural quotes. Columnists wrote from a

Christian perspective and based their writings on the Christian ethic. The entire sermon of a leading cleric would be printed on Monday in the papers. Now, consider today: the newspapers—and other sources of information and entertainment—have mostly become fortresses of opposition to Christianity.

The Need for Christians to Get Involved in the Media

I think we need to realize that our culture's Christian bashing is in part a result of a misguided attitude on the part of Christians earlier this century. For decades we retreated from our culture. We left the media, for the most part, to unbelievers.

Let me, by way of a caveat, say that there are, of course, a number of Christians who are working in the "desert wasteland" of the media, trying to do what they can, but their task is very difficult. Now and again they get fired for refusing to play a particular role, for refusing to say certain lines, for refusing to write something a different way. Dean Jones, perhaps best known as the star of *The Love Bug* and other Disney classics, is a committed Christian. A few years ago he declined to play a role in a movie because of one lewd scene. He really liked the character in the script, but in good conscience, he couldn't play the part because it had him in a bathtub with an unmarried woman. He tried to talk the producer out of including the gratuitous scene, but she wouldn't hear of it. So he gave up a lucrative offer at a time he really needed the money.[20]

I have talked to writers of newspapers and magazine articles who have told me, "I know that my editor or publisher wants something more negative, but I hope that I can get this in." They feel constrained to write negative things about Christians or about ministers, knowing that oftentimes if they don't, the editors won't even publish their material.

We need to have more Christian anchorpersons, newswriters, editors, publishers, producers, and directors, since these people are in a position to influence the thinking of so many others in our culture. Christian parents could encourage their children to pursue such careers if they were so inclined. But, of course, we must always make sure we change the media and not that they change us!

Michael Medved, the only major movie critic who appears to have a Judeo-Christian worldview, said recently that people of faith can have a positive impact in the movies and on TV: "We need less complaining and more creating, less confrontation and more communication, less attitude and more gratitude."[21]

Christians changing the media is not going to happen overnight, if it happens at all, but over a period of decades. Nor is it easy for Christians to enter this field. Sometimes those who naively set out to change Hollywood get corrupted by Hollywood.

Nonetheless, Christians in the secular media can have a great impact. In such a secularized culture they must be discerning in what they say. They must be wise as serpents and as innocent as doves.

I would challenge your church to take as a project a newspaper, a television station, or a radio station and begin to pray for them and witness to them. I have made it a part of my ministry to try to witness to every person in a place of influence that I possibly can. Their souls are of no more value in the sight of God than the drunks on skid row, but their influence may be fifty million times greater.

Also, another opportunity to fight back against anti-Christian bigotry in the media is to work from the top down. You could invest in the stock of media companies and express your opinion in the meeting of their boards. There are many such opportunities we could use to glorify God in the media.

Support the Alternative Media

What further steps can we take to fight the war against Christ and Christianity that is being waged on TV, on the radio, and in the movies? We can support the growing conservative "alternative media." These are mostly Christians involved in the media, using their talents to serve the Lord. The alternative media have become a virtual lifeline today. If you're interested in learning about news of relevance to Christians, you're much better off to listen to the daily newscast of *Family News in Focus*[22] than you are the daily network news. Listen to Dr. Dobson's *Focus on the Family*,[23] *The Rush Limbaugh Show* (which I recommend with caution because of his occasional crudeness), *Point of View* with Marlin Maddoux,[24] *Prime Time America* with Jim Warren or *Open Line* with Chris Fabre (two programs on the Moody Broadcasting Network),[25] and, if I may, my own radio broadcasts, *Truths That Transform* and *The Kennedy Commentary*.[26] Today there are some 1,300 radio stations preaching the gospel and featuring local and national talk shows, and they are having a positive impact in our land!

Television shows that will inform you of today's news from a Christian perspective are *The 700 Club*,[27] and *The John Ankerberg Show*,[28] and again, if I may, *The Coral Ridge Hour*.[29] Recommended reading includes *World* magazine,[30] and (with caution) the *Washington Times*[31] and *National Review*.[32]

Millions of Americans get their information from these alternative sources. It behooves us to support these sources or networks and not to follow blindly along with the agenda of "the dominant media culture" (to borrow a phrase from Congressman Bob Dornan).

A Loss of Influence

There are signs that the influence of the dominant media culture is waning—largely because of the alternative media. In his book *Politically Incorrect*, Dr. Ralph Reed, founder and president of the Christian Coalition, pointed out,

> Talk radio and cable television, dominated by conservative voices like Rush Limbaugh and Pat Robertson, now rivals or eclipses the establishment press in shaping the nation's political agenda. . . . We are standing on the threshold of the most dramatic transformation of technology and politics since the advent of television.[33]

Reed has given a label to this growing phenomenon of the alternative media slowly beginning to have power that rivals that of the networks: "technopopulism."[34]

Conclusion

The days of merely complaining among ourselves about the Christian bashing in movies and TV are over. It's time to act. It's time to make our voices heard to those still engaged in anti-Christian bigotry. It's time to write those letters to the editor. It's time to put our money where our mouths are. It's time to pray for those in the media and to lead more people to Christ, including those in the media. And it's time for Christians to boldly enter the media.

I was interviewed on a television station in one of our cities by a young Christian woman who was the coanchor for the news. She began to ask me questions about the very heart of the Christian life—the sort of things not usually asked on network television. Finally, she said: "Do you know that there are a lot of people out there watching our program right now that do not really know what a Christian is or what it means to be 'born anew'? Why don't you explain that to them." And so I explained what it means to be a Christian. Afterward, during a commercial, I said: "Do you know that they are never going to run this?" She said, "Of course they will. It's live." I said, "You had better look for a new job because you are going to get fired." She said, "I won't get fired. I'll tell you why later."

After the program she said, "I'll tell you why I won't get fired. Do you see that man over there behind the camera? Five years ago I led him to Christ. I led my coanchor to Christ three years ago. I led my station manager to Christ two years ago. I led the owner of this station and five other stations to Christ four years ago." She said, "I can do anything I want and say anything I want." Now that is the Great

Commission! What an influence that station has been in their city. If more and more Christians were to take her attitude, we could see major changes in this country! If more Christians could exhibit even a portion of the faithfulness to Christ that she does, we would see our culture cease from the relentless Christian bashing that now plagues us.

Salt for a Decaying Culture

Yet in all these things we are more than conquerors
through Him who loved us.
—Romans 8:37

A few years ago, Bill Jack of the Caleb Campaign—a ministry to reach children in the public schools—spoke in a church and told of Christopher Columbus's Christian motivation to sail to the Indies. Columbus wrote,

> It was the Lord who put into my mind (I could feel His hand upon me) to sail to the Indies. All who heard of my project rejected it with laughter, ridiculing me. There is no question that the inspiration was from the Holy Spirit, because He comforted me with rays of marvelous illumination from the Holy Scriptures. . . . Our Lord Jesus Christ desired to perform a very obvious miracle in the voyage to the Indies.[1]

A girl in that audience was later taking a test during which she was asked to write about Columbus's motivation for his classic voyage. She answered correctly that it was the Lord who put it into his mind to do it, as she had learned about this from Bill's presentation. The teacher deducted ten points from her grade for that answer. She wept as she told the youth pastor's wife she would never "express her faith in school" again. Bill Jack learned about this, and he patiently told her to ask the teacher to consult Columbus's *own* writings and then reevaluate her grade. So she made this request, and the teacher was big enough to look into the matter. When he did, he came across the truth about Columbus and then gave her back the ten points. Strengthened by this experience, the student was even able to write an extra-credit report on how the Bible impacted the Declaration of Independence and the Constitution![2]

We *can* be light in this dark world and make a substantial difference in the attack on Christ in America. Just like that teenage girl and Bill Jack, if we hold our ground, we can win more often than not—for God's glory, not ours. In this chapter, we will look at some important things to know to recover our lost freedoms and heritage.

As an introductory point, let me begin by clearly denouncing any and all violent vigilantism. In the last couple of years we have seen the tragic instances of demented people who profess Christ with their lips but take the law into their own hands by shooting abortion providers. This is not the way of Christ. This is not pro-*life*. This is a violation of what Jesus said to His followers when He taught us we are to love our neighbor (Mark 12:31) and *our enemy* (Matt. 5:44)—and therefore, everybody in between.

The effect of misguided vigilantism is also self-defeating. One violent pro-lifer (isn't that an oxymoron?) justified shooting an abortion doctor because it stopped abortions that day; in effect, he actually contributed heavily to the abortion industry. The pro-abortion forces' coffers are filling up; the large undecided middle part of America that is neither pro-life nor pro-abortion rights is moving toward favoring abortion rights after these shootings. These gunmen have inadvertently given the abortion forces the equivalent of a winning lottery ticket. They may slow abortions that day, only to greatly accelerate them in the future. "Christian" vigilantes just give the other side more ammo to try and get the federal government to close churches and seize their assets.

I saw this happen recently with a pastor in my own area. His church almost had to disband so they could sell their prime property in order to pay legal fees for a suit they lost. The suit grew out of their having aided and abetted Operation Rescue some five years before.

To those who think the pro-life movement is totally discredited because of these tragic and misguided shootings, we would ask: Did the violence of Nat Turner[3] or John Brown[4] discredit the abolition movement? Ralph Reed of the Christian Coalition points out that the Civil Rights movement rightfully distanced itself from the violence of the Black Panthers.[5]

So when I talk about regaining lost territory in the culture war, I am not advocating violence in the least. If you know someone who has been inclined to such action or has been contemplating such, tell them to put down their weapons and surrender to Jesus Christ. He *will* conquer this world, but the Prince of Peace will do it in *His* time and *His* way. His is *not* the way of violence. As the Bible says so clearly: "'Vengeance is *Mine, I* will repay,' says the Lord" (Rom. 12:19, emphasis mine).

A Silent Minority

Several years ago, I had lunch with an outstanding missionary who had been in South America for a good many years. He said to me, in effect, "How is it that when I occasionally return to the States, I see that there is an apparent evangelical awakening, a revival of sorts—superchurches, tremendous television and radio ministries, great crusades and conferences—yet I still see the moral fiber of the country continuing to slip? Why is there still the increasing pornography, the increasing ungodliness in the laws that are passed, the unconcern for human life?"

I said to him, "You will remember that as recently as 1960 we had a presidential election that was decided by less than 1 percent of the vote. Of course, when we have an election that is determined by less than 1 percent of the vote, we give the winner slightly more than half of the White House and the loser gets the rest, just slightly less, or 49 percent. The winner gets most of the power and the loser gets slightly less. Isn't that the way that we do it? Or am I mistaken? Did I miss something? Obviously, I am grossly in error. The fact is that the winner, though he may win by 1/10th of 1 percent, takes it all! And the loser is Mr. Alsoran, whoever he might have been."

The problem is that though there are many Christians in this country, though we can say that about 36 percent of adults claim that they have had a conversion experience,[6] and though that number is growing, that is still a minority. It just so happens that evangelical Christians are not making the laws in the Senate or in the Congress; they are not the ones running our television networks; they are not the ones printing pornographic material, nor allowing the laws which permit it. Though Christianity is growing in this country, it is still far from being the controlling force.

Render unto Caesar

Someone once asked me, "Do you think Christians should be involved in politics? That's dirty business." I said, "Of course not, you should leave it to the atheists; otherwise, you wouldn't have anything to complain about." Well, we have got plenty to complain about today, because that is exactly what we've done.

We have been commanded by Christ to render unto Caesar the things that are Caesar's. But how do we do that? First, we should pray regularly, faithfully, and daily for those who are in power—for our president and vice president, for our Cabinet, the Supreme Court, the Congress, the Senate, the House, and those who rule locally.

Secondly, we must register to vote. A lady who works in one of our precincts said that the average turnout in her precinct is 10 percent. Furthermore, it's amazing that up until the last decade and a half, huge blocs of people in the Church were not even *registered* to vote. In fact, according to a study about fifteen years ago, eighteen and a half million evangelical Christians were not even registered to vote! Half of those who were registered never voted, and a good number of those few who did, didn't even know what they were voting for; they were not informed. Do you realize that those eighteen and a half million people could have totally changed every election that has taken place in the last fifty years? Bill Clinton squeaked by with only 43 percent of the vote, but he still beat George Bush by about 4 percent.

Christians have had it in their power to change all of these things that we lament and complain and grumble about, and we just haven't done it. Providentially, we saw in the 1994 elections that this abysmal situation has begun to change significantly. We have come a long way; we still have more to go. Even though we have made progress, there is still a large group of evangelicals not registered to vote. Some of the greatest letters I've received from my television audience are those from elderly viewers that tell me they hadn't voted for many decades, until they saw one of my broadcasts. I thank God that He's using these television programs for positive change.

The Church is like a sleeping giant that is beginning to arouse from slumber. It's not totally alert yet, but it is awake. About five years ago, author and former political liaison for President Bush, Doug Wead, once said this of the Church and politics when he was asked if politicians take evangelicals seriously: "I think they kind of treat the evangelical movement like a seven-foot tall high schooler who can't play basketball. If he ever learns how to play, he's going to be awesome. In the meantime, they'll do everything they can to take advantage of his awkwardness."[7]

Voting, for non-Christian Americans, is a privilege and a responsibility; for Christians, it is a *duty* that we should fulfill.

Third, we should become informed so we don't simply walk into voting booths and close our eyes and punch holes in cards. At election time, look for the biblically oriented candidate scorecards. They are very helpful. You should get your information from many sources. Then get involved.

Do more than just vote. Support candidates of your choice. There are many Christians who have run for office who have lamented that they have received very little help from other Christians. Support candidates. Work for them. Run for office. I am grateful that I have people in my own congregation who have run for office and who have been elected. I hope more and more Christians will consider doing the same thing.

The Christian Coalition

One exciting force that has begun to emerge in our culture is the Christian Coalition, which is uniting people of faith and mobilizing them at the grassroots level. The Christian Coalition, headed by Ralph Reed, was the brainchild of Pat Robertson and was an outgrowth of his 1988 run for the presidency. Clearly, the Coalition played a big, positive role in the 1994 elections. Chapters of the Christian Coalition have been formed in many different states throughout the country. As more and more Christians get involved in this organization or in similar activities, we will indeed be able to not only fight back in the attack on Christ, but we will be able to help set the agenda. For too long we have been on the defensive; it's time we have a Christian offensive.

The Christian Coalition has raised much ire. But that's to be expected when you stand up for righteousness in an unrighteous culture. They have accomplished quite a bit in a short time. Indeed, it is "regarded as one of the most effective grassroots citizen organizations in America."[8] Wherever you are, chances are there is a Coalition chapter in your area, or if there's not, you may be able to start one. More Christians of each political party are needed to join in the political process, to be salt in this decaying culture.[9]

Being Salt and Light in the Public Schools

What can be done about the Christian bashing in our schools? How can the public schools be reformed and revived in order to provide an education compatible with Christian values? The key is in understanding how our local public schools are controlled.

Where are the seats of power in our public education system? Once we determine these, it is simply a matter of placing committed Christians into these positions and having them influence the policy and practice of the schools.

Power in the public school system has three sources: the Supreme Court and its decisions concerning education, the local school boards, and the teachers in the classroom. If Christians can wield influence in these three areas, public schools can be transformed in their religious and philosophical foundations.

The first seat of power in American education is the Supreme Court. So much of the secularizing of American education and of the public square in general began with the Supreme Court. Therefore, improving the Court would go a long way to reverse the trend.

The second (and perhaps greatest) source of power influencing the public school system is the local school board. One of the great glories of American education is that it has historically been under the control of parents and concerned citizens in the local community. Because this is still true, we have an excellent opportunity to ensure that the positions on the school board are held by committed Christians who clearly understand how to think and make decisions based on their faith.

Since local elections often have poor participation, it would be easy for a determined Christian community to elect godly men and women to influence the public school policy in nearly every community in our nation. From these positions, they could accomplish a great deal in establishing godly policies and in encouraging the selection of textbooks that are favorable to a Christian philosophy.

Finally, we must encourage the thousands of Christian public school teachers to learn new and more effective ways of integrating their Christian faith into their teaching. They are usually playing against a stacked deck. In some schools, depending on the principals, teachers can do very little of a positive, pro-faith nature—except perhaps to be "silent witnesses." And yet, there are still subtle ways they can at times integrate faith and learning when appropriate. For example, English teachers dealing with literature that contains references to the Bible can legally incorporate reading biblical passages to help the students understand the backdrop of the story.

In many school districts, because of Christian influence on the school boards, teachers can exert a more direct Christian witness. Christian teachers in the public school classroom need our prayers; they are the salt that remains in the public schools.

Many of these teachers perceive the public schools as their mission field and have been reaching out to young people for years. The effective Christian teacher must be an expert in apologetics and Christian philosophy.

At this time many teachers are leaving the schools because of the discipline problems and the lack of fulfillment. We have a golden opportunity to train an army of dedicated Christian teachers that can enter the public school classrooms. They can place a shield around the children in their care to protect them from the rampant secular philosophy that has become embedded in our public schools.

Christian teachers, arise! Stand firm for the faith of God! You are on the front lines of the battle for the minds of the youth of our nation. You can help turn back the tide of secularism in our schools.

What about Prayer in the Public Schools?

I am definitely in favor of school prayer. I favor a voluntary, student-led prayer. I believe the Jew should have the right to pray to God in his way, the Muslim to Allah, and the Christian to Jesus Christ. I think there's a definite need for us to develop a little tolerance in this country about religion and not feel we have to throw a tantrum every time somebody prays in a way that we don't particularly approve or like. Our culture is always blasting people who are intolerant, but when it comes to religion, it seems to be OK to be intolerant. Figure that out.

I think that one of the benefits of having school prayer would be the opposite of what the side effects of banning school prayer have been. There have been many, many indirect consequences of the Supreme Court's decisions to ban school prayer, not the least of which has been to turn our schools into virtual "religion-free zones." The fallout from these decisions has amounted to expelling God in toto from our entire school system and, beyond that, from the public life of America.

An amendment allowing for voluntary school prayer would, I think, send a signal across the country that God is not unconstitutional and He is not to be ruled out of the public life of Americans. And so I believe, as I've reflected on this, that the indirect consequences of school prayer would be more valuable, perhaps, than the direct consequence of it.

To those biblical purists who oppose school prayer on the grounds that the God of the Bible is not pleased with idolatrous prayer—which is absolutely correct—I would simply point out that this is not a theocracy, and I am not advocating that we have a theocracy. What I am advocating is freedom and religious liberty, which means that anyone may have the right to express his or her religious beliefs. I believe it's time for a constitutional amendment for voluntary, student-initiated, student-led school prayer so that in a land of free speech, "God talk" is no longer perceived as criminal activity.

The Education Revolution

The secular education establishment is now being threatened by a grassroots rejection of their social program. Christian parents are rising up by the millions and refusing to allow their children to be secularized before their eyès. Even many *non*-Christian parents have become upset about some of the abuses of the public schools and are beginning to seek educational alternatives or reform in the present public school system. Unfortunately, these non-Christian parents have not yet seen that the best answer to the problems in education exist in an educational system based on Christian principles that are consistently applied in every facet of the educational process.

As alternatives to the present public school system, new Christian schools are opening all the time, and thousands of parents each year are beginning to educate their children at home. Although they face an uphill climb, many bold parents throughout America are challenging school boards and teachers about the immoral and anti-Christian nature of many of their textbooks. And People for the American Way calls these concerned parents "censors." But as Jesus said, "Blessed are you when they revile and persecute you, and say all kinds of evil against you falsely for My sake" (Matt. 5:11). I'll take the opinion of Jesus Christ any day over that of Norman Lear!

The educational elite have noticed the rising tide of Christian resistance—though they view it as a rejection of their "enlightened" approach to the world; nevertheless, they are beginning to admit its growing social power and impact. Such a recognition of this "Christian revolution" in education can be heard from Terry Herndon, former executive director of the National Education Association (NEA), as he unabashedly slanders parents who are trying to make this change:

> I say to you that a cohort of chronic tax resisters, congenital reactionaries, dangerous witch hunters, energized super patriots, wayward dogma peddlers, and vitriolic race haters have coalesced into a sophisticated political force that has nearly overwhelmed a too comfortable and too stale progressive political movement.[10]

The group he is speaking of is largely made up of godly parents and teachers who are resisting the secularization of American education. (Note that I'm not supporting tax resisters or the like; but if one opposes tax hikes to support the public school system, which is failing by every criteria, then all of a sudden he is labeled a "tax resister.") The progressive political movement that Herndon perceives as good, but which is being overwhelmed, is the National Education

Association—one of the main groups attempting to push a secular and humanistic philosophy into our public schools.

If the Christian Church, Christian educators, and Christian parents are faithful in resisting the philosophy of secular humanism and providing Christian alternatives, within both public and private education, the days of the domination of America's education by secularism are numbered. Christ *must* rule over every thought, every action, every plan, in every area of life.

Citizens for Excellence in Education

One organization that is having a powerful impact for Christ in this realm is Citizens for Excellence in Education, which was founded in 1983 by Dr. Robert Simonds. Dr. Simonds, who has had thirty-three years of experience in the public education system, has a tender heart for children in the public schools. About forty-two million children (approximately 90 percent of the children in this country) attend public schools, including the vast majority of those from Christian homes. The atmosphere these children face is often hostile to Christianity. But CEE is beginning to make a difference. They have 250,000 concerned parents involved in CEE and 1,600-plus chapters around the country.

Dr. Simonds wrote a very influential book, *How to Elect Christians to Public Office*. One of CEE's goals is to get conservative Christians elected to local school boards. When concerned parents first started running for school boards, they had only 250 people win in 1989. In 1990, 454 CEE members were elected to school boards. In 1991, that number jumped to 1,157. In 1992, it was 3,611. In 1993, 7,153 and in 1994, 10,111! So, although the anti-Christian nature of the public schools continues, it will not go unchallenged. It seems a mighty force is moving forward to "replace faith-destroying curricula with programs that support moral values and create a climate emphasizing strong academics."[11] From all that I can tell, CEE is doing an outstanding job.

Parents and concerned citizens are encouraged to get involved with CEE. The future of our nation rests with our schoolchildren.[12]

Opting Out of NEA Dues

There are approximately two million teachers, administrators, and support personnel of public schools paying dues to the National Education Association. This is the largest union in the nation. While the NEA lobbies on behalf of these employees for good salaries, they also spend a significant amount of the monies for left-wing lobbying. They are pro-abortion and pro-homosexuality, and unfortunately many Christians indirectly support that through their dues. But there is a way out!

The National Right to Work Legal Defense Foundation in Northern Virginia has been winning court case after court case, all the way up to the Supreme Court, establishing the right for employees to opt out of the union or to opt out of paying that portion of their dues that is used for lobbying. This applies to Christian teachers and school personnel as well as others. This organization, a division of the National Right to Work Committee, provides free legal aid to people opting out of the NEA or out of paying for the NEA's lobbying. Many Christian teachers are going this route, so as not to violate their conscience. More and more are needed to stop funding the other side.[13]

Exciting things are happening at this time. Things are not as bleak as they sometimes seem.

The Biblical Basis for Christian Involvement

I believe we can overcome the attack on Christ in America, that we can change the direction of this country. We can eradicate the laws spawned by ignorance that have left us vulnerable to destruction. We can change this country only if we are willing to be faithful witnesses for Jesus Christ. Unless people come to a living faith in Christ, we will never see this nation exalt and honor God again.

The final barrier we must overcome in order to see our nation return to Christian values is to take all the potentialities of this country—in other words, every element of its culture and every one of its institutions—and bring them under the control of Christ and His Word. As we seek to dedicate our lives to the work to which God has specifically called us and we attempt to do that work to the glory of God, then God will use our efforts to bring our entire culture under the control of biblical principles.

We need to regard no area of life as secular, that is, divorced from God. Every sphere of life needs to be regenerated by the saving message of Christ. This means that government is not a secular island, free from the claims of Christ. Government, like all institutions in this world, is responsible to God.

It is at this point that many Christians have problems. They have accepted the teaching that to be spiritual they must withdraw into some sort of pietistic ghetto and wait to be taken out of this evil world. They strongly and sincerely believe that Christians must not be involved in political and social issues if they are to be pure in spirit.

I know that many feel this way because I receive hundreds of letters from sincere Christians who are troubled because I speak out sometimes on social issues. They feel that when I do this I am failing to teach the Word of God and have become involved in worldly affairs. Is this true? Is the Bible just a road map to Heaven? These are crucial questions we must answer if we are going to effectively fight in the present battle for the soul of America.

I believe a careful study of Scripture will clearly teach us that a faithful Christian *must* be involved in the political and social issues of his or her time. There are five biblical principles that lead me to this conclusion:

1. The cultural mandate commands mankind to rule the earth for the glory of God. "Then God blessed them, and God said to them, 'Be fruitful and multiply; fill the earth and subdue it; have dominion over the fish of the sea, over the birds of the air, and over every living thing that moves on the earth'" (Gen. 1:28). This mandate includes the function of government.

2. God commands men to form civil governments to stem the growth of violence by administering the death penalty (Gen. 9:6). From this flow all other powers and functions of government.

3. The vast majority of all the godly men mentioned in the Old Testament were either godly rulers or were prophets who warned the government and nation to repent. Almost no saint in the Old Testament can be named who was not somehow politically involved in government. It is clearly taught that men like Joseph, Samuel, David, and Daniel were called by God to be *political* leaders.

4. The New Testament call to repentance did not demand men to leave the sphere of military and political activity, but only to conduct themselves in such offices in a just manner (Luke 3:14).

5. The teaching of Christ and the apostles denied government the right to demand obedience if contrary to God's commands, yet it also acknowledges that government is part of Christ's kingdom and therefore has legitimate authority (Acts 4:19; Rom. 13:1–7). There is no reason for Christians not to serve in the political realm to restrain evil and encourage good. And, in fact, who does these things better, as the history and growth of our country shows?

From this cursory examination of the teaching of the Scriptures, we find a clear affirmation that involvement in social concerns and government is not intrinsically evil, but rather a required service to Almighty God. As Christian citizens, who, by the providence of God, have been enabled to control and direct our nation, we should do all we can to have it ruled by Christian principles. This is clearly the will of God for each and every Christian.

But what the world wants from us is something entirely different. As former Vice President Dan Quayle said, "What the media wants and what the media demands of Christians is very simply this: your silence."[14] And we have been all too willing. But I, for one, will be silent no longer. I will not be ashamed of Him upon whom my hopes of Heaven depend. I will speak the name of Christ and not be ashamed. I will speak for the principles of Christ.

More Power Than We Think

Too often we have allowed the world to intimidate us. But in reality, we have *much* more power than we think. On the spiritual level, we can do all things through Christ who gives us strength (Phil. 4:13). "We are more than conquerors through Him who loved us" (Rom. 8:37). We have our faith in Him who has overcome the world (John 16:33). We'll address the spiritual power we have through prayer in just a moment.

We also have *much* leverage on the human level. The anti-Christians who are attacking Christ in America may temporarily have control of many key institutions in this country—the media, the education establishment, the universities, the law schools, and many important political posts—but we have the people and lots of them. And many of them are beginning to get involved in the political process for the first time.

While the lawsuits against things Christian are often well publicized, there are a number of significant victories we never hear about. Victories that show when we resist the onslaught, we often win. And we fight back, again for the sake of the furtherance of the gospel, that it might spread unfettered. Let's consider some of the many victories of which you may or may not be aware.

When Audrey Pearson, a handicapped girl from Northern Virginia, was ten years old, she learned an important lesson in religious liberty. Because of her condition, she had to take an hour-long bus ride, one-way, each day to school. Despite her mental limitations, she loved the Lord and enjoyed reading the Bible. She started to bring her Bible with her to read it on her long bus ride. The principal got wind of this and instructed her mother that Audrey could no longer do this. Audrey was crushed and very confused when this happened—especially as her mother had been trying to teach her about authority and that it ultimately comes from God. Fortunately, Audrey's mother found out about the work of the Rutherford Institute (see the Appendix); she tracked them down and called them. A representative of the organization wrote a letter to the principal, pointing out that Audrey was totally within her rights to read her Bible on the bus, and the principal backed off, allowing Audrey to read her copy of the Scriptures on the bus.[15]

In Ottawa, Illinois, there's a public park that was the sight of the Lincoln-Douglas debates. In our time the same park was the center of another debate—a debate about religious liberty. A series of paintings based on the life of Christ had been donated to the city by the artist. Since 1956, they had been erected by volunteers at Christmastime each year, until one atheist in town complained to the ACLU in the late 1980s. The ACLU sued the city; a federal judge agreed with them, and the paintings came down—to the chagrin of the vast majority of the people of Ottawa. But the National Legal Foundation got involved, as did generous viewers of the *Coral Ridge Hour*, and a federal appeals court reversed the earlier decision. The entire court (the seventh Circuit Court of Appeals) voted *unanimously* in favor of the National Legal Foundation's position. Although they had been in storage for a few years, today those paintings are again erected in Ottawa Park at Christmastime.[16] Furthermore, this case (*Doe v. Small*) has set a positive precedent in religious speech cases; it has already been cited in numerous cases involving religious expression in the public square.

Often, all it takes to fight back and win is simply a phone call or letter from an attorney to the school board or the city. Frequently in these cases, the law is on our side. We just need to act against religious bigotry.

An important point to be underscored is that the ACLU and groups like it are often more of a paper threat than anything else. They often win by intimidation, by merely *threatening* to sue, even if they might be totally unconstitutional in their position.

There are numerous cases in which Christians have stood their ground for the gospel's sake and won. As we fight back in love, we need to realize there are sometimes hidden opportunities in the attacks against Christianity. Here's an example that happened in my own community. Coauthor Jerry Newcombe received a slick, full-color homosexual magazine from a friend who had picked it up free from the main branch of the public library. It was part of a large display for "Gay Pride Month." In that magazine were two derogatory references to me and Coral Ridge Church. When Jerry said to me that somebody should call the library about this, I said, "Go ahead." Jerry did call and spoke with a library official, who stood by the display in general but claimed that she had not cleared the magazine, nor would she have, given its negative slant. Then he asked her, since the gays had their display, bashing the Church, would it be possible to have a display at Christmastime complete with literature on the true meaning of Christmas? She agreed to it, and the following December the display went up. We have more power than we think. We just need to use it for the sake of Christ.

In the spring of 1994, some members of Congress tried to pass a law that would have effectively broken the back of the home-schooling movement. It would have forced all parents who teach at home to be fully accredited by the state. The bill, known as H.R. 6, came to the attention of some of the leaders in the home-schooling movement, who alerted their own. The alarming aspects of this bill were spread only through Christian talk radio (Marlin Maddoux's *Point of View* and Dr. Dobson's *Family News in Focus* were among the biggest heroes in this fight) and churches and word of mouth. Nonetheless, Congress received more than a million phone calls on this—almost all against H.R. 6. So many calls came in that the switchboard was effectively closed down for a day. Although it was the biggest response to any bill in recent memory, there was hardly a peep about this from the mainstream press, the "dominant media culture," as Congressman Bob Dornan (R-Calif.) likes to call them. Media attention or not, the victory against H.R. 6 reveals once again that we have the numbers and if mobilized properly, the Christian community in this country can have a far-reaching positive impact!

The Equal Employment Opportunity Commission drew up guidelines in 1993 that, if adopted, would have disallowed evangelism and the public display of religious symbols in the American workplace. Fortunately, the outcry against this injustice was great. The EEOC received more than 100,000 letters against these proposed restrictions. The Senate voted 94-0 against these guidelines, and they were dropped. The amazing thing is that the EEOC was way behind on their normal workload at the time they drew up this proposal. The *Sarasota Herald-Tribune* ran a front-page story on November 26, 1994, that declared: "Backlog of Cases Mounts at EEOC; Complaints Wait on the Shelf for 19 Months before Investigators Can Reach Them."[17] It's revealing, isn't it? For months they actively pursued an anti-Christian agenda, while not keeping up with their main responsibility!

The U.S. Postal Service announced in late 1994 that they would discontinue Christmas stamps of Madonna and child. This had been a tradition for nearly three decades; and it wasn't because of lack of sales that they were to be canceled. But again the public outcry was great. I personally wrote a letter remonstrating this, as did many others. Thankfully, the decision was reversed.

As Christians in this culture watch the ongoing attack against Christ and His Church, it's easy to feel like the legendary boy of Holland who plugs up the holes in the dike with his fingers. He barely finishes plugging one when another leak emerges. So it is in our battle against anti-Christian bigotry. We do battle on one front, sometimes winning, sometimes losing. But we barely finish one battle before another one emerges. This has created the need for Christian legal services. Thankfully, that need is beginning to be filled.

Legal Organizations Fighting Anti-Christian Bigotry

God has raised up a number of legal organizations that preserve the rights of Christians, churches, and various ministries. Today there is, writes Mark Curriden in an article entitled "Defenders of the Faith" for the American Bar Association, "a growing number of lawyers who focus entirely on religious liberty cases in at least eight full-time public interest law firms. With five firms organized within the past four years, the money they have been able to raise also has skyrocketed."[18] Many of them have begun to use the strategy of making these religious-freedom cases matters of free speech. As Mat Staver, head of Liberty Council, one of these organizations, said, "We were beating our heads against the wall by arguing most of these cases as 'establishment clause' and 'free exercise.'"[19] But when they instead argued them as *free-speech* cases, they achieved greater success. Curriden writes, "Some time in the late 1980s, a light bulb went off and religious-freedom lawyers discovered the free speech clause of the First Amendment."[20] This strategy has led to greater victory in fighting anti-Christian bigotry.

I have compiled a listing of the phone numbers and addresses of these many Christian legal groups in the Appendix of this book. No Christian should have his or her constitutional rights trampled on again. Help is out there and is available for the asking.

Not with Flesh and Blood

Finally, we have to remember that this is a spiritual battle. While we need to be engaged in the type of battle that the Christian legal groups are waging, and while we need to be salt and light in a decaying school system, there is a spiritual dimension to fighting back against anti-Christian bigotry. We need to have a balanced approach in this—working as if everything were up to us and praying as if everything were up to God.

We are engaged in spiritual warfare. Because it is an invisible war, because it is a war that is different from that which we generally call war, many people are not aware of its progress. They are not even aware of the fatalities and the injuries of that war, so numerous as to make any previous war pale by comparison. We are under attack by spiritual beings, Paul tells us in Ephesians 6. We wrestle not with flesh and blood but with principalities and powers, wickedness in high places, against beings that are more mighty, more powerful, more wise, more cunning, and more malicious than we are. We are told in this great passage (Eph. 6:10–18) that there are two things we need. First of all, the armor of God. Second, we need a power to go with that armor.

What Paul is telling us is that physical power, intellectual power, and moral power are all powers to be found in the natural world, and they are all absolutely useless in the warfare in which we are engaged. We are not to be ignorant of the wiles of the devil. I am afraid, however, that many Christians are indeed unaware of his wiles. How many Christians are trying to fight a spiritual war with natural weapons? We are engaged ultimately in supernatural warfare!

We are dealing with principalities and powers. These are angels, Paul is telling us. These are the angels that God created who have fallen with Lucifer and now form the demonic host. These angels are something to reckon with. The Old Testament tells us that one angel in one night destroyed 185,000 fully-armed Assyrian soldiers (2 Kings 19:35). Which of you would like to take him on?

We are engaged in a supernatural, spiritual, and invisible warfare, and we need a supernatural power if we are to survive and succeed and be victorious. The King James Bible says, "Be strong in the Lord" (Eph. 6:10). But that is not quite what Paul says. The verb in the Greek is passive. It means "be ye made strong" or "be ye strengthened in the Lord." It is in the Lord, in the power of His might, that we are to be strengthened. "The power of His might"—these are the same Greek words that were used in the first chapter of Ephesians to describe the power God used to raise Jesus Christ from the dead and the same terms used to describe the power God used to quicken us from the deadness of sin. It is the might of Him who said, "All power is given unto me in Heaven and earth. Go and preach the gospel to every creature" (Matt. 28:18–19, my paraphrase). Strengthened with the power of His might, we are to go.

Thus, as trite as this may sound, sincere prayer is the *ultimate weapon* we have in our arsenal for combating the attack on Christianity in our culture. Also, fasting, a lost spiritual discipline in our instant-gratification culture, is exceedingly powerful. I encourage more and more Christians to discover the effectiveness of fasting and prayer.

On this front, we are happy to report some exciting developments. For example, David Bryant's organization, Concerts of Prayer, is organizing more and more groups to pray for our country. Recently, in December 1994, there was a historic prayer meeting in Orlando where some "600 churchmen gathered for one purpose—to pray! They prayed for the nation and the fulfillment of the Great Commission. They asked God to come against an immoral media and racism."[21]

My good friend Bill Bright called this meeting and also asked the participants to fast for forty-eight hours.

More recently, in November of 1995, thousands of Christians from ninety different countries came to Los Angeles for six separate events (most of which were simultaneous) that were dedicated to prayer, fasting, repentance, and strengthening of their Christian outreach. One of these events was aptly titled "Fasting & Prayer '95."[22] Who knows the potential long-range impact of these kinds of meeting?

The *Critical* Need for Evangelism

In the long run, if we really want to change the world for good, what we need to do is to evangelize! We need to proclaim the gospel of Christ to every creature. Nothing will change the world as powerfully and as effectively as letting people know Jesus Christ and Him crucified (1 Cor. 1:23). When individuals get converted it changes everything. Thus, to prevail in this conflict, we must become effective witnesses.

What is the problem with all of the ungodly people, the people who hate Christ and hate Christians and hate His Word? The problem is simple: They have never been converted. They don't know what it's like to fall in love with Jesus, to be set free from sin. We have, because of our own neglect and our own failure to obey the Great Commission, allowed a growing number of heathen to spring up so that they now occupy many places of power and use that power against the Church.

Conclusion

Dr. Ralph Reed, president of the Christian Coalition, was in a debate a few years ago and the invariable issue of church and state came up. Reed was asked, "If you are allowed to pass laws based on your religious beliefs, where do you draw the line?" I conclude this chapter with Reed's noteworthy response:

> What good is religious liberty, I asked, if it can only be practiced behind stained-glass windows on Sunday? If one desires to pass a law to prohibit people of faith from engaging in political action based on their beliefs, one would need to take a knife to our history books and cut out the pages on the antislavery crusade, the temperance movement, the women's movement, the civil rights struggle, and the anti-Vietnam War protests. All these social movements flowered in their day because religious people believed that the ideas of right and

wrong they found in the Bible should be reflected in our laws. . . . The United States of America was founded on religious principles by religious people. Our society works best when we remember that fact and welcome into the public square those who act in its finest traditions.[23]

Soldiers of Christ

No soldier in active service entangles himself in the
affairs of everyday life, so that he may please
the one who enlisted him as a soldier.
—2 Timothy 2:4 NASB

Question: Who is the best-known person in the world today? I recently asked our officers at church if they knew the answer to that. Somebody said Billy Graham. Billy Graham has spoken to countless millions of people, but he is not the one. Someone else said Muhammad Ali. He has been seen by millions, but he is not the most recognized person in the world. Another guessed the Pope. No, not the Pope. Someone else volunteered, "I know. The king—Elvis." No, not Elvis Presley.

Then who? Perhaps, Jesus of Nazareth, the King of kings and Lord of lords? Unfortunately, it is not.

Do you think you know?

The answer is Mickey Mouse! Mickey Mouse? Yes, the most recognized "person" in the world, according to a survey is a mouse. (I use the term "person" in the broadest sense. I suppose if *Time* magazine could make a computer "Person of the Year," then we could say that Mickey is a person.)

I want you to know that offends me; that should grieve every Christian. Mickey is fifty years old. The gospel has been preached almost two thousand years. That should send us to our knees in repentant prayer.

Dear friends, does it grieve your heart that Jesus Christ is not the best-known, most recognized person on the face of this earth? It should. If you belong to Him, it no doubt will. Jesus Christ is the King of kings. He is a real, living person, and He does more than entertain us for a moment—He promises us eternal paradise in that place He has gone to prepare for us, in that house of many mansions. This survey result underscores our need to get out all the more and proclaim the good news of Christ, even to a culture hostile to what they think the gospel is.

Soldiers of Christ

We are called to be soldiers of Christ, and to bear His name in America will require greater commitment and self-sacrifice in the days ahead. If we are to reclaim lost ground, we need to avoid compromise and incessant flirting with the world. We are in a serious battle with great issues at stake.

If you are in the army of Christ, then service is not optional; every member must serve his General. Unfortunately, there are too many who claim to be members, but who are AWOL (Absent Without Leave). Since you're with me this far in reading this book, I would doubt you are one of them.

We have a tremendous opportunity! God has clearly shown us the way to see the victory of Christ manifested in our nation, in our time. He has left us with a command to live lives of holiness, to proclaim His Word by our lives and actions, and to bring all of creation under His control.

This is not an option; it is not an elective, in which Christians may choose not to participate. It is the command of our General. It is the marching orders of the army of Christ. If we claim to be soldiers in that army, then we are under orders to do all we can to bring this nation back to God.

Some may say, "It's too much. There are too many of them. They are too well entrenched." My friends, remember World War II. The Japanese forces took over almost all of the Pacific; it seemed there was no stopping them. They moved into Korea, China, Midway, and the Philippines. They were on their way into Australia. The panzer division of the blitzkrieg of Hitler crushed Poland and Czechoslovakia. They moved through France, and it looked like they were going to take all of Europe, and England as well.

Then, in the providence of God, there was the battle at Midway, and the backbone of the Japanese carrier fleet was destroyed. There was that great D day, when the largest armada in the history of the world landed on the shores of Normandy. There was the Battle of the Bulge, the crossing of the Rhine, and all of a sudden the tide was turned, and the forces of liberty soon rejoiced in victory.

We, too, may see a turning point in the battle for the soul of America. But it's going to take a stronger commitment on the part of Christians.

Out of the Closet

What Christians need this day is courage. We live in a time when just about everyone is coming out of the closet. The homosexuals have come out of the closet and are marching down the streets in Gay Pride Week. The prostitutes have come out of the closet and are walking the streets demanding their rights. Unfortunately, in many closets, if you move back the overcoat and look behind the suitcase, you might find cringing there . . . a Christian. Alas! It is time for the Christians to come out of the closet. Bob Briner, author of *Roaring Lambs*, asks: "Why does it seem so stupid to openly be who we are? Why should it be fashionable to keep the most important aspect of our lives in a closet? Gays don't. Radical feminists don't. . . . Can we be all Christ expects us to be in a closet?"[1]

It is time for Christians not to be ashamed of Jesus Christ. People scream and yell and become hysterical at football and baseball games and are called "fans." But if you get a little enthusiastic for Christ, people call you a "fanatic." It is not so! Christ is the only person in the world who is really worth getting excited about because He frees us from our sins; He gives us a purpose for living (*the* purpose for living!); He gives us an abundant life; and He promises an eternity in His presence! This reminds me of that anonymous phrase that goes something like this:

My past is forgiven.
My present is abundant life in Christ.
My future is heaven, forever with Him.

We have great news to share with the rest of the world. We need to be bold in its proclamation.

In this day of so much Christian bashing, we need Christians who are courageous. We need preachers in pulpits who are courageous, who are not afraid to step on toes, who will challenge their people and call a spade a spade.

Don Wildmon, a bold Christian who, through the American Family Association, has provided much salt and light in our dark and decaying culture wrote an excellent column titled "300,000 Silent Pulpits" that's worth reprinting:

Today, 4,000 innocent precious lives of unborn babies were snuffed out . . . .

And 300,000 pulpits are silent. . . .

The networks make a mockery of Christians, the Christian faith and Christian values with nearly every show they air. Greed, materialism, violence, sexual immorality are standard fare. Program after program, movie after movie contains anti-Christian episodes and plots. News articles condescendingly refer to the "fundamentalist, right-wing Christians." Those who speak out for the sacredness of life are branded as extremists.

And 300,000 pulpits are silent.

Teenage suicide is the highest it has ever been. . . . Christian morality cannot be taught in schools but atheistic immorality can. . . .

And 300,000 pulpits are silent.

Rape has increased 700 percent in the last fifty years, and that takes into consideration the population growth. . . .

And 300,000 pulpits are silent.

Rock music fills the airwaves and our children's minds with music which legitimizes rape, murder, forced sex, sadomasochism, adultery, satanic worship, etc.

And 300,000 pulpits are silent.

A majority of states now have lotteries. We have eliminated that crime by making it legal and putting it under the control of the state.

And 300,000 pulpits are silent.

What important matters are being dealt with in our churches?

The church bulletin says there will be a meeting to plan the church-wide supper. We are raising money to put a new floor cover on the kitchen. (The old one doesn't match the new stove and refrigerator.) The sermon subject last Sunday was "How to Have a Positive Attitude." We are organizing a softball team.

At a meeting of church officials a program was announced to recruit new members. We need the new program because we are losing membership. The new program was worked out by some of the very top professionals, people who have had success in gaining new members for the Lions Club, the Civitan Club and other organizations. We really need professionals to do the job.

Sometimes blasphemy comes unnoticed.[2]

Thankfully, not all 300,000 pulpits are silent! And many more are now speaking out, certainly more than those at the time Don wrote this in the mid-1980s. Nonetheless, it underscores a pathetic truth. We can no longer abandon our call to be salt to a decaying culture.

"I Can't Get Involved at This Time"

Years ago one American said to another American, "We need your help. We need your leadership."

And the second American replied, "I really can't, because I have a family and my business is growing, and I have to give myself to that. I have my own personal needs and I must take care of those needs. I just can't get involved."

"But, General Washington, what will we do if you don't lead us?"

That conversation never took place, but what if it had? Where would we be? If some Christians today were in Washington's shoes, that's exactly what they would have said. We don't care about the larger concerns—concerns that will affect our nation.

This attitude was rampant in 1919–33 in the Weimar Republic in Germany. The Pietistic Movement had become very big at that time. They didn't want to be concerned with what was happening out there. They hardly noticed when somebody named Adolf began to move into prominence and took over.

As a result of the assault on Christianity, the Christian faith has been isolated more and more into a tiny private sector of life and removed from the whole public spectrum of America. Christians have got to wake up to the fact that they have been deluded, deceived, and outmaneuvered. We have got to assert the truth of what our Constitution means. As could be expected, some who have spoken up in recent decades have been told to sit down and shut up. I think of Jerry Falwell and the Moral Majority, which was a lightning rod for all sorts of criticisms. Many involved in that movement or involved in pro-life work have experienced burnout because of the constant pressure from a culture moving away from God. Therefore, for lasting change, more and more Americans must become Christians.

Every Christian to Be a Witness

I estimate that there are more than 65 million evangelical Christian *adults* in this country.[3] If every one of those would simply win one other person to Christ within the next twelve months, we could dramatically increase our influence in this country. Think about that. That would be more than 130 million. That is not a difficult goal. All you have to do is win one person this year. I am thankful for someone who said he was determined that no week in the year was going to go by without his witnessing to someone for Jesus Christ. In one sense, winning one person a year for Christ is very little. We should win many in a year if we are faithful witnesses for Jesus. Will you make this your goal?

I can tell you that there is no greater joy than leading someone to faith in Jesus Christ. Even if they reject your message, it still feels great to obey Christ. Yet regardless of how we feel, we need to remember this is what He has commanded. Besides, since we have the spiritual counterpart to the cure for cancer, how can we be content to just keep it to ourselves? How can we only think about ourselves?

Suppose you are walking down the street one night and pass by a neighbor's house. Suddenly you see flames pouring out of the children's bedroom window! You might say to yourself, "Now I really ought to shout and tell my neighbor that their house is on fire. But I would sound rather strange standing here in the street shouting. People might think I'm some sort of a fanatic. Best that I just go home, get down on my knees, and pray about it." There is not a person reading this book who would do that. Rather, you would rush up, pound on the front door, and exclaim, "Fire! Fire! Your house is on fire!" Why? Because you believe those flames are real.

Jesus Christ, who came to save us from perdition, said that unbelievers shall go into everlasting torment; they shall be cast into a lake of fire (Rev. 20:15). But coiled in the soul of many who profess Christianity is the serpent of unbelief that doesn't really believe those things at all.

Sometimes we lack boldness to share the gospel because we say to ourselves, "Ah, there is no point. Certainly, this hardened reprobate will never change." I think of a young man who was a professional musician. He was a pretty rowdy sort of fellow. But his brother went to West Point and there became a Christian. He came home and talked to his rowdy brother and he, too, became a Christian.

This professional musician had a very good friend with whom he had caroused many a time, and he said to himself, "I think that I shall go speak to my friend." But then the doubts crept into his mind: "Ah, no, that would be to no avail. Nothing good would come of that. That fellow is such a reprobate and such a hard-hearted sinner that he would probably take me by the scruff of my neck and throw me out of his office." And so he never went. The name of that musician was Robert Shirley, and the name of his hard-hearted, reprobate friend was Jim Kennedy.

I am often sobered by the thought that my best friend considered me a lost cause, beyond the reach of the grace of God. I am glad that God did not share that opinion!

This is a time when every Christian should overcome the fear of witnessing, a time when every Christian should be willing to share the gospel and be equipped to do so boldly and courageously. If you have not received that training, I hope you will request that your pastor train you to do that. If your church needs more information on how to get that training, then by all means I encourage you to write to me. I'll send you more information about Evangelism Explosion, the lay-witnessing program originated here at Coral Ridge Presbyterian Church, now used by thousands of churches around the globe.[4]

Lord and Savior

Jesus Christ demands to be both Lord and Savior. As Savior, He went to a cross, and there He suffered, bled, and died. But as Lord, He demands His rightful place as King on the throne of our hearts. We are to submit our wills to Him.

You probably know what an oxymoron is. If not, an oxymoron is a combination of contradictory words. Awful pretty, jumbo shrimp, idiot savant, deafening silence—all are examples of oxymorons. One part cancels out another.

The oxymoron I would like you to consider is the phrase: "No, Lord." You cannot say, "No, Lord," and mean both words; one annuls the other. If you say no to Him, then He is not your Lord. There is one person to whom you never say no, and that person is your Lord.

Someone cleverly wrote the following letter and response—from Christ to His Church and the latter's reply. It creatively communicates the oxymoron of saying "No, Lord."

Dear Christians,

I have been given all power and authority in heaven and earth. Go then to all people and make them My disciples. Baptize them in the name of the Father and the Son and the Holy Spirit and teach them to observe, obey, and respect everything that I have commanded you. I will be with you always, even to the end of the age. Shalom,

With all My love,
Jesus Christ

And the church board replies:

Dear Jesus, Our Lord,

We hereby acknowledge receipt of Your memorandum. The proposal is very interesting, and we feel that we should probably undertake this project—not immediately, of course, but as soon as it may seem feasible. Due to the shortage of personnel and several other financial and personal obligations, we do not feel that we can give it proper emphasis at this time. A committee, however, has been appointed to study the plan, and we should have a report in a few months. In the meantime, we are honored to know that You have considered us for this task, and we appreciate Your offer to serve as our resource person should we choose to undertake this project. You may rest assured that it will be given careful consideration by our committee, and we hope to have an answer at our earliest convenience.

Your Obedient Servants,
The Christians[5]

That is a classic example of an oxymoron and a rebellious, faith-lacking spirit.

In our day, the need for Christians to lovingly and effectively share the gospel could not be greater. If you, in sincerity, before God Almighty, will determine "Yes, I am going to do more to try to present the gospel to more people in this country," and "I am going to do something to try to impact this culture for God and for Christ," and if you are willing to do something more than you've done before, I'm going to ask you right now to put down this book for a moment and commit this to the Lord. Again, I am talking about making a renewed (or for some, a first time) commitment to witness for Christ and to positively impact our culture for Christ.[6]

The Potential Impact of Active Christians on Our Culture

I pointed out earlier that there are more than 65 million adults who claim to be born-again Christians in this country. Meanwhile, homosexuals represent a very small population in this country. In fact, homosexuals (men and women) and bisexuals represent at most only about 2.1 percent of the U.S. adult population, according to the recent, exhaustive survey *Sex in America*, under the auspices of the University of Chicago.[7] Yet with their 2.1 percent, homosexuals still have a stranglehold on the media. That's because the media concur with the homosexual agenda and they disagree with ours. However, they also would like to have a paycheck on Friday. If there were enough Christians *who really were concerned,* then boycotts would be devastating, and could close them down or cause them to have to lay off a lot of people. They would then listen more carefully.

Ultimately, you're not going to have a Christian morality in a pagan nation where most of the people are unbelievers and where the Christians are only a minority. Christian morality can't be imposed (nor should it be) by a Christian minority upon a vast majority of non-Christians. That's not going to happen. Although, you *can* take 3 percent of the people and impose communism on a country because "political power comes out of the barrel of a gun," as Chairman Mao said, or as Hitler said in *Mein Kampf,* "what is refused to amicable methods, it is up to the fist to take."[8] But Christians don't use machine guns or the fist. All we have is a ballot, and we're not up to 51 percent of the population. Yet.

I can think of an example or two where a Christian minority won an election but were unable to impose their agenda on a district largely uninterested in their agenda. A few years ago in a local town here in Florida, some conservatives got together, got organized, and elected a whole slate of conservative city commissioners. They went in and changed everything in that city, and they put in a lot of conservative measures. But what they simply did was to awaken the beast: when the bear (the large majority of the population) woke up, it swept the conservatives out of office in the following election.

Recently, in Jacksonville, a similar thing happened. This time it wasn't conservatives; it was Christians—Christian conservatives who got together in their local churches. They won seats on the city commission, on the school board, and so on. They put into the schools abstinence-based sex education, the teaching of creation, and other Christian teachings, etc. When the next election came along, they lost the majority on the school board. So now all those things are going out.

You can organize and be active while the beast is asleep; but when you win the election, you're going to wake them up. And they're going to sweep you right out of their lair. What you need to do is to win more people to Christ. That way, if you have, say, 55 percent on your side, even if you do wake up the secularists, they'll be too weak to stop the cause of Christ.

In the case of the courts, we've seen many situations where the overwhelming majority favor a particular initiative—only to see it overturned by some liberal judge. To make a difference in that realm is a much more long-term process. That's not going to happen with one election. Just suppose that 60 percent of the people in this country were conservative, born-again Christians. Then add the other conservatives in the nation. You would have conservative Christians elected to office all over the place. They would be appointing judges, and they wouldn't be ACLU-type judges. They wouldn't be judges like those that killed Amendment 2. (Amendment 2, you may recall, was a measure that denied granting homosexuals *special* rights in the state of Colorado; the majority of the citizens voted the measure in, but it was nullified by some liberal judges.)

A conservative majority would be appointing judges who had Christian convictions and believed in Christian principles, such as John Jay, the first chief justice of the U.S. Supreme Court and an outspoken evangelical. It's going to take time to replace those liberal judges who sit on the bench now. It's going to take a solid majority, not just a charismatic Ronald Reagan who gets in for a little while and makes some positive changes, only to see the liberals come back in and undo it.

The only way to have long-term change in this country is through *evangelism*. May God empower and embolden more and more of His Church today to live up to our lofty calling!

We Can Change America!

People made America what it is, and we can make it what it ought to be. Do we really believe that? Paul said, "I can do all things through Christ. . . ." (Phil. 4:13), and Jesus Christ tells us to be faithful citizens of this country (Mark 12:17). Remember those men who worked indefatigably, who pledged their lives, their fortunes, and their sacred honor[9] on producing this country—men who were willing to sacrifice everything. Many gave their lives that we might enjoy freedoms and the blessings of this nation, but we are letting it slip through our fingers like sand.

I wonder what people will say to their grandchildren if they ask, "Grandaddy, where were you when America lost its freedom? What were you doing? What were you doing when America became a godless nation? What did you do to stop that?" We *can* stop it and we *can* change it if we will simply be obedient to what Jesus Christ has told us to do and fulfill our responsibilities as Christian citizens.

Here is my dream. I believe it is possible with all my heart. I hope you believe it is possible that we can see a nation . . .

. . . where babies can be conceived and born without the possibility of being hacked to pieces in their mother's womb;

. . . where this vile ocean of pornography can be cleaned up and removed from our land;

. . . where nativity scenes can be publicly exhibited at Christmastime;

... where children can voluntarily pray in the public schools and not get suspended or otherwise punished;

... where the First Amendment free-speech rights of the students and teachers will not be stifled when it comes to religious speech in the public schools;

... where Scripture can be quoted in the courtroom and not penalized;

... where the president, lawmakers, judges, and all magistrates throughout this land will once again recognize the true King of kings and Lord of lords, Jesus Christ;

... where we can see a film without worrying about what is going to be contained in it;

... where we can turn on the television and not expect to hear the name of Christ blasphemed or see all sorts of unseemly things;

... where we can have a society in which drugs are not rampant and where it is safe to walk the streets again.

These things are the blessings that Christians can bring to a nation. All the blessings that this nation has enjoyed have come from Jesus Christ, and it's up to us to bring Him and His teachings and His gospel back to this country.

Each of us must root our lives and actions in this conviction: *Christ rules over all!* The Scriptures clearly teach that secular humanism, communism, socialism, and all the false religions of the world will be overcome and destroyed by the truth that is in Jesus Christ.

It's great to know that we are on the winning side. Think of that before you talk to the next person about Jesus Christ. We are *winning*, but, of course, the battle is not over. We have a long way to go. The war's outcome has not yet been rendered in the present. But we know that our Christ has *already* won! We are winning! With your help—as part of the mighty army of Jesus Christ—we will win, to the glory of God.

A Challenge

There is a stirring story from the annals of history that has long challenged my life. It is about a bold and courageous man who lived three hundred years before Christ. His name was Alexander. We call him "The Great." He had conquered the whole world by the time he was thirty and then wept because there were no more worlds to conquer.

One day he was conducting court for his army in a great palace. Soldiers were lined up along each wall with their spears at their sides, standing at attention. Alexander, the king of the world, was sitting on a golden throne, and one after another the soldiers were brought before him. He swiftly pronounced sentence upon them, and there was none that could deliver them out of his hand for he was the sovereign of the earth.

Finally, there was brought before him a young man who was about seventeen years old. He was a Macedonian; he was unusual in his appearance in that he was blond and blue-eyed—a very handsome lad. Alexander looked at him and his countenance softened somewhat. The soldiers thought that perhaps he had taken a fancy to the young lad. Alexander asked what his crime was, and the sergeant at arms read the charge. He had been found cringing in a cave, having fled from the face of the enemy in battle.

If there was one thing Alexander could not tolerate, it was cowardice, because there was not a cowardly bone in his body. On his great white horse, Bucephalus, Alexander had ridden out in front of his army, and all of the Persian spears and arrows had not been able to bring him down.

When he heard what this young man had done, he looked at him stonily. But as he looked at this young man who was so handsome and seemed so young, Alexander's face softened again and he said to him: "Young man, what is your name?" Everyone in the room breathed a sigh of relief, and they knew that he had won the king's heart. The young man sighed also and said, "Alexander."

With that the smile left the king's face, and he said to him, "*What* is your name?" The young man snapped to attention and said, "Alexander, sir." The king crimsoned and said again, "*What is your name?*" The boy began to tremble and stammer, and he said, "A-A-A-Alexander, sir." With that the king exploded out of his chair. He grabbed the boy by the tunic, picked him off his feet, threw him on the ground, and said to him, "Soldier, change your conduct or change your name!"

How about you? "What is your name?" "Christian, my Lord." "*What is your name?*" "Christian, my God." "Dare you take upon yourself the name of Him who set His face as a flint unto Jerusalem and went to a cross? You, who have never opened your lips to bear witness to Him? You, who have maintained a yellow and craven silence in the face of adversaries who have dragged His name in the mud? Man! Woman! Change your conduct or change your name!"

Always to Triumph!

*Now thanks be to God who always leads us in triumph
in Christ, and through us diffuses the fragrance
of His knowledge in every place.*
—2 Corinthians 2:14

Many television programs and movies have a predictable outcome. You know from the outset that the good guy is going to win and the bad guy is going to lose. No matter how thorny it may get for the hero or heroine, there is no real question what the outcome will be. So, too, we need to always remember who will win the cosmic conflict between good and evil, between God and Satan, between Christ's Church and the forces of Hell. In the big picture the Christian Church is always to triumph!

Though Satan seems to be winning sometimes, we know the Lord has *already* won. The second verse of the well-known Thanksgiving hymn "We Gather Together" is a helpful reminder:

> *Beside us to guide us, our God with us joining,*
> *Ordaining, maintaining, His kingdom divine.*
> *So from the beginning, the fight we were winning.*
> *Thou, Lord, be at our side. All glory be Thine.*

There it is: "From the beginning, the fight we were winning"! Knowing we've already won gives us great hope to continue.

The "Obituary" of the Religious Right

But we don't always win every battle. For example, in 1989 Jerry Falwell announced that he was closing down the Moral Majority (the first major wave of modern political involvement on the part of conservative Christians). "Our mission," he said at the time, "has been accomplished."[1] This caused many liberals to happily write up what Ralph Reed calls "the obituary of the so-called 'religious right.'" With the Moral Majority gone, with some of the major televangelists shaken from power, with Pat Robertson's unsuccessful bid for the presidency, it looked like conservative evangelicals and Catholics were politically dead. But says Reed: "What these critics did not realize was that even as they danced on the grave of the Moral Majority, a new pro-family movement was rising, phoenix-like, from its ashes. Falwell had accomplished his objective of reawakening the slumbering giant of the churchgoing vote."[2] This second wave of modern-day Christian involvement helped bring about a major shift in American politics in our day.

The Christians Are Coming

It seems that we're moving in the right direction in terms of Christians becoming a majority in this country. To wit: on November 8, 1994, a great political earthquake took place in this nation, which, as one writer said, if measured on a political Richter scale of one to ten, it would have registered a twelve. The event? The House, Senate, and gubernatorial elections.

There have been endless analyses of what that election meant, but few looked at it from a spiritual angle. What spiritual lessons underlie that political event? Jesus rebuked the Pharisees who could discern the weather from the sky and the various phenomena in the heavens, but they could not perceive the signs of the times (Matt. 16:3). There was a great spiritual work in their day, and they were blind to it. Well, there is a great spiritual work in our time, and I am afraid that most Americans are blind to it.

Yes, it was a political revolution. But what really happened? We have heard all sorts of reasons for the change in the American political picture. I am going to tell you now what really happened on November 8, 1994, and what I think will continue to happen in the future if the present growth of the Christian movement carries on.

On Tuesday night, November 8, 1994, after the election, Market Research Institute asked a number of questions to voters. One of them was, "Are you an evangelical born-again Christian?" A pretty specific designation. To give you a little historical background for comparison, let me say that when that question was asked in 1988, just six years before, the results were that 18 percent of those who voted said they were "evangelical born-again Christians." In 1992 that figure had risen to 24 percent. But just two years later, in the year of 1994, that figure had risen to 33 percent of those who actually voted![3] Yes, my friends, the spiritually significant event is that the sleeping giant of evangelical Christianity is at long last shaking itself awake. That is what happened in the recent elections.

And this was viewed as the top religion story of the year. A poll taken among the Religion Newswriters Association (RNA) at the end of 1994 revealed that they thought the number one story dealing with religion that year was the "role conservative religious groups such as the Christian Coalition played in getting out voters to contribute to the GOP election landslide."[4] This election showed the power of grassroots involvement.

Voting a Biblically Informed Conscience

I wrote a letter after the elections to our senators, representatives, and governors informing them of these statistics, their meaning, and what they portend for the future—especially when you bring to bear several other pieces of information. First of all, how did these people vote? Sixty-nine percent in the House races voted Republican. Sixty-eight percent in the Senate races, and 71 percent in the gubernatorial races, for about an average of 70 percent, voted Republican. Why did they vote that way? Because they believe that that party more closely represented the values of faith, family, and free enterprise that they believe are important. They were voting a biblically informed conscience. This does not mean that all Christians are Republican or all Republicans are Christians. It simply means that as things stand *now*, the Republican Party platform is perceived by most voting evangelicals as being closer to biblical morality than the alternatives.

Fulfilling the Cultural Mandate

Thankfully, many Christians are entering the political arena in our time. Why is that? Several reasons leap to mind. One, that spiritual leaders, ministers, and others in this country for the last decade or two have been telling Christians that it is vital that they become involved in their culture; that Christ says that we are not only to be the light of the world (to proclaim the gospel), but also the salt of the earth (to prevent the nations from utterly corrupting themselves) (Matt.

5:13–16). We are to fulfill not only the Great Commission of sharing the gospel with everyone, but we are also to fulfill the cultural mandate of bringing the teachings of Christ to bear on every sphere of society.[5] At last it appears that many Christians are understanding and responding to that message.

Stung by Liberal Politicians and the Media

The second reason Christians are entering the political arena is because they have been awakened by the sting of liberal politicians and the media. Liberals, for example, like columnist Molly Ivins, who has labeled politically active evangelicals as (and how is this for a pejorative label?) "Shiite Baptists."[6] Christians have been called Khomeinis, Hitlers, Fascists, and every other ugly name. Even the *New York Times* published an editorial piece in 1993 that asserted that the religious conservative movement "confronts us with a far greater threat than the old threat of Communism."[7] Can you believe that? Where have these people been? Do they not realize that religious, conservative, evangelical Christians are the people who founded America? You would think we were some aliens who recently arrived on this planet from who knows where!

So why all the hostility from these columnists? William J. Bennett, former secretary of education and the editor of *The Book of Virtues: A Treasury of Great Moral Stories*, provides a clue. He delivered a speech at the Heritage Foundation of Washington, D.C., on "What Really Ails America," in which he said: "America's only respectable form of bigotry is bigotry against religious people. And the only reason for hatred of religion is that it forces us to confront matters many would prefer to ignore."[8]

Whatever the correct reason, the bigotry carries on and *is stinging evangelicals awake*. When the evangelicals became significantly visible in the Republican party, one of the columnists in the *New York Times*, Garry Wills, said: "The crazies are in charge. The fringe has taken over."[9] The results of the 1994 election show that that fringe is really the *core* of the electorate. Whereas another syndicated columnist, even more acerbic, suggested (though I won't use his word) that "we tax the [expletive deleted] out of the churches if they open their holy yaps one more time about abortion, prayer in the schools, or anything else."[10] A friendly fellow, noted for his tolerance, very opposed to bigotry, unless it is bigotry directed against Christians, and tolerant of anyone except Christians who should open their "holy yaps" about anything dealing with moral and political issues.

In a now infamous article, the *Washington Post* once described followers of the religious right as "largely uneducated, poor, and easy to command,"[11] but at least they did print a retraction later, labeling the derogatory characterization as "without basis in fact."[12]

Ramon Mestre of the editorial board of the *Miami Herald* unapologetically said this about Ralph Reed and the Christian Coalition:

> The Constitutional Convention's leading luminaries would have been aghast to learn that two centuries after the first states ratified the Constitution, a slick Puritan named Reed would be hellbent on refashioning America as a "city on a hill"—a 17th Century invention of totalitarian Massachusetts colonists. Call it, if you like, the rise of the free spirit's Ebola.[13]

Mestre said in the same article that he loses less sleep over the Ebola virus (which is killing people in Africa) than he does over the Christian Coalition!

To its credit, the *Wall Street Journal* published an intriguing editorial called "Those Troublesome Christians," in which they pointed out the hypocrisy of those who seem to want democracy for all, except members of the religious right:

> There is something, it must be said, wonderful in the spectacle of all these defenders of democracy and pluralism, now busy alerting the nation to the menace of the Christian Right. For the menace, in their descriptions, all comes down to the same remarkable charge: namely that Evangelicals and other Christians have committed the crime of getting into politics to make their views heard. In the strange view of the defenders of pluralism, getting into public politics is equal to extremism.[14]

Yes, indeed, the columnists have done their best to sting the evangelical Christian giant awake. If that wasn't enough, the politicians themselves have jumped in to awaken that giant. For example, California Congressman Vic Fazio, who at the time of the election was chairman of the Democratic Congressional Campaign Committee, called those on the religious right "fire-breath[ing]" fanatics.[15]

The summer before the 1994 election, David Wilhelm, the chairman of the Democratic party, said that they should no longer call evangelicals the "religious right" (as if that was not pejorative enough), but call them the "radical religious right." Immediately after that I noticed that particular phrase repeated in numerous columns and editorials. Is it any wonder that Christians are tempted to feel marginalized by these desperate attempts of those in the media and politics who find their influence diminishing by the second?

But we don't want to pick on the Democrats. Let's look at the Republicans. One of the first contestants to cast his hat into the ring for the Republican presidential nomination, Arlen Specter of Pennsylvania, set out right from the very beginning to bash Christians. He didn't know, apparently, what had happened in the election. I wrote him a letter! In fact, as I said, I wrote every representative, senator, and governor a letter telling them what really happened on November 8, 1994, so that they might act in accordance with the realities of our time. Coral Ridge Ministries even put a full-page ad in *USA Today* within weeks of the new Congress taking charge to remind our politicians to stay on track and to remember who really put them in office.

The Stench of Rotting Culture

So we see that religious leaders have begun to awaken Christians. We see that hostile politicians and a hostile media have begun to *sting* them awake. But there is also a *stench* that has disturbed the sleep of the evangelical Christian giant: the stench of a culture rotting all around us, and that is the third reason Christians are waking up and entering the political arena. I think that Dr. Ralph Reed put that very well when he said this:

> We live in a country in which one out of every three children is born out of wedlock, one out of every two marriages ends in divorce, one out of every three pregnancies ends in abortion, and one out of every four high school students drops out of school without graduating. We have 90 million functional illiterates in our society. Murder is the leading cause of death for African-American males aged eighteen to thirty-four, and a minority adolescent male living in our nation's capital has a higher likelihood of being killed than an American soldier did in Vietnam. And yet, there are still some who believe that the most frightening thing that could happen in America is for people of devout faith to become involved in public life.[16]

This is what our critics have produced! I guess they are afraid evangelical Christians are going to clean America up. Sin has become very profitable for many.

Yes, the stench of the country, the attacks of the media and politicians, and the urging of Christian leaders, it seems, have all combined to awaken the sleeping giant of evangelical Christianity in America. We have seen that percentage of voters go from 18 percent six years ago to 33 percent today. Evangelicals are now the largest voting bloc in the country! I think that percentage will probably grow to almost 40 percent in 1996 because Christianity is growing faster than ever, and Christians are becoming involved in the political process more than ever.

Christians, in my opinion, should be confined to no political party. They should be confined to the Word of God. They should search the Scripture, learn what the Bible says about any issue facing our nation, and then they should vote their biblically informed conscience. As Martin Luther said, "My conscience is captive to the Word of God. . . . Here I stand, I cannot do otherwise."[17] That is how Christians ought to vote!

But I can say this, if either of our major political parties wakes up and smells the coffee, understands the signs of the times, perceives what is happening, and embraces the moral biblical agenda of Christians—which has been the agenda upon which this country was built for hundreds of years—that party will be in power for the next century. That is the significance of what really happened on November 8, 1994. I guarantee you never heard that on CBS, NBC, ABC, or CNN.

We should not seek power for power's sake. We should only seek to influence this country for good. But there is much in America that is not good. It is fashionable to be sinful and wicked today. All you have to do is tune in to almost any talk show on television today and you will find the most current depths of depravity that could be dredged up that week.

There is a little couplet that I like so much, and it contains a good word, forgotten by many today—the word *mien* (pronounced "mean"). It means countenance or appearance. Listen to the couplet:

> *Vice is a monster of such horrible mien,*
> *that to be hated needs but to be seen.*
>
> *But seen too oft, grown familiar with its face,*
> *first we endure, then we embrace.*[18]

Familiarity with the face of the monster of vice is the very essence of just about every talk show on television I have seen or know anything about (except the news or Christian-oriented ones). We need to see America changed, and what we want to do is restore moral sanity and spiritual responsibility to this nation, which, indeed, has fallen so far from what it was.

For whom should Christians vote? For those who embrace their moral, spiritual, and political values as informed by the Scripture.

Have you ever heard the point made that Christians in this Christian nation should select and prefer Christians for their rulers? That sounds like it came right from the lips of Jerry Falwell, doesn't it? That's a biased, un-American, radical right-fringe statement if I ever heard one. At least, I am sure that is the way the *Washington Post* would describe it. But the interesting thing is, Jerry Falwell never said it. It was said by John Jay.[19] John Jay was the first chief justice of the first Supreme Court of the United States. He was appointed to that august position by the father of our country, George Washington, who obviously held him in the highest esteem. John Jay, with Madison and Hamilton, authored the Federalist Papers, which explained the meaning of the new Constitution and sold the states on ratifying and adopting it as the law governing the United States. Thus, Jay was one of the central founders of America, and he said, "Providence has given to our people the choice of their rulers, and it is the duty, as well as the privilege and interest of our Christian nation to select and prefer Christians for their rulers."[20]

This was and is a Christian nation. Thus it was established: 99.8 percent of the people, as late as 1776 professed themselves to be Protestant or Catholic Christians.[21]

Isn't it interesting, as Dr. Ralph Reed says, that only in recent times have religious conservatives, or religious people of any kind, been viewed as trying to transform this country into something that critics do not want to admit that it always has been: namely a Christian nation.

But now we are beginning to see some tremendous signs of an awakening of evangelical Christians to their responsibilities to the culture in which they live. Political philosopher Russell Kirk put it very well when he pointed out that "culture" comes from the same root as "cult"—cult in the general sense meaning "religion"—and that no culture can thrive if it is severed from the religious vision that gave it birth.[22] That is exactly what the atheists, the secularists, and the humanists have been doing for the past forty years. They have done their very best to sever this culture from the religious vision of the Pilgrims, Puritans, and the Founders of this country.

I believe a time is coming and soon will be upon us when we shall return to that vision of the Founders of America. Christians should be encouraged. We should be encouraged to realize that we are not losing, and defeated, and discouraged, and marginalized. Rather, just the opposite is true. We need to realize we *can* make a difference—we can make a determinative difference in the direction of this country. We have had forty years of secular humanistic principles imposed upon this country, and these principles have delivered chaos and corruption. I think American Christians are waking up to say, "Enough is enough! We are going to change America back to what it once was."

How can this be accomplished? By fulfilling the Great Commission. By obeying the cultural mandate, which means to take all the potentialities of this world—in other words, all of its spheres and institutions—and bring them all to the glory of God. By being both light and salt. By rendering unto God the things that are God's and unto Caesar the things that are Caesar's.

C. S. Lewis, the great author from Oxford and Cambridge, put it so interestingly: "He who converts his neighbour has performed the most practical Christian-political act of all."[23] I couldn't agree with him more. But second to that is that we become involved in our culture and regraft it into that vision that gave it its original life.

We need to be able to discern the signs of the times, and our politicians and cultural elites had better discern them, because . . . the Christians are coming!

So from the beginning, the fight we were winning.
Thou, Lord, be at our side. All glory be Thine.

Greater News

As good as all the above news is, I think the worldwide growth of the Church in our time is even greater news. As the gates of Hell continue to buffet the Church, just think, tomorrow there will be more than 100,000 souls added to Christ's kingdom![24]

In the first chapter, we saw the incredibly encouraging statistics that show that Church growth, worldwide, is taking place like never before. Let's look at the exponential growth of the Church in our time in a different way—by the number of professing converts to the faith on a *daily* basis. This information comes from the U.S. Center for World Missions in Pasadena, California. This is reported to be the number of people per day who are being converted to Christ, who are being brought to a saving knowledge of Christ. Think about this the next time you see some vicious attack against Christianity in prime time!

- In A.D. 100, 100 persons a day worldwide were being converted to Christ.

- By 1900, the number of conversions was 943 per day.

- By 1950, that number grew to 4,500. It began to outstrip the population explosion.

- By 1980, that 4,500 had grown to 20,000 per day.

- By 1993, it had risen to 86,000 converts per day, making Christianity the fastest growing religion in the world, by far.

- By 1995, the figure of those converted to Christ has reached in excess of 100,000 per day.

- By 2,000, it is estimated to reach about 200,000 per day.[25]

An incredible two-hundredfold increase in one century! Amazing! God is doing a marvelous thing in our time. In Latin America, Africa, and parts of Asia, hundreds of thousands are becoming Christians every week. Christians in South Korea now have a greater burden to reach the rest of Asia by the year 2000 than most Christians in America do!

George Otis, Jr., comments on the relatively new aspect of this spurt of growth in the worldwide Church: "About 70 percent of all progress toward completing the great commission has taken place since 1900. Of that, 70 percent has occurred since World War II. And 70 percent of that has come about in the 1990s alone."[26]

Worldwide Evangelism Explosion

One of the forces—by no means the only one—helping to spread the gospel worldwide is Evangelism Explosion, the lay witness program that was begun at Coral Ridge Presbyterian Church. It has quietly multiplied itself into every state in this union, has crossed all of the oceans of the world, and is at work across the globe. And lives are being changed everywhere as a result.

Take the example of a young man in our community. He had broken up with his wife and had moved out of the house. He was at the grocery store to stock up his new bachelor's apartment when an Evangelism Explosion team from our church met him and shared the gospel with him. He was converted that night, and he reestablished communication with his estranged wife. She agreed to go to church with him and even attend counseling with him. But she was still resolute about divorcing him, despite his change of heart and despite their two small children.

On the day she was going to the courthouse for the divorce, he asked friends at church to pray for him that God would somehow intervene. As she and a friend drove to see the judge, they got stuck waiting for a freight train. Then at the courthouse, they drove around in circles in the parking lot trying to locate a space. And then in the courthouse building they were delayed waiting for an elevator that seemed to take forever. Normally a very punctual person, she was so late (forty-five minutes) that the judge ruled she had to make another court date. She never rescheduled! Lives are being changed in this country through lay evangelism, and lives are being transformed all over the world.

Evangelism Explosion is now on all continents and, as of this printing, is in about two hundred nations of the world. Around the world, people are sharing the good news of Christ. You can go to Invercargill, the southernmost city in New Zealand, or to the northern island of Iceland and Reykjavik, and there you will find people going out day by day, week by week, sharing the gospel of Jesus Christ.

You can visit the former cannibals of Irian Jaya and New Guinea or the city sophisticates of London or Los Angeles, and you will find that there are people who are going out day by day, week by week, sharing the gospel of Jesus Christ and seeing people set free, transformed, born again.

You can travel several thousand feet down into one of the great diamond mines in the southern tip of Africa, and you will find that during the lunch break Christians are teaching other Christians how to share the gospel with the thousands of people who work in those dark caverns.

Wherever you go, with whatever kinds of people, on whatever continent, you will find people who are going out every day of the week sharing the gospel of Jesus Christ because of Evangelism Explosion. And pretty soon, perhaps by the time you are reading this book, this ministry will have reached our lofty goal to be active in every nation on earth. The growth of the spread of Evangelism Explosion to other nations has been very exciting. Look at this progress:

Total in 1989: 89 nations

Total in 1990: 103 nations

Total in 1991: 117 nations

Total in 1992: 137 nations

Total in 1993: 155 nations

Total in 1994: 174 nations[27]

As of this writing, that figure is up to more than 200 nations (of the 211 on earth)! Within months, we anticipate that Evangelism Explosion will be active in every nation on earth.

To my knowledge, this marks the first time in two thousand years of Church history that any ministry—much less one that mobilizes *lay*people to witness—could be found in every country of the world! So not only will the gates of Hell not prevail, but we are always to triumph! And all of history is moving to its ultimate climax—the discipling of every nation and the return of Jesus Christ.

The Second Coming of Christ

This phase of history we're in is really just the time between two outstanding events: the first and second comings of Christ. And all of history is moving toward this inevitable climax. What an awesome thing when you consider all those busily engaged against His kingdom now.

The apostles declared that there would come scoffers who would deny the second coming of Jesus Christ saying, "Where is the promise of His coming?" (2 Peter 3:4). "Behold," said the apostle John in the Apocalypse, "He is coming with clouds, and every eye will see Him, even they who pierced Him. And all the tribes of the earth will mourn because of Him" (Rev. 1:7).

This second advent of Christ is the great hope of the Christian. It will climax history, being the final exclamation point to the last page of the last volume of history that will be written. When Jesus Christ appears again in all His glory in the sky, the drama of the ages will be brought to a glorious conclusion.

How will it be? How will He come? Unfortunately, it is true many fanatics have labored over their charts to set their dates and hours and seasons for Christ's return. Others have divided the people of God on all the minutiae connected to the Second Coming. And often they are woefully wrong in these details.

Meanwhile, some Christians do nothing to fight back against the onslaught against the faith because they think that it's all just a part of fulfilled prophecy. Things will just get worse and worse and then Christ will come. They feel like we should do nothing to preserve our culture from sliding away from Christ and deeper and deeper into the sewer—despite the call of Jesus for us to be *salt* as well as light.

Why should we fight against anti-Christian bigotry, wonder these people, since it's all going to get worse and worse anyway? Why polish the brass on the Titanic, since it's sinking anyway? I don't agree with the analogy that we're on a sinking ship; but even if I did, I'd like to say to such people, "we might not want to polish the brass, but at least we should unclog the toilets! The stench in our culture stinks to high heaven."

Every Eye Will See Him

When Jesus Christ returns in all the glory of His Father, He will eclipse the sun. "Every eye will see Him" (Rev. 1:7). Paul has told us that not only will the living see Him, but the dead will see Him. From out of their tombs they will rise (1 Thess. 4:16–17). From out of the crystal sarcophagus of the oceans they will rise. Westminster Abbey will give forth its honored dead, the catacombs of Rome will disgorge theirs, and the mummies of Egypt will be unwrapped and revealed. Every eye will see Him.

Those who pierced Him will see Him. All the kindreds of the earth will wail because of Him.

Come now, Judas! Now you know where He is. There He looms in the midst of the air in all His glory. Now run, go quickly to the high priests and betray Him once more for you know where He is. What is the matter, Judas? Will not your legs move?

Come now, Caiaphas, tell us once more that it is expedient that this man die, that the whole nation perish not. Come! Tell us how we should take Him with rough hands and skewer Him to a cross. Are your hands so busily engaged blocking the bright effulgence of His glory from your eyes that you cannot touch Him? Come now, Pilate! Call for a basin to wash your hands, and tell us once more that you will have nothing to do with this man. No one can find any place where he will have nothing to do with this man. Indeed, people will call upon the hills to cover themselves and for the mountains to fall upon them that they may hide from the face of Him who sits upon the throne and from His wrath. He will come visibly and every eye will behold Him.

Come now, ACLU! Will you try to haul Him off to court and declare His kingdom unconstitutional, although the Constitution was largely based on His Word? Will you attempt to oppose every public mention of Him, although He is the Creator of all? Will you still be proud of having kept many from finding eternal life in Him?

Glory Unveiled

Jesus will come gloriously. Someone once said to me, "I suppose that if Jesus Christ were to come again and He were to walk around Ft. Lauderdale or Chicago or London in a business suit, we would probably take Him and crucify Him once more."

How little he understood what the second advent of Christ really means! Jesus will not come again in humility. He will come in glory and in the power of His Father with all of His mighty angels attendant, with ten thousand times ten thousand of His saints, with the sound of a trumpet that shall wake the dead; with the voice of the archangel He shall come!

No one will dare to lift a hand against Him, for this time He will come undisguised. When Jesus came before, He came with His deity disguised: the disguise seen by the Bethlehem caravansary, the disguise of the mausoleum in stone, the disguise of the seamless robe and the sandals, the disguise of face, the disguise of voice, the disguise of eyes. This next time He will come undisguised.

He will come with His glory unveiled, and people will see Him as He really is. His glory will eclipse the brightness of the sun! Ten thousand of the most glorious sunsets or sunrises will pale into insignificance when He comes with myriads of angels attending.

And He will return, triumphant over His foes and His enemies. For Christians that will be a day of great rejoicing, but for those who have not believed, the day of the glory of Christ's power will be a day of great wailing, the *Dies Irae*—the day of wrath. They will tremble when He comes "in flaming fire taking vengeance on those who do not know God, and on those who do not obey the gospel of our Lord Jesus Christ" (2 Thess. 1:8). They will be destroyed with everlasting destruction when He comes.

I am utterly and unshakably convinced that Jesus shall reign. The gospel of Christ *will* continue going forth in victory. Every single weapon devised by man to destroy it has utterly failed and *will* utterly fail. Nothing can stand before it. And I am sure the pagan philosophies and religions of this nation and of the entire world will crumble before the advent of the gospel of Christ. He who sits upon the white horse that goes forth conquering and to conquer will continue until every nation, tribe, and tongue upon this earth shall offer their praise to the Savior. Jesus Christ is building His Church on earth, and the gates of Hell shall not prevail against it!

The third verse of the great hymn "Onward, Christian Soldiers" puts it so well:

> *Crowns and thrones may perish, kingdoms rise and wane,*
> *But the Church of Jesus constant will remain;*
>
> *Gates of Hell can never 'gainst that Church prevail;*
> *We have Christ's own promise, and that cannot fail.*
>
> *Onward, Christians soldiers, marching as to war,*
> *With the cross of Jesus going on before.*[28]

Amen.
Soli Deo Gloria!

Appendix

Legal Resources to Fight Anti-Christian Bigotry

Here are some brief descriptions, phone numbers, and addresses of those organizations that can help you fight against religious bigotry. If you know of anyone whose religious liberty has been jeopardized, feel free to contact any of these not-for-profit organizations. There is usually no cost to the client for these services, as these groups derive their income from donations. Share these phone numbers with anyone who needs them. Virtually all of them were started and are run by Christians. Most of them will help non-Christians if their religious rights are also "under fire."[1] These are listed in alphabetical order.

1. **Alliance Defense Fund,** P.O. Box 54370, Phoenix, AZ 85078-4370, tel. 602-953-1200, 800-TELLADF.

The Alliance Defense Fund is a servant organization, geared to help all other religious liberty groups in the country. The ADF has the triple purposes of

- strategic planning to bring together the best and brightest of legal minds to fight for religious freedom,

- raising funds for fighting religious liberty cases, and

- enlisting and training more Christian attorneys in the cause of preserving religious freedom.

The ADF was launched in early 1994 and is headed up by attorney Alan Sears.[2] The board of ADF consists of many leading evangelicals, drawn together by the common goal of preserving religious freedom. The founding members of the board include James Dobson, Larry Burkett, John Ankerberg, Bill Bright, Don Wildmon, Marlin Maddoux, and myself. ADF has been a model example of Christians working together in harmony. This unity has come about because the anti-Christian hostility has reached such a high pitch. Indeed, the ADF is an organization whose time has come.

You will want to call the ADF if

- you're an attorney willing to donate time to serve the body of Christ in critical religious liberty battles;

- you would like to donate funds to the cause of religious freedom (they will make sure that your donation goes to wherever it's needed most);

- you need assistance in your own legal struggle pertaining to religious liberty.

Working with attorneys and organizations across the nation—thus, knowing the big picture—the Alliance Defense Fund can refer someone needing legal help in a case involving religion to the most appropriate agency of which they're aware.

2. American Center for Law and Justice, P.O. Box 64429, Virginia Beach, VA 23467, tel. 804-579-2489.

Founded by Pat Robertson, the ACLJ persuasively fights for religious liberty. The chief litigant of the ACLJ is the aggressive Jay Sekulow, a young man from a Jewish background who came to accept Jesus as his Messiah when he was in college. Jay is also the founder and director of CASE (Christian Advocates Serving Evangelism), a separate organization that helps preserve the right of people to evangelize, primarily students, in the public schools. Jay Sekulow has argued nine times before the Supreme Court, and he has won all nine times! Because of his success in aggressively arguing the case for religious freedom, Pat Robertson called on Jay to head the ACLJ. Keith Fournier is the executive director of the American Center for Law and Justice.

The ACLJ describes itself as "pro-life, pro-liberty, and pro-family." With a network of approximately twenty-four attorneys throughout the U.S., they are actively engaged in litigation to preserve religious liberty. They are involved in First Amendment issues, students' rights (primarily in the public school system), and pro-life issues.

3. American Family Association Law Center, P.O. Drawer 2440, Tupelo, MS 38803, tel. 601-844-5036.

Don Wildmon founded the American Family Association (originally known as the National Federation for Decency) in order to clean up the airwaves. In the early 1990s he saw the need to start a legal branch of the same organization to fight for religious freedom. The general counsel is Scott Thomas. The AFA Law Center deals with First Amendment, constitutional-rights, and freedom-of-speech cases.

4. **Liberty Counsel**, P.O. Box 540772, Orlando, FL 32854, tel. 407-875-2100, 800-671-1776.

The Christian civil liberties group, the Liberty Counsel, was founded by a former minister. Mat Staver served as a pastor for many years in Kentucky, but he became frustrated over the "erosion of our religious rights." He thus went to law school and then established this legal organization in 1989. They, too, have argued some cases before the Supreme Court. Staver has written a book that gives up-to-date information on the civil rights of religious people, *Faith and Freedom: A Complete Handbook for Defending Your Religious Rights* (Crossway, 1995).

Susan Engel of the Liberty Counsel highlights their work: "Based in Orlando, Florida, Liberty Counsel provides education and legal defense throughout the nation on First Amendment free speech and religious liberty issues such as students' and teachers' rights on public school campuses, equal access, religion in public places, and political activity of nonprofit organizations."[3]

5. **National Legal Foundation**, 6477 College Park Square, Suite 306, Virginia Beach, VA 23464, tel. 804-424-4242, 800-397-4242.

The National Legal Foundation is a small but effective organization; they manage to get a lot of work done on a shoestring budget. Dr. Robert Skolrood, a gentle giant, has been the head of the NLF for years until very recently. Although he is now devoting more time to writing, he's still affiliated with the NLF, which he led for more than a decade. On some occasions Coral Ridge Ministries has joined forces with the NLF to fight specific cases. The Ottawa story written up in Chapter 13 is one such case. Skolrood has practiced law for thirty-eight years and is a fellow in the prestigious American College of Trial Lawyers.[4] The biggest victory of the National Legal Foundation was probably the 1990 *Mergens* case, which established the principle of equal access for voluntary, student-led Bible studies at public schools during nonclassroom hours. The NLF took the case all the way to the Supreme Court, and then Jay Sekulow was brought in to argue the case before the Court. The decision was a resounding victory for religious liberty. If you feel your religious rights are being threatened in any way, call the National Legal Foundation.

6. **The Rutherford Institute**, P.O. Box 7482, Charlottesville, VA 22906-7482, tel. 804-978-3888.

The oldest legal group mentioned in this lineup that fights for religious liberty is the Rutherford Institute.[5] Constitutional attorney and prolific author John Whitehead is the founder and director of Rutherford. Their name is derived from the seventeenth-century Puritan divine of Scotland, Samuel Rutherford, who wrote *Lex Rex*, wherein he promoted the then-subversive idea that the law is king, as opposed to "Rex Lex," the prevailing concept that the king was law.

Early in his career Whitehead had actually served with the ACLU, seeing it as an organization that helped people. But as he drew close to Christ, he not only stopped that, he considered dropping out of law altogether to pursue the ministry. But the teachings of Francis Schaeffer showed him he could pursue ministry through law. In 1982, as religious liberty began to come under serious fire in this country, John founded the Rutherford Institute to preserve religious freedom.[6] The Rutherford Institute has a network of chapters all across the country (and even some chapters in other countries).

You will want to call the Rutherford Institute if in any way your religious liberties are being infringed upon. Whitehead says, "We don't turn down any case. If one of our salaried lawyers cannot do it, we try to find someone else to handle the case."[7] Whitehead reports that they average one thousand calls a month for legal help.[8]

7. Other organizations worth mentioning:

a. The Christian Legal Society's **Center for Law and Religious Freedom**, tel. 703-642-1070. They file important friend-of-the-court briefs on behalf of religious freedom.

b. **The Beckett Fund for Religious Liberty**, tel. 202-955-0095, founded in 1994 by Kevin Hasson, who served as church-state counsel in the Department of Justice from 1987 to 1988.

c. **Christian Law Association**, tel. 813-399-8300, which is a part of David Gibbs's law firm in central Florida. "It has focused on issues facing religious schools."[9]

d. **Western Center for Law and Religious Freedom**, with offices in California, Oregon, and Washington, tel. 503-588-2532. It was established in 1990 and deals primarily with cases in states along the Pacific Coast.

e. **The Home School Legal Defense Association**, tel. 540-338-5600, for those homeschoolers needing legal help; membership is a prerequisite for receiving help. This effective organization was quite active in defeating H.R.6 (as discussed in Chapter 13).

These are the major organizations of which I'm aware. I encourage Christians to support these groups as they keep religious freedom alive. They also provide newsletters to keep their supporters or friends up to date on the cases they're fighting. Please keep these phone numbers and addresses handy and give them out to people whose religious rights are trampled on. As more and more Christians stand up for what's right, we can regain our lost freedom. Know your rights. Hold your ground. There's a lot at stake.

Notes

Introduction

1. Updated and based loosely on a story heard in a sermon delivered by Dr. James O. Speed of the First Presbyterian Church, Marietta, Ga., summer 1977.

2. Ramon Mestre, "Christian Coalition: A Free Spirit's Ebola," *Miami Herald*, 26 May 1995.

3. John Foxe, *Foxe's Book of Martyrs* (Springdale, Pa.: Whitaker House, 1563, 1981), 1.

Chapter One

1. David B. Barrett and Todd M. Johnson, *Our Globe and How to Reach It: Seeing the World Evangelized by AD 2000 and Beyond* (Birmingham, Ala.: New Hope, 1990), 56. In their 1990 book, authors Barrett and Johnson list the number at a rounded-off figure of 1.8 billion. With the rapid growth rate of the Church, it's not unreasonable to extrapolate that today there are nearly two billion professing Christians. In fact, it may well exceed that figure!

2. Ralph Reed, *Politically Incorrect: The Emerging Faith Factor in American Politics* (Waco, Tex.: Word, 1994), 5. Used by permission.

3. Philip Schaff, *The History of the Christian Church*, vol. 2 of *Ante-Nicene Christianity, A.D. 100–325* (Grand Rapids: Eerdmans, 1910), 22.

4. Ralph Winter, Phil Bogosian, Larry Boggan, and Frank Markow, "The Amazing Countdown Facts!" (fact sheet) U.S. Center for World Missions, Pasadena, Calif., 1992, 4.

5. I am indebted to the U.S. Center for World Missions in Pasadena, Calif., for most of these statistics.

6. Quoted in David Bryant, *The Hope at Hand: National and World Revival for the Twenty-first Century* (Grand Rapids: Baker, 1995), 27.

7. "The Growth of the Gospel!" *Mission Frontiers* 16, July–August 1994, 5.

8. Ibid.

9. Dr. David Barrett cited by Vern Dueck, Manager of the Mission Resource Center for World Missions of the U.S. Center for World Missions, who told Jerry Newcombe this via telephone on June 14, 1995. Newcombe asked Dueck if the Center ever publishes books on the phenomenal growth of the Church in our time. Dueck replied that such a book would be out of print by the time it came off the presses!

10. "The Growth of the Gospel!"

11. Richard N. Ostling, "In So Many Gods We Trust," *Time*, 30 January 1995, 72.

12. "College Revival Spreading from Campuses," *National & International Religion Report*, 15 May 1995; 10 July 1995.

13. George Barna, *Absolute Confusion: How Our Moral and Spiritual Foundations Are Eroding in This Age of Change* (Ventura, Calif.: Regal Books, 1993), 86–87.

14. Ibid., 87.

15. Philippians 2:11.

16. Based on Hebrews 13:5.

17. Based on 2 Corinthians 2:14.

18. Based on Revelation 19:16.

19. Based on Revelation 19:11–21.

20. Bill Stearns, "What in the World Is God Doing? A Global Glimpse of God's Harvest Today," *Discipleship Journal*, 78 (1993): 66.

21. Ibid.

22. Ibid.

23. Bryant, *The Hope at Hand*, 223.

24. Ibid., 227.

25. Barrett and Johnson, *Our Globe and How to Reach It*, 54.

26. Bryant, *The Hope at Hand*, 223.

27. Ibid.

28. Ibid., 225.

29. Ibid., 227.

30. Ibid., 224.

31. Barrett and Johnson, *Our Globe and How to Reach It*, 60.

32. Ibid.

33. Bryant, *The Hope at Hand*, 238.

34. Alister McGrath, "Why Evangelicalism Is the Future of Protestantism," *Christianity Today*, 19 June 1995, 18.

35. Ibid., 22.

Chapter Two

1. "Tabloid Psychics' Forecasts Flop Again," *Washington Times*, 7 January 1995.

2. Ibid.

3. I've written an entire book on the subject of Jesus fulfilling messianic prophecies. It's entitled *Messiah: Prophecies Fulfilled* (Ft. Lauderdale, Fla.: Coral Ridge Ministries, 1985).

4. Lee Strobel, *Inside the Mind of Unchurched Harry and Mary: How to Reach Friends and Family Who Avoid God and the Church* (Grand Rapids: Zondervan, 1993), 36–37.

5. Peter Stoner, *Science Speaks* (Chicago: Moody Press, 1963), 109, quoted in Josh McDowell, *Evidence That Demands a Verdict* (San Bernardino, Calif.: Campus Crusade for Christ, 1972), 167.

6. Strobel, *Inside the Mind of Unchurched Harry and Mary*, 37.

7. Ibid., 36.

8. See James C. Hefley, *What's So Great about the Bible?* (Elgin, Ill.: David C. Cook, 1969), 17–20.

9. Ibid., 17.

10. Ibid., 18.

11. C. S. Lewis, *Mere Christianity* (New York: Macmillan, 1960), 56.

12. Barrett and Johnson, *Our Globe and How to Reach It*, 56.

13. Josh McDowell, *Evidence That Demands a Verdict: Historical Evidences for the Christian Faith* (Nashville: Thomas Nelson, 1979), 209.

14. Quoted in ibid., 214.

15. Ibid., 223.

16. Foxe, *Foxe's Book of Martyrs*, 6–13.

17. Josh McDowell, interviewed by Jerry Newcombe, *The Coral Ridge Hour*, Ft. Lauderdale, Fla.: Coral Ridge Ministries-TV, 15 April 1988.

18. McDowell, *Evidence That Demands a Verdict*, 179.

19. Ibid., 236–39.

20. *Principal Hill, Lectures in Divinity*, vol. 1, 47–48, quoted in William Taylor, *The Miracles of Our Saviour* (New York: Hodder and Stoughton, 1890), 21–22.

21. Ibid., 233.

22. Quoted in McDowell, *Evidence That Demands a Verdict*, 244.

23. Ibid., 248–55.

24. John A. T. Robinson, *Redating the New Testament* (London: SCM Press, 1976).

25. One of the reasons he came to believe this was because John 5:2 says, "Now there *is* in Jerusalem by the Sheep Gate a pool" (emphasis mine). When the Roman Titus came in A.D. 70, he thoroughly destroyed Jerusalem and much of Israel. So Robinson believed, therefore, that John—the final Gospel to be written—was penned before A.D. 70.

26. Foxe, *Foxe's Book of Martyrs*, 6–13.

27. McDowell, *Evidence That Demands a Verdict*, 81–87.

Chapter Three

1. Hy Pickering, *One Thousand Tales Worth Telling: Mostly New, Strictly True, Suitable for You* (London: Pickering and Ingles, n.d.), 20.

2. John 20:1–18.

3. Luke 19:1–10.

4. See 1 and 2 Peter.

5. Foxe, *Foxe's Book of Martyrs*, 13.

6. Mark 3:17.

7. Foxe, *Foxe's Book of Martyrs*, 6.

8. Mark 5:1–19.

9. Acts 7; 9; 13.

10. St. Augustine, *The Confessions of St. Augustine*, trans. John K. Ryan (Garden City, N.Y.: Doubleday, 1960), 65–66.

11. J. M. Roberts, *History of the World* (New York: Oxford University Press, 1993), 235.

12. J. D. Douglas, ed., *The New International Dictionary of the Christian Church* (Grand Rapids: Zondervan, 1978), 752.

13. Ibid., 964.

14. Ibid., 45.

15. Ibid., 386–87.

16. G. K. Chesterton, *St. Francis of Assisi* (New York: Doubleday, 1924, 1990), 127–28.

17. John D. Woodbridge, ed., *Great Leaders of the Christian Church* (Chicago: Moody Press, 1988), 253–56.

18. *Encyclopaedia Britannica*, s.v. "William Wilberforce." See also Ford K. Brown, *Fathers of the Victorians: The Age of Wilberforce* (Cambridge: Cambridge University Press, 1961).

19. Woodbridge, *Great Leaders of the Christian Church*, 320–24.

20. Eugene Myers Harrison, *Giants of the Missionary Trail: The Stories of Eight Men Who Defied Death and Demons* (Chicago: Scripture Press, 1954), 65–68.

21. Lee Lambert, *Basic Library of the World's Greatest Music* (Ft. Lauderdale, Fla.: Basic Library of the World's Greatest Music, 1986), 44.

22. Catherine Marshall, *A Man Called Peter: The Story of Peter Marshall* (New York: McGraw-Hill, 1951), 15.

23. Lloyd Billingsley, *The Generation That Knew Not Josef: A Critique of Marxism and the Religious Left* (Portland, Ore.: Multnomah, 1985), 72–77.

24. David Wilkerson with John and Elizabeth Sherrill, *The Cross and the Switchblade* (Old Tappan, N.J.: Spire Books, 1963).

25. Nicky Cruz with Jamie Buckingham, *Run, Baby, Run* (South Plainfield, N.J.: Bridge Publishing, 1968).

26. Quoted in Chuck Colson, *Born Again* (Old Tappan, N.J.: Spire Books, Fleming H. Revell, 1976), 57.

27. That first program aired 6 November 1967. Phil Donahue & Co., *Phil Donahue: My Own Story* (New York: Simon and Schuster, 1979), photo caption, opposite 112.

28. William J. Murray, *My Life without God* (Nashville: Thomas Nelson, 1982), 14.

29. Ibid., 232–33.

30. Ibid. See also William J. Murray, interviewed in *The Coral Ridge Hour*, Ft. Lauderdale, Fla.: Coral Ridge Ministries-TV, 25 June 1989. Why would an atheist read the Gospel of Luke? Murray had read the novel *Dear and Glorious Physician* by Taylor Caldwell. At the end of the book, Caldwell refers her readers to the Gospel of Luke for more information. So Murray picked it up. By that time, he was so sick of the dysfunctional world of atheism he had experienced in his family, that he was open to the gospel.

31. John Perkins, *Let Justice Roll Down: John Perkins Tells His Own Story* (Glendale, Calif.: G/L Regal, 1976).

32. Bio on Jeffrey C. Fenholt, Jeffrey Fenholt Outreach, Uplands, Calif.

33. Jeffrey C. Fenholt, *From Darkness to Light* (Tulsa, Okla.: Harrison House, 1994).

34. Carol Everett with Jack Shaw, *Blood Money: Getting Rich off a Woman's Right to Choose* (Sisters, Ore.: Multnomah, 1992). "Playing for the Other Team" is the title of chap. 14.

35. Johnny Hart, interviewed in *The Coral Ridge Hour*, Ft. Lauderdale, Fla.: Coral Ridge Ministries-TV, 27 March 1994.

36. Source: Creators Syndicate, Los Angeles, Calif.

37. Sy Rogers, "The Man in the Mirror," *The Last Days Magazine*, 1991, 2.

38. Marcia Montenegro, interviewed in *The Coral Ridge Hour*, Ft. Lauderdale, Fla.: Coral Ridge Ministries-TV, 2 January 1994. For additional reading on her testimony, see Marcia Montenegro, "From Astrology to Christ: The Personal Testimony of Marcia Montenegro," *The Shantyman*, July–August 1993, 6–7.

39. Richard D. Lumsden, "Professing to Be Wise . . . a Scientist's Salvation," unpublished, Los Angeles, 1994, 9.

40. Ibid., 9–10.

41. Dr. Lumsden teaches creationism part-time at Master's College in Los Angeles and part-time at the Institute for Creation Research in San Diego.

42. Dr. Donald Gray Barnhouse, pastor of the Tenth Presbyterian Church of Philadelphia, on a weekly radio broadcast airing on a Tampa radio station in the early 1950s. See Dr. Herbert Lee Williams, *D. James Kennedy: The Man and His Ministry* (Nashville: Thomas Nelson, 1990), 48–53.

43. Paul Little, *Paul Little's Why & What Book* (Wheaton, Ill.: Victor Books, 1970, 1980), 123.

44. Frank S. Mead, *The Encyclopaedia of Religious Quotations* (Old Tappan, N.J.: Fleming H. Revell, 1965), 308.

45. Lyrics from familiar hymn "Rock of Ages," Augustus Toplady and Thomas Hastings.

46. Paul Lee Tan, *Encyclopedia of 7,700 Illustrations: Signs of the Time* (Rockville, Md.: Assurance Publishers, 1984), 530.

47. Write to me: James Kennedy, Box 40, Ft. Lauderdale, FL 33302, and ask for *Beginning Again* or call 954-772-0408.

Chapter Four

1. Samuel Valentine Cole, "Hammer and Anvil," quoted in Vernon C. Grounds, *The Reason for Our Hope* (Chicago: Moody Press, 1945), 41–45.

2. Hefley, *What's So Great about the Bible?*, 46.

3. The International Council on Inerrancy met from 1978 to 1988. The purpose was to clearly affirm that when the autographa, the original writings of the Scriptures, were first written, they were inerrant. They were breathed out by God (2 Tim. 3:16) and therefore were without error.

4. James Montgomery Boice, interviewed by Debra Revitzer, Ft. Lauderdale: Coral Ridge Ministries-TV, Fla., 4 December 1994.

5. Ibid.

6. In a literal sense, higher critics analyze the Bible against outside sources; lower critics analyze the text against itself. However, many "higher critics" are merely human judges who have set themselves in judgment on the veracity of the Word of God.

7. Term cited by R. C. Sproul, interviewed in "The Bible: Fable, Fraud, or Fact?" *The Coral Ridge Hour*, Ft. Lauderdale, Fla.: Coral Ridge Ministries-TV, 4 December 1994.

8. Grounds, *The Reason for Our Hope*, 61.

9. Werner Keller, *The Bible as History: A Confirmation of the Book of Books*, trans. William Neil (New York: Bantam Books, 1956, 1976), xx–xxi.

10. Ibid., xix, xxiii.

11. Norman Geisler and William Nix, *A General Introduction to the Bible* (Chicago: Moody Press, 1986), 195.

12. Gleason Archer, Jr., *A Survey of Old Testament Introduction* (Chicago: Moody Press, 1994), 173–76.

13. Joseph Reither, *World History at a Glance* (New York: New Home Library, 1942), 7.

14. Roberts, *History of the World,* 40.

15. Keller, *The Bible as History,* 12.

16. Josh McDowell, *More Evidence That Demands a Verdict: Historical Evidences for the Christian Scriptures,* vol. 2 (San Bernardino, Calif.: Campus Crusade for Christ, 1975), 309.

17. Keller, *The Bible as History,* 107.

18. Ibid., 106–11.

19. McDowell, *More Evidence That Demands a Verdict,* 308.

20. Quoted in Grounds, *The Reason for Our Hope,* 63.

21. "Bible's Right, Study Says—Jericho's Walls Did Tumble," *Miami Herald,* 22 February 1990.

22. Ibid.

23. Bryant G. Wood, "Did the Israelites Conquer Jericho? A New Look at the Archaelogical Evidence," *Biblical Archaeology Review,* March–April 1990, 44–59.

24. Keller, *The Bible as History,* xxiii.

25. Ibid., 384.

26. Ibid., 383–84.

27. Dr. Clifford Wilson, interviewed in "The Bible: Fable, Fraud, or Fact?" *The Coral Ridge Hour,* Ft. Lauderdale, Fla.: Coral Ridge Ministries-TV, 4 December 1994.

28. Quoted in McDowell, *Evidence That Demands a Verdict,* 65.

29. "How True Is the Bible?" *Time,* 30 December 1974, 41.

30. Boice, interview.

31. Grounds, *The Reason for Our Hope,* 65–66.

32. Lew Wallace, *Ben-Hur: A Tale of the Christ* (New York: Buccaneer Books, 1880, 1983), 216–17.

33. McDowell, *Evidence That Demands a Verdict,* 190.

34. Frank Morison, *Who Moved the Stone?* (London: Faber and Faber, 1930), 9.

35. Ibid., 5.

36. Ibid., 192.

37. Strobel, *Inside the Mind of Unchurched Harry and Mary,* 22–24.

38. Ibid., 26, 33.

39. Quoted in Grounds, *The Reason for Our Hope,* 45–46.

Chapter Five

1. Pat Buchanan, "Hollywood's War on Christianity," *Washington Times,* 27 July 1988.

2. In our previous book, we address the cruelty and unChristian nature of the Crusades, but we also make the point that these black marks on the Christian record in history shouldn't be exaggerated the way they often are. Some social critics talk as if the credibility of Christianity has been forever lost because of these bloody episodes, which ended six hundred years ago. For a Christian perspective on them, see D. James Kennedy and Jerry Newcombe, *What If Jesus Had Never Been Born?* (Nashville: Thomas Nelson, 1994) chap. 14 "The Sins of the Church."

3. Ibid., 207–8.

4. Reviewers have called it "a full frontal assault on the New Testament." See *National & International Religion Report* (21 September 1992): 5.

5. Philip Weiss, "Outcasts Digging in for the Apocalypse," *Time*, 1 May 1995, 48.

6. See Kennedy and Newcombe, *What If Jesus Had Never Been Born?* 151–52.

7. Gary Bauer, interviewed in "Crisis in Character," *The Coral Ridge Hour*, Ft. Lauderdale, Fla.: Coral Ridge Ministries-TV, 16 October 1994.

8. Quoted in David Barton, *The Myth of Separation: What Is the Correct Relationship between Church and State? A Revealing Look at What the Founders and Early Courts Really Said* (Aledo, Tex.: WallBuilder Press, 1992), 50. This is a theme we will flesh out in Chapter 9. For now, a pronouncement from the Supreme Court will suffice. In 1892, the U.S. Supreme Court, after poring through all the major founding documents of this nation, declared in the Trinity Decision: "This is a Christian nation."

9. For a fascinating treatment of the biblical record of the conflict between God and Satan, see Donald Gray Barnhouse, *The Invisible War* (Grand Rapids: Zondervan, 1953).

10. For a thoroughly documented treatment of this subject, see our previous book, *What If Jesus Had Never Been Born?*

11. Ravi Zacharias, interviewed by Debra Revitzer, Ft. Lauderdale, Fla.: Coral Ridge Ministries-TV, June 1994.

12. James Dobson and Gary L. Bauer, *Children at Risk* (Dallas: Word, 1990), 36.

13. See Thomas Johnson, "How Prime Time Boxes in Religion," *American Family Association Journal* (June 1994): 5.

14. Movie critic Michael Medved of *Sneak Previews* on PBS says the anti-Christian slant of Scorsese's *Cape Fear* was the director's revenge on the fundamentalists who opposed his earlier work, *The Last Temptation of Christ*.

15. "Losing My Religion," by the group R.E.M, on the CD *Out of Time*, Warner Brothers, 1991.

16. John Whitehead, *Religious Apartheid* (Chicago: Moody Press, 1994), 154.

17. *Stone v. Graham*, 1980.

18. Chuck Colson, "Mother Teresa, the Mobster," *Breakpoint* (April 1994): 1.

19. See Thomas J. Billitteri, "The Gospels: Was Jesus Misquoted?" *St. Petersburg Times*, 29 January 1994.

20. Jay Sekulow, "Canada: A Step in the Right Direction!" *ACLJ Casenote* (November 1994).

21. *Washington Times*, 1 December 1994, quoted in *Christian News*, 26 January 1995, 2.

22. Don Feder, "Christian Bashing Reaches New Heights," *Christian American* (April 1993): 6.

23. Don Feder, *A Jewish Conservative Looks at Pagan America* (Lafayette, La.: Huntington House Publishers, 1993), 150. Used by permission.

24. "Cross Examined: Television's Anti-Religion Bias," *TV, Etc.* (May 1991): 1.

25. Jesus said, "He who does not believe is condemned already" (John 3:18b).

26. Hefley, *What's So Great about the Bible?*, 53.

27. Matthew Henry, *Commentary on the Whole Bible*, ed. Leslie F. Church (Grand Rapids: Regency Reference Library, 1961), 1287.

Chapter Six

1. Tan, *Encyclopedia of 7,700 Illustrations*, 1509.

2. Cal Thomas, letter to Jerry Newcombe, 15 April 1995.

3. We are indebted to Don Wildmon for his *American Family Association Journal* and to L. Brent Bozell III, the founder and director of the Media Research Center of Alexandria, Virginia. Both the American Family Association and the Media Research Center carefully monitor what's on television, and the picture is not good when it comes to the portrayal of Christianity.

If you want to reach these organizations and subscribe to their excellent publications, write to: American Family Association, P.O. Drawer 2440, Tupelo, MS 38803, telephone 601-844-5036 for the *AFA Journal*; or the Media Research Center, 113 S. West Street, Second Floor, Alexandria, VA 22314, telephone 713-683-9733 for *TV, etc.* (on entertainment programming) or *MediaWatch* (on news programming).

4. Episode of *Picket Fences*, 3 December 1993, cited in Johnson, "How Prime Time Boxes in Religion."

5. Episode of *Martin*, 11 February 1993, ibid.

6. Review of *Grace Under Fire*, quoted in *American Family Association Journal*, January 1995.

7. "Network Programs Continue to Denigrate Christian Faith, Diminish Traditional Family, Promote Sexual Perversions," *American Family Association Journal* (February 1993): 5.

8. Johnson, "How Prime Time Boxes in Religion," 5.

9. Ibid.

10. Ibid.

11. Media Research Center, "Second 'Faith in a Box' Study," *American Family Association Journal* (June 1995): 11.

12. Ibid.

13. Ibid., 12.

14. Ibid.

15. Ibid.

16. S. Robert Lichter, Linda S. Lichter, and Stanley Rothman, with the assistance of Daniel Amundson, *Prime Time: How TV Portrays American Culture* (Washington, D.C.: Regnery Publishing, 1994), 422.

17. The Branch Davidians, you will recall, was the name of the cult in Waco, Texas, centered around David Koresh. Koresh was a self-proclaimed messiah who allegedly had multiple conjugal relationships with some of the women in the compound. The cult was besieged by the federal government for several weeks reportedly because of its cache of firearms; it went up in flames in the spring of 1993, killing some eighty people.

18. Barbara Reynolds, "Religion Is Greatest Story Ever Missed," *USA Today*, 16 March 1990, 13.

19. Ibid.

20. Ibid.

21. George W. Cornell, "Media See Religion as Private Matter," *American Family Association Journal* (June 1994): 20.

22. Ibid.

23. Ibid.

24. Ibid.

25. Ibid.

26. Ira Glasser, interviewed in "Taking Liberties: The Legacy of the ACLU," *The Coral Ridge Hour*, Ft. Lauderdale, Fla.: Coral Ridge Ministries-TV, 14 April 1991.

27. Michael Novak, "The Revolt Against Our Public Culture," *National Review*, 4 May 1984, 48.

28. Ostling, "In So Many Gods We Trust," p. 75.

29. Barna, *Absolute Confusion*, 86–87.

30. C. V. Garnett, "Some Things You Never See on Television," *Signs of the Times* (December 1985): 21.

31. Gregg Lewis, "Telegarbage," quoted in *Looking Ahead*, vol. 87, no. 2 (Elgin, Ill.: David C. Cook, 1982). See also Lewis, *Telegarbage,* (Nashville: Thomas Nelson, 1977).

32. Modern secular man protests God's prohibitions related to sex perhaps more than anything else in the Bible. But the fact is that God's laws are for our good. Promiscuous sex, homosexuality, and adultery are harmful spiritually, socially, emotionally, and often physically. For a full treatment of this—showing how God's commands are for *our* good—see our *What If Jesus Had Never Been Born?* chapter 9.

33. Benjamin J. Stein, "TV: A Religious Wasteland," *Wall Street Journal*, 9 January 1985.

34. "Disney Helps Push Homosexual Agenda" [by repeatedly advertising on programs that promote homosexuality], *American Family Association Journal* (June 1994): 6.

35. "Network Programs Continue to Denigrate Christian Faith," 5.

36. *American Family Association Journal* (June 1993): 6.

37. Paul Johnson, *Modern Times* (New York: Harper and Row, 1983), 729.

38. "Bible Is Cop's Defense in Letting Homosexual Fellow Officer Die," *American Family Association Journal* (July 1993): 7.

39. Media Research Center, press release, 2 May 1991.

40. One could argue that the same is true of other public figures. But it seems to me that when a Christian falls, the media have a field day.

41. To any student of history that is a very inaccurate statement. From its birth to the present, Islam spread by the sword, conquering even many Christian lands. Muslims are free to practice their religion in this land; Christians have made it that way. The same liberties are not afforded Christians in Islamic lands. Dan Rather's report, of course, neglected to show Muslims in a negative light—which is not being requested. What is being requested is a little bit of fairness—to stop focusing on negatives when dealing with Christianity.

42. Lichter, et al., *Prime Time*, 422–24.

43. Ibid.

44. "Is Hollywood Getting More Conservative?" *Movieguide*, 7 August 1992.

45. Roseanne Arnold, *HBO Comedy Hour*, 20 June 1992, quoted in *TV, etc.* (July 1992): 3.

46. Quoted in *American Family Association Journal* (November/December 1991): 3.

47. Rosie Perez, quoted in *TV, etc.* (August 1994): 3.

48. Donald E. Wildmon, "It Is Time to End the Religious Bigotry," *American Family Association Journal* (July 1995): 21.

49. *The Jerry Springer Show*, 8 May 1995.

50. Bob Greene, "TV and Movies Teach Violence," in *American Family Association Journal* (September 1993): 5.

51. "Study: Prime-Time Profanity Way Up," *USA Today*, 2 March 1995, reported in *American Family Association Journal* (May 1995): 3.

52. "Advertisers Pay Big Bucks to Get to You," *Daily Variety*, 1 June 1993, quoted in *American Family Association Journal* (September 1993): 4.

53. Reed, *Politically Incorrect*, 58.

54. "What's Right about Television," *TV, etc.*, (June 1995): IV.

55. Ibid. This police drama contains some rough elements, but the Media Research Center recommends it on balance because it portrays police as "competent, capable, and dedicated to their profession. The commissioner, compassionate both on and off the job, was shown to be a dedicated family man."

56. "*Christy* Scores Big," *Movieguide* (June 1994): 18.

57. Kerrie L. Mahan, "Cause for Celebration," *TV, etc.* (December 1994): 6.

58. Dave Geisler, "A Hollywood Surprise," *Focus on the Family*, December 1994, 10.

59. Ibid.

60. "Christy's Swan Song," *American Family Association Journal* (September 1995): 8.

Chapter Seven

1. These contributions of Christianity to civilization are detailed and documented in our previous book, *What If Jesus Had Never Been Born?*

2. *Time*, 14 February 1995, 17.

3. James D. Davis, "*Priest*: As It Begins to Be Shown in Theatres, the Movie Elicits Discomfort and Strong Reactions," *Sun-Sentinel*, 19 April 1995.

4. Michael Medved, *Hollywood vs. America* (Grand Rapids: Zondervan, 1992), 59. Used by permission.

5. See John Eidsmoe, *Columbus and Cortez, Conquerors for Christ: The Controversy, the Conquest, the Mission, the Visions* (Green Forest, Ark.: New Leaf Press, 1992).

6. Medved, *Hollywood vs. America*, 57.

7. Quoted in ibid., 58.

8. Ibid., 67.

9. Thomas Bosse, review of *The Quick and the Dead, Movieguide* (March 1995): 15.

10. This is a far cry from the respect shown Christianity in one of the most moving episodes of the original *Star Trek* series, "Bread and Circuses," episode 43. "Bread and Circuses" gave a creative twist on how the Son of God conquered in love the brutal Roman Empire.

11. *Movieguide* is a biweekly publication of the Christian Film and Television Commission. Their address is P.O. Box 190010, Atlanta, GA 31119; their phone number is 404-825-0084.

12. "Top 100 Movies by Total Viewers" (compiled by *Entertainment Weekly*), *Movieguide* (June 1994): 17.

13. "Jesus Film in 200 Languages," *Christian News*, 21 November 1994, 1 (emphasis mine).

14. Medved, *Hollywood vs. America*, 51, 53.

15. This one is particularly grievous. A woman with a rough past seems to be getting her life together after an alleged Christian conversion. She takes her daughter out to the desert awaiting the rapture and return of Christ. Disappointed, she shoots and kills her little daughter.

16. Medved, *Hollywood vs. America*, 64.

17. Ibid. (emphasis mine).

18. Michael Medved, *Hollywood vs. Religion*, prod. and dir. Michael Pack, 60 min., Dallas, Tex.: Chatham Hill Foundation, 1994, video documentary.

19. Buchanan, "Hollywood's War on Christianity."

20. Feder, *A Jewish Conservative Looks at Pagan America*, 149.

21. Lloyd Billingsley, *The Seductive Image: A Christian Critique of the World of Film* (Westchester, Ill.: Crossway Books, 1989), 119.

22. Ted Baehr, interviewed via telephone by Jerry Newcombe, 6 January 1995.

23. Jim Impoco with Monika Guttman, "Hollywood: Right Face; Under Siege, Filmmakers and TV Bosses Become More Family Friendly," *U.S. News & World Report*, 15 May 1995, 66–72.

24. Ibid.

25. "Critic Says Hollywood Finding Religious Values," *Christian News*, 24 April 1995, 2.

26. Quoted in Eric Holmberg's video, *Hell's Bells, the Dangers of Rock 'n Roll*, part 2, Gainesville, Fla.: Real-to-Reel Ministries, 1989.

27. "Rolling Stones Tour Earns $121M," Associated Press, 29 Dec 1994.

28. Ibid.

29. C. S. Lewis, *Mere Christianity* (New York: Macmillan, 1960), 51.

30. Holmberg, *Hell's Bells*, part 2.

31 Ibid.

32. Quoted in Tan, *Encyclopedia of 7,700 Illustrations*, 1619.

33. Quoted in Mead, *The Encyclopaedia of Religious Quotations*, 57.

34. Quoted in Tan, *Encyclopedia of 7,700 Illustrations*, 649.

35. Quoted in Mead, *The Encyclopaedia of Religious Quotations*, 50.

36. Quoted in McDowell, *Evidence That Demands a Verdict*, 129.

37. Quoted in ibid., 132–33.

38. Quoted in Mead, *The Encyclopaedia of Religious Quotations*, 51.

39. Quoted in ibid., 56.

40. Quoted in David A. Noebel, *The Marxist Minstrels* (Tulsa, Okla.: American Christian College Press, 1974), 103.

Chapter Eight

1. Francis Schaeffer, *How Should We Then Live? The Rise and Decline of Western Thought and Culture* (Old Tappan, N.J.: Fleming H. Revell, 1976), 122.

2. *Funk & Wagnalls New Encyclopedia*, 1979, s.v. "French Revolution."

3. This happened to ten-year-old Joshua Burton on 8 March 1995 at Columbia Elementary School in Orange County, Florida. See *The Liberator* (April 1995): 2.

4. Quoted in James C. Dobson's Focus on the Family Monthly Letter, January 1995.

5. Andres Tapia, "Communities Put Brakes on Churches in Poor Areas," *Christianity Today*, 15 May 1995, 49.

6. For more details on this, see the next chapter and see *Religion in the Public Schools: A Joint Statement of Current Law* available for $3.00 and a self-addressed, stamped envelope to the National Association of Evangelicals, Office of Public Affairs, 1023 15th Street NW, Suite 300, Washington, D.C. 20005. See also Mat Staver, *Faith & Freedom: A Complete Handbook for Defending Your Religious Rights* (Westchester, Ill.: Crossway Books, 1995).

7. Nancy Gibbs, "Has the Separation of Church and State Gone Too Far?" *Time*, 9 December 1991, 62.

8. Rush Limbaugh's television program, 9 June 1994.

9. Rush Limbaugh III, *The Way Things Ought to Be* (New York: Pocket Books, 1992), 274–75.

10. Quoted in Larry Witham, "Christmas Debate Has Been Going On for a Long Time," *Washington Times*, 24 December 1994.

11. Stephen L. Carter, *The Culture of Disbelief: How American Law and Politics Trivialize Religious Devotion* (New York: Basic Books, 1993), 4–5.

12. Rod Dreher, "Jackson Hit for Slurs on 'Religious Right,'" *Washington Times*, 8 December 1994.

13. Garry J. Moes, "The Separation of Culture and State: Should Government Endow the Arts?" *The Rutherford Institute Journal* (January 1992): 1.

14. This was overturned on appeal, but that doesn't change the fact that a jury came to this absurd decision.

15. "The Coming Nuclear Attack on Christianity in America," Action Sheet for *Truths That Transform*, Ft. Lauderdale, Fla.: Coral Ridge Ministries (radio), 25 January 1990. The seminar was conducted May 4–5, 1989, in San Francisco.

16. Lynn Buzzard, founding director of the Christian Legal Society, used this phrase when interviewed for Coral Ridge Ministries-TV's "The Constitution in Crisis," 20 September 1987.

17. In the 8 February 1991 interview by Jerry Newcombe for Coral Ridge Ministries-TV, Ira Glasser, ACLU's executive director, admitted he was uncomfortable with the Union's actions in this incident.

18. Quoted in "ACLU Uses Hyde's Christianity as Basis for Suit," *NFD Journal* (August 1986): 14.

19. Quoted in ibid.

20. For example, a tooth thought to be that of an ape-man was later determined to be that of an ancient pig.

21. Clarence Darrow, quoted in L. Sprague de Camp, *The Great Monkey Trial* (Garden City, N.Y.: Doubleday, 1968), 492.

22. Quoted in Peggy Lamson, *Roger Baldwin: Founder of the American Civil Liberties Union* (Boston: Houghton Mifflin, 1976), 192. The Communist leanings of the ACLU in its early years are well documented. (See 180–234). Baldwin said of the Soviet Union in its earlier years that he and fellow travelers "regard the Russian Revolution as the greatest and most daring experiment yet undertaken to recreate society in terms of human values" (141). In fairness to Baldwin, he did eventually lose faith in the Soviet Union—but not until Stalin made a deal with Hitler in the Russo-German nonaggression pact of 1939.

23. William A. Donohue, *Twilight of Liberty: The Legacy of the ACLU* (New Brunswick and London: Transaction Publishers, 1994), 124.

24. "Workplan 1994: Defending the Abiding Values of American Democracy," ACLU Foundation, 3.

25. Ibid., 1.

26. John Whitehead, interviewed by Jerry Newcombe, Ft. Lauderdale, Fla.: Coral Ridge Ministries-TV, December 1990.

27. John Eidsmoe, *Christianity and the Constitution* (Grand Rapids: Baker, 1987), 81–92.

28. Karl Day, "We Met the Enemy—They Are Us?" *American Family Association Journal* (June 1995): 20.

29. "Liberal Leader Kropp Dies," Associated Press, 12 June 1995.

30. Day, "We Met the Enemy," 20.

31. "Christian Coalition Biography," Christian Coalition, Chesapeake, Va., September 1995.

32. Ibid.

33. David Cantor, *The Religious Right: The Assault on Tolerance & Pluralism in America* (New York: The Anti-Defamation League, 1994).

34. Abraham H. Foxman, national director of the ADL, in his foreword, ibid., v.

35. Paid political advertisement, *New York Times,* 2 August 1994.

36. Mona Charen, "The ADL Betrays Its Mandate," Creators Syndicate, 30 June 1994.

37. For a detailed description of much of the shoddy research, see the Christian Coalition's special report: *A Campaign of Falsehoods: The Anti-Defamation League's Defamation of Religious Conservatives* (Chesapeake, Va.: The Christian Coalition, 28 July 1994).

38. *National Review,* 1 August 1994, 10.

39. *Time* magazine points out about the public schools: "This has always been the central battleground for church-state conflict in America" (9 December 1991, 65).

40. "School Prayer's Bad Day in Court," *U.S. News & World Report,* 17 June 1985, 9.

41. Cited in "The Constitution in Crisis," *The Coral Ridge Hour,* Ft. Lauderdale, Fla.: Coral Ridge Ministries-TV, 20 September 1987.

42. See Gary Habermas, *Ancient Evidence for the Life of Jesus: Historical Records of His Death and Resurrection* (Nashville: Thomas Nelson, 1984) or McDowell, *Evidence That Demands a Verdict.*

43. *National & International Religion Report,* 19 September 1994, 1–2.

44. As told by Sonia Van Ostrand of Foster City, Calif., to Jerry Newcombe on 6 December 1994. Jerry encouraged her to call the Rutherford Institute. She did, and Rutherford was able to get the school to change its mind.

45. Lynn Buzzard, interviewed in Kennedy, "The Constitution in Crisis."

46. Tamara Henry, "Schools Get a Directive on Religion," *USA Today*, 22 August 1995.

47. Benjamin Rush, "The Bible in Schools" (American Tract Society, c. 1830, reprinted Garland, Tex.: 1994).

48. O. L. Davis, Jr., Gerald Ponder, Lynn M. Burlbaw, Maria Garzia-Lubeck, Alfred Moss, *Looking at History: A Review of Major U.S. History Textbooks* (Washington, D.C.: People for the American Way, 1986), 3.

49. Dobson and Bauer, *Children at Risk*, 35.

50. William L. Shirer, *The Rise and Fall of the Third Reich* (New York: Simon and Schuster, 1960), 249.

51. Quoted in ibid.

52. Quoted in ibid.

53. Allan Turner, "Where Is Madalyn Murray O'Hair?" *Miami Herald*, 12 November 1995.

54. "Bible Makes Comeback in Public Schools," *Impact* newsletter for Coral Ridge Ministries, September 1995, 3.

55. Stan Oakes, Christian Leadership Ministries, a division of *Campus Crusade for Christ*, letter to supporters, November 1994.

56. Ibid.

57. Kennedy and Newcombe, *What If Jesus Had Never Been Born?* 51–53.

58. Reverend Peter Gomes, pastor of the Campus Memorial Church, declared himself gay a few years ago. The conflict between Christians and gays at Harvard University is dealt with very well in the 1993 PBS special "Campus Culture Wars." See Michael Pack, filmmaker, *Campus Culture Wars: Five Stories About PC* (Santa Monica: Direct Cinema Limited, 1993).

59. John Avant, pastor of Coggin Avenue Baptist Church in Brownwood, Texas, quoted in *National & International Religion Report*, 10 July 1995.

60. "One Nation under God: Has the Separation of Church and State Gone Too Far?" *Time*, 9 December 1991, 64.

61. Ibid., 68.

62. Feder, *A Jewish Conservative Looks at Pagan America*, 51–52.

Chapter Nine

1. Ken Roberts, interviewed in *The Coral Ridge Hour*, Ft. Lauderdale, Fla.: Coral Ridge Ministries-TV, 2 July 1989.

2. "In regard to this great book, I have but to say, it is the best gift God has given to men. All the good the Saviour gave to the world was communicated through this book. But for it we could not know right from wrong."

Abraham Lincoln, "Remarks upon the Holy Scriptures, in Receiving the Present of a Bible from a Negro Delegation," 7 September 1864. In Marion Mills Miller, ed., *Life and Works of Abraham Lincoln: Centenary Edition*, vol. 5 (New York: The Current Literature Publishing Co., 1907), 209.

3. Quoted in Verna M. Hall, *The Christian History of the Constitution of the United States* (San Francisco: Foundation for American Christian Education, 1966), 372.

4. Quoted in Barton, *The Myth of Separation*, 135.

5. Quoted in ibid., 83.

6. Larry Witham, "'Christian Nation' Now Fighting Words," *Washington Times*, 23 November 1992.

7. Gary DeMar, *America's Christian History: The Untold Story* (Atlanta: American Vision, 1993), 2.

8. Jay Sekulow, interviewed in "Taking Liberties: The Betrayal of Our Heritage," *The Coral Ridge Hour*, Ft. Lauderdale, Fla.: Coral Ridge Ministries-TV, 23 August 1994.

9. Erwin Lutzer, *Hitler's Cross* (Chicago: Moody Press, 1995), 70.

10. Barton, *The Myth of Separation*, 25–29.

11. Lynn Buzzard, interviewed in "The Constitution in Crisis," *The Coral Ridge Hour*, Ft. Lauderdale, Fla.: Coral Ridge Ministries-TV, 20 September 1987.

12. "Student Sent to Detention for Praying at Lunch," press release from the Rutherford Institute, 18 April 1994.

13. "Workplan 1994," 5.

14. Robert Cord, *Separation of Church and State: Historical Fact and Current Fiction* (Grand Rapids: Baker, 1988), 4.

15. Ibid., 7.

16. Saul K. Padover, *The Complete Madison* (New York: Harper and Bros., 1953), 306, quoted in Cord, *Separation of Church and State*, 8.

17. Cord, *Separation of Church and State*, 15.

18. Ibid., 23.

19. Limbaugh, *The Way Things Ought to Be*, 274.

20. George Washington, *The Writings of Washington*, vol. 30, 321, quoted in Barton, *The Myth of Separation*, 113.

21. Ira Glasser, interview.

22. Quoted in Lynn Buzzard and Samuel Ericsson, *The Battle for Religious Liberty* (Elgin, Ill.: David C. Cook, 1982), 81.

23. Cord, *Separation of Church and State*, 18.

24. "Has the Separation of Church and State Gone Too Far?" Gibbs, 64.

25. "The Supreme Court," *Time*, 6 July 1962, 7.

26. "While Most Believe in God . . ." *Newsweek*, 9 July 1962, 44.

27. Ibid.

28. Benjamin Hart, "The Wall That Protestantism Built: The Religious Reasons for the Separation of Church and State," *Policy Review* (Fall 1988): 44.

29. See David Barton, *America: To Pray or Not to Pray* (Aledo, Tex.: WallBuilder Press, 1988, 1991).

30. William Rehnquist's dissent in the 1985 decision, *Wallace v. Jaffre*, reprinted as a special supplement to *The Journal of the American Center for Law and Justice*, 8, (emphasis mine).

Chapter Ten

1. Edmund W. Robb and Julia Robb, *The Betrayal of the Church: Apostasy & Renewal in the Mainline Denominations* (Westchester, Ill.: Crossway Books, 1986), 25, 28, 184–86.

2. The substance of much of *Foxe's Book of Martyrs* deals with that unhappy fact.

3. Sproul, interview.

4. Don Feder, "Annihilation of the Soul at the Harvard Divinity School," Creators Syndicate, 4 April 1994.

5. Ibid. (emphasis mine).

6. Ibid.

7. Billitteri, "The Gospels: Was Jesus Misquoted?"

8. Robert Funk, Roy Hoover, and the Jesus Seminar, *The Five Gospels: What Did Jesus Really Say?* (New York: Macmillan, 1993).

9. "Jesus: A Divorced Father of Three? Latest Blast of Post-Christianity Selling Like Mad in Australia, U.S." *The Christian Challenge*, November 1992.

10. Richard N. Ostling, "Jesus Christ, Plain and Simple," *Time*, 10 January 1994, 38.

11. N. T. Wright, "The New, Unimproved Jesus: An Eminent Scholar Investigates the Recent, Intriguing Attempts to Find the 'Real' Jesus," *Christianity Today*, 13 September 1993, 22–26.

12. *The U.S. Book of Facts, Statistics & Information for 1968*, (New York: An Essandess Special Edition, 1967), officially published by the U.S. Government as *Statistical Abstract of the United States* (Bureau of the Census, U.S. Department of Commerce), 42.

13. *The World Almanac and Book of Facts 1995* (New York: Funk & Wagnalls, 1994), 729.

268   Notes

14. *The U.S. Book of Facts, Statistics & Information*, 5.

15. *The World Almanac 1995*, 373.

16. "Statistical Record of Membership," PCUSA, *The Presbyterian Lay Committee*, Springfield, Pa., fax dated 1 September 1995.

17. McGrath, "Why Evangelicalism Is the Future of Protestantism," 18.

18. Lutheran professor Leif Vaage of Lima, Peru, cited by Gayle White, "Christ Was 'No Goody Two Shoes' Says Organizer of Jesus Seminar," *Atlanta Journal*, 30 September 1989.

19. White, "Christ Was 'No Goody Two Shoes' Says Organizer of Jesus Seminar."

20. Ibid.

21. Boice, interview.

22. Sproul, interview.

23. Michael J. Wilkins and J. P. Moreland, eds., *Jesus under Fire: Modern Scholarship Reinvents the Historical Jesus* (Grand Rapids: Zondervan, 1995).

24. Ibid., 43–44.

25. Karen Augustine and Nancy Reynolds, "Interview with Luke Sissyfag," *Rutherford*, July 1994, 16.

26. Contrary to the accusations of some, we don't hate homosexuals. We love them. We want to see them freed from the bondage of homosexuality. We want to see them spared from the heartbreak of AIDS or other illnesses that are the natural by-product of their unnatural acts. Many former homosexuals have found freedom in Christ. If you or someone you know is struggling with this, contact Exodus, International for the local group near you. The numbers are 415-454-1017 or 407-629-5770.

27. Robert H. Knight, "Homosexual Magazine's Attack on Christ One of the Ugliest Ever," *Kansas Christian*, 11 January 1995.

28. See Chuck and Donna McIlhenny with Frank York, *When the Wicked Seize a City* (Lafayette, La.: Huntington House Publishers, 1993).

29. Reverend David Innes (pastor of Hamilton Square Baptist Church, San Francisco), interviewed for Action Sheet of *Truths That Transform*, Ft. Lauderdale, Fla.: Coral Ridge Ministries (radio), 26 April 1994.

30. Mel White, *Stranger at the Gate: To Be Gay and Christian in America* (New York: Simon and Schuster, 1994), 269, 285.

31. Richard Culbertson, interviewed via telephone by Jerry Newcombe, 31 August 1995.

32. To get more information on CASA, call 410-268-3442 or write CASA, P.O. Box 3612, San Rafael, CA 94912-3612.

33. I've never agreed with that term. What choice do the unborn have in the matter? What choice do many of the girls have who abort, who are rail-roaded into it by their boyfriends, husbands, or parents? He who frames the debate often wins the debate. Choice per se is as American as apple pie. Choice in the case of abortion is as wrong as the sky is blue. A much more fair term would be "pro-abortion-rights."

34. *Miami Herald*, 1 April 1993.

35. Jules Loh, "KKK's Power Is Close to Dead," Associated Press, 17 December 1994.

36. Jack Miller, *Terror in the Night: The Klan's Campaign Against the Jews* (New York: Simon & Schuster, 1993), 12.

37. Ibid., 242, 26.

38. Quoted in ibid., 246.

39. John Perkins and Thomas A. Tarrants III with David Wimbish, *He's My Brother: Former Racial Foes Offer Strategy for Reconciliation* (Grand Rapids: Chosen Books, 1994), 194.

40. Quoted in Susan Cyre, "Women's Conference Re-imagines New God," *Rutherford*, August 1994, 19.

41. Ibid.

42. "Onward Christian Sophists," *National Review*, 18 April 1994, 19.

43. "Re-imagining Alive and Well," *American Family Association Journal* (September 1995): 11–12.

44. George Archibald, "Anti-Vatican Group Says Bible Backs It," *Washington Times*, 1 September 1995.

45. C. S. Lewis, *The Screwtape Letters* (New York: Collier Books, 1961, 1982), 12.

46. To any seeker of God's kingdom, I would refer you back to Chapter 3, Part 2, which explains how one can become a Christian and receive the assurance that he or she is going to Heaven.

47. Quoted in Philip Schaff, *Person of Christ: The Miracle of History* (Boston: The American Tract Society, undated, c. 1900), 323, 328.

Chapter Eleven

1. Their opinions can be found in Barton, *The Myth of Separation*, 1995 edition.

2. Keep in mind that at least fifty-two of the fifty-five men who wrote the Constitution were churchgoing Christians in good standing with their Trinitarian, Bible-believing churches. See M. E. Bradford, *A Worthy Company* (Marlborough, N.H.: Plymouth Rock Foundation, 1982).

3. Benjamin Franklin, *The Works of Benjamin Franklin*, ed. Jared Sparks (Boston: Tappan, Whittemore and Mason, 1840), 10: 281–82, (emphasis mine).

4. "Culprit Rewrites History" (Ft. Lauderdale) *News Sun-Sentinel*, 6 September 1986.

5. Ron Grossman, review of *The Oxford Illustrated History of Christianity*, *Chicago Tribune*, 10 March 1991.

6. In one sense, you could argue that there were attacks on Christ before He even came to the world—centuries before Herod's slaughter of the innocents; for instance, Pharaoh's decree to kill the Hebrew babies. Another example is when Haman tried to kill all the Jews in 731 B.C. Had he succeeded, it is unlikely Jesus could have come. Haman's attempts were thwarted; they comprise much of the book of Esther. Other attacks against the Jews prior to Jesus' coming can in one sense be viewed as attacks against Christ, for they were attacks against God, and Christ is God. Haman is like an eighth-century-B.C. version of Hitler. His plans came to nothing.

7. Foxe, *Foxe's Book of Martyrs*, 18, 26.

8. Ibid., 18.

9. Quoted in Schaff, *The History of the Christian Church*, vol. 2.

10. Alan F. Johnson, *The Freedom Letter* (Chicago: Moody Press, 1974), 136 (emphasis mine).

11. Schaff, *The History of the Christian Church*, 43.

12 . Ibid.

13. Ibid.

14. Ibid., 77.

15. Tertullian, quoted in ibid., 41.

16. Ibid.

17. Will Durant, *Caesar and Christ: A History of the Roman Civilization and of Christianity from Their Beginnings to A.D. 325* (New York: Simon and Schuster, 1944), 652.

18. In one sense, only the Western half of the Roman Empire fell; the Eastern half continued for another millennium—no longer as Rome, but as the great Christian civilization of Byzantium. They were finally destroyed by the Turks (Muslims) when Constantinople fell in 1453.

19. Henry Charles Lea, *A History of the Inquisition of the Middle Ages*, 3 vols. (New York: Harper and Bros., 1888), 1: 450.

20. Barrett and Johnson, *Our Globe and How to Reach It*, 18.

21. Billingsley, *The Generation That Knew Not Josef*, 82.

22. Quoted in Marvin Olasky, "One Man's Religious Odyssey from Marxism to Christianity," *American Family Association Journal* (September 1995): 14.

23. Aleksandr Solzhenitsyn, *The Mortal Danger* (New York: Harper and Row, 1980).

24. David B. Barrett, *Cosmos, Chaos, and Gospel: A Chronology of World Evangelization from Creation to New Creation* (Birmingham, Ala.: New Hope, 1987), 51.

25. Ibid., 60.

26. Testimony of Miguel Bolanos before the U.S. House of Representatives in early 1984.

27. E. Calvin Beisner, *Prosperity and Poverty: The Compassionate Use of Resources in a World of Scarcity* (Westchester, Ill.: Crossway Books, 1988), xiv–xv, 67.

28. Armando Valladares, *Against All Hope: The Prison Memoirs of Armando Valladares*, trans. Andrew Hurley (New York: Ballantine Books, 1986), 50.

29. David Lee Ralston, letter to the editor, *Washington Times*, 17 February 1987.

30. "How the East Was Won," *National Review*, 22 January 1990.

31. Chuck Colson, "A Baby in the World," *Breakpoint*, February 1994, 21.

32. See Laszlo Tokes, with David Porter, *The Fall of Tyrants: The Incredible Story of One Pastor's Witness, the People of Romania and the Overthrow of Ceausescu* (Wheaton, Ill.: Crossway Books, 1990).

33. Ragnhild Kjeldaas Ulrich, U.S. director of the Bridge International, letter to author, 28 March 1990.

34. Barrett, *Cosmos, Chaos, and Gospel*, 60.

35. Bryant, *The Hope at Hand*, 225.

36. David Barrett, quoted in Tetsunao Yamamori, *God's New Envoys: A Bold Strategy for Penetrating "Closed Countries"* (Portland, Ore.: Multnomah Press, 1987), 43.

37. "Mao's Presence Wanes," The Associated Press, 3 January 1995.

38. Schaff, *Person of Christ: The Miracle of History*, 323, 328.

39. Andrew Wark, "New Hope along the Mekong," *Moody Monthly*, February 1994, 24.

40. Ibid., 22.

41. William McGurn, "Good Morning Vietnam," *National Review*, 15 May 1995, 53.

42. "KGB's Warriors Come in from the Soviet Cold," *Washington Times*, 15 November 1992.

43. Feder, *A Jewish Conservative Looks at Pagan America*, 54.

44. Clarence Macartney, *Macartney's Illustrations* (New York: Abingdon, 1946), 54.

45. Quoted in Tom Dowley, gen. ed., *A Lion Handbook: The History of Christianity* (Oxford: Lion Publishing, 1977, 1990), 589–90.

46. Quoted in ibid., 600.

47. Shirer, *The Rise and Fall of the Third Reich*, 240.

48. Ibid.

49. Quoted in Armin Robinson, ed., *The Ten Commandments: Ten Short Novels of Hitler's War against the Moral Code* (New York: Simon and Schuster, 1943), xi.

50. Unfortunately, many Church leaders in Germany were fooled by Hitler, and they went along with the Nazis until it was too late. Erwin Lutzer wrote an excellent book on this and the lessons to be learned from compromising with the world. See Lutzer, *Hitler's Cross), 153.* Lutzer made a great point about the gates of hell: "What do we make of Hitler's apparent victory in crushing the church? Did the 'gates of Hades' prevail? To put the question differently, Did God win, even in Nazi Germany? Yes, God always wins, even when He appears to lose. *He does not to have to win numerically to win spiritually.*"

Chapter Twelve

1. Doug LeBlanc, "Alice Cooper Plugged In: The Once-Wayward Son of a Preacher Comes to His Senses," *World*, 27 August 1994, 20.

2. Quoted in ibid.

3. Ted Baehr, interviewed in *The Coral Ridge Hour*, Ft. Lauderdale, Fla.: Coral Ridge Ministries-TV, 1 March 1992.

4. George Barna, *The Barna Report, 1992–1993, An Annual Survey of Life-styles, Values and Religious Views: America Renews Its Search for God* (Ventura, Calif.: Regal Books, 1992), 125.

5. Quoted in Craig Massey, *Adjust or Self-Destruct* (Chicago: Moody Press, 1977), 17.

6. Quoted in Charles Colson with Ellen Santilli Vaughn, *Against the Night: Living in the New Dark Ages* (Ann Arbor, Mich.: Vine Books, 1989), 35.

7. "Executive Style Survey," *Wall Street Journal*, 20 March 1987, cited in Steffen T. Kraehmer, *Time Well Spent* (New York: Prentice Hall Press, 1990), 57–58.

8. Wilkerson, *The Cross and the Switchblade*, 11–12.

9. Note: the addresses of the advertisers are always listed in the *American Family Association Journal*.

10. "Defeating Donahue," *Truths That Transform*, 29 March 1995. See also Richard Neill, *Taking on "Donahue" and TV Morality* (Portland, Ore.: Questar/Multnomah, 1995).

11. Ibid.

12. Ibid.

13. Elaine Graybill, "Must Men Hate? Sigmund Livingston . . . kept asking the question," *On the Frontline* (September 1993): 14.

14. The address of the American Family Association is P.O. Drawer 2440, Tupelo, MS 38803, or call 601-844-5036.

15. The address of the Media Research Center is 113 S. West Street, Second Floor, Alexandria, VA 22314, or call 703-683-9733.

16. "Taking Liberties: The Legacy of the ACLU," 14 April 1994.

17. William Donohue, interviewed via telephone by Jerry Newcombe, 6 January 1995.

18. Ibid.

19. The address of the Catholic League is 1011 1st Ave., New York, NY 10022, or call 212-371-3191.

20. Dean Jones explains this story on my "Character and Destiny" special, Coral Ridge Ministries-TV, Ft. Lauderdale, Fla., 1994.

21. "Critic Says Hollywood Finding Religious Values," *Christian News*, 24 April 1995, 2.

22. For times and station listings, write to Focus on the Family, Colorado Springs, CO 80995, or call 719-531-3400.

23. Ibid.

24. For times and station listings, write to Point of View, Box 30, Dallas, TX 75221, or call 214-484-2020.

25. For more information, write to the Moody Bible Institute, 820 N. La Salle, Chicago, IL 60610, or call 312-329-4300.

26. For times and station listings, write to Coral Ridge Ministries, Box 40, Ft. Lauderdale, FL 33302, or call 954-772-0404.

27. For times and station listings, write to The 700 Club, 700 CBN Center, Box 64303, Virginia Beach, VA 23463, or call 804-424-7777.

28. For times and station listings, write to The John Ankerberg Show, Box 8977, Chattanooga, TN 37414, or call 423-892-7722.

29. For times and station listings, see address in note 26 for Coral Ridge Ministries.

30. For information on *World*, write Box 2330, Asheville, NC 28802, or call 704-253-8063.

31. For more information, call 202-636-3000.

32. For more information, call 212-679-7330.

33. Reed, *Politically Incorrect*, 159, 168.

34. Ibid., 159.

Chapter Thirteen

1. Christopher Columbus, *The Book of Prophecies*, quoted in Eidsmoe, *Columbus and Cortez, Conquerors for Christ*, 90.

2. Bill Jack, "The First Amendment Works for Christians Too," *Christian Herald*, September 1988, 18.

3. Nat Turner (1800–1831) was a slave who led a violent revolt against slavery.

4. John Brown (1800–1859) was a militant abolitionist. He and a handful of other vigilantes unsuccessfully tried to seize the U.S. arsenal at Harper's Ferry, Virginia (today it's in West Virginia). He was hanged. It turned out that Brown's raid was on the eve of the U.S. Civil War.

5. Reed, *Politically Incorrect*, 59.

6. Barna, *Absolute Confusion*, 86–87.

7. Quoted in Robert P. Dugan, Jr., *Winning the New Civil War: Recapturing America's Values* (Portland, Ore.: Multnomah, 1991), 187.

8. Reed, *Politically Incorrect*, 200.

9. If you would like to reach the Christian Coalition, the address is 1801-L Sara Drive, Chesapeake, VA 23320, or call 804-424-2630.

10. Quoted in *Restoring the Truth: A Monthly Commentary by Dr. D. James Kennedy*, Coral Ridge Ministries, Ft. Lauderdale, Fla., 1985, 16.

11. *Building a Brighter Future for Your Family*, brochure, Citizens for Excellence in Education, Costa Mesa, Calif., n.d.

12. The address is Citizens for Excellence in Education, Box 3200, Costa Mesa, CA 92628, or call 714-251-9333.

13. You can reach the National Right to Work Legal Defense Foundation at 8001 Braddock Road, Springfield, VA 22160. The telephone numbers are 703-321-8510 and 800-336-3600.

14. Dan Quayle, speech at the Reclaiming America for Christ Seminar, Coral Ridge Presbyterian Church, Ft. Lauderdale, Fla., 22 January 1994.

15. "Taking Liberties: The Legacy of the ACLU," 14 April 1991.

16. Ibid.

17. Peter T. Kilborn, "Backlog of Cases Mounts at EEOC," *Sarasota Herald-Tribune*, 26 November 1994.

18. Mark Curriden, "Defenders of the Faith; The Growth of Public-Service Christian Law Firms Is Sending the Message That Threats to Religious Freedoms Will Not Go Unchallenged," *ABA Journal* (1994).

19. Ibid., 3.

20. Ibid.

21. H. B. London, Jr., "Historic Prayer Summit," *The Pastor's Weekly Briefing*, vol. 2, no. 49 (Colorado Springs: Focus on the Family, 9 December 1994): 1.

22. "Christians Pray, Fast & Repent in Los Angeles," *National & International Religion Report* (27 November 1995): 1–3.

23. Reed, *Politically Incorrect*, 131–32.

Chapter Fourteen

1. Bob Briner, *Roaring Lambs: A Gentle Plan to Radically Change Your World* (Grand Rapids: Zondervan, 1993), 68–69.

2. Donald E. Wildmon, "300,000 Silent Pulpits," Citizen's Bar Association Bulletin, vol. 3, no. 12.

3. This number is based on George Barna's statistic that 36 percent of adults in America claim to be born-again (Barna, *Absolute Confusion*, 86–87). Assuming there are roughly 186 million adults (Americans older than 18, based on the 1990 U.S. census), that means we would have about 66.9 million self-proclaimed evangelicals in this country.

4. For more information about Evangelism Explosion, write to me at: D. James Kennedy, Evangelism Explosion III, International, 5554 N. Federal Highway, Ft. Lauderdale, FL 33308, or call 954-491-6100.

5. This anonymous letter was circulating in evangelical circles in this country at least as early as 1976 (source unknown).

6. I highly recommend you get involved in a structured witnessing program, preferably at your local church. Again, if you want more information about Evangelism Explosion, write to me at the address in note 4. Or you can read my book *Evangelism Explosion* (Wheaton, Ill.: Tyndale House Publishers, 1970, 1977). God bless you as you endeavor to serve Him by sharing the best news the world has ever heard.

7. Philip Elmer-Dewitt, "Now for the Truth about Americans and Sex; The First Comprehensive Survey Since Kinsey Smashes Some of Our Most Intimate Myths," *Time*, 17 October 1994, 64.

8. Adolf Hitler, *Mein Kampf* (Boston: Houghton Mifflin, 1943), 139, quoted in Shirer, *The Rise and Fall of the Third Reich*, 83.

9. This phrase comes from the last line of the Declaration of Independence.

Chapter Fifteen

1. Quoted in Reed, *Politically Incorrect*, 191.

2. Ibid., 192.

3. Reported in "Religious Conservatives Increase Influence in National Election Data, Pro-Family/Pro-Life Candidates Account for Most of GOP Gains," Christian Coalition press release, 8 November 1995.

4. "Christian Coalition's Role in Elections Is Year's Top Story," *Washington Times*, 31 December 1994.

5. God told man at the very beginning of time, "Be fruitful and multiply; fill the earth and subdue it; have dominion over the fish of the sea, over the birds of the air, and over every living thing that moves on the earth" (Gen. 1:28).

6. Quoted in Reed, *Politically Incorrect*, 57.

7. Quoted in ibid., 54.

8. William J. Bennett, "What Really Ails America," speech delivered at the Heritage Foundation, Washington, D.C., 7 December 1993.

9. Quoted in Reed, *Politically Incorrect*, 54.

10. Quoted in ibid.

11. *Washington Post*, February 1993, quoted in *National & International Religion Report*, 5 April 1993, 2.

12 . *National & International Religion Report*, 5 April 1993, 2.

13. Mestre, "Christian Coalition: A Free Spirit's Ebola."

14. "Those Troublesome Christians, " editorial, *Wall Street Journal*, 30 June 1994.

15. Quoted in Reed, *Politically Incorrect*, 61.

16. Reed, *Politically Incorrect*, 10.

17. Quoted in Roland H. Bainton, *Here I Stand: A Life of Martin Luther* (New York: Mentor, 1950), 144.

18. Alexander Pope, *Essay on Man*, Epistle 2.

19. On October 12, 1816, John Jay said: "Providence has given to our people the choice of their rulers, and it is the duty, as well as the privilege and interest of our Christian nation to select and prefer Christians for their rulers" Quoted in *The Correspondence and Public Papers of John Jay*, vol. 4, ed. Henry P. Johnston (New York: Burt Franklin, 1970), 393.

20. Ibid.

21. Hart, "The Wall That Protestantism Built," 44.

22. Russell Kirk, "Civilization without Religion," speech for Heritage Foundation, Washington, D.C., 24 July 1992. See also Russell Kirk, *The Roots of the American Order* (LaSalle, Ill.: Open Court, 1974).

23. C. S. Lewis, *God in the Dock*, part 2, "Meditation on the Third Commandment," ed. Walter Hooper (Grand Rapids: Eerdmans, 1990), 199, quoted in

Wayne Martindale and Jerry Root, eds., *The Quotable Lewis* (Wheaton, Ill.: Tyndale House, 1989), 479.

24. This statistic is based on David Barrett's 1990 figure of 38.7 million Christian net increases per year (gains minus losses). See Barrett and Johnson, *Our Globe and How to Reach It*, 56.

25. U.S. Center for World Missions, Pasadena, Calif.

26. Quoted in Bryant, *The Hope at Hand*, 116.

27. "A New Year and a Challenge of Particular Magnitude," *Explosion Energizer* (January 1995), 1. The number of unreached nations as of January 1995 is thirty-seven.

28. Lyrics from the familiar hymn "Onward Christian Soldiers," Sabine Baring-Gould and Arthur S. Sullivan.

Appendix

1. The name of John Whitehead's short radio feature is "Freedom under Fire." Constitutional attorney John Whitehead is the founder and director of the Rutherford Institute, the oldest of the religious-liberty organizations listed here.

2. Alan Sears was the executive director of the Attorney General's Commission on Pornography, under the direction of Ed Meese. Despite hostile media reaction against it, this commission played an important role in cleaning up a lot of the nation's illegal, hard-core pornography.

3. Susan Engel, fax to Jerry Newcombe, 21 December 1994.

4. It is by invitation only; less than 1 percent of attorneys are ever invited.

5. The Christian Legal Society is older than the Rutherford Institute, but Rutherford has been fighting for religious liberty longer. Only in recent years has there been a branch of the Christian Legal Society to fight for religious freedom.

6. Carol Whitehead, "Looking Back at the Early Days," *Rutherford*, January 1994, 14.

7. Karen Augustine, "Interview [of John Whitehead]," *Rutherford*, January 1994, 12.

8. Ibid.

9. Curriden, "Defenders of the Faith," 4.

INDEX

SCRIPTURE INDEX

ABOUT THE AUTHORS

From the team that brought you
What If Jesus Had Never Been Born? . . .

D. James Kennedy, Ph.D., is the Senior Minister of Coral Ridge Presbyterian Church in Ft. Lauderdale, Florida and speaker for the international *Coral Ridge Hour* telecasts.

Dr. Kennedy also serves as President of Evangelism Explosion International and Chancellor of Knox Theological Seminary.

The Kennedys have one daughter.

Jerry Newcombe is an award-winning producer for Coral Ridge Ministries, the television outreach of Coral Ridge Presbyterian Church.

The Newcombes have two children, a daughter and a son.

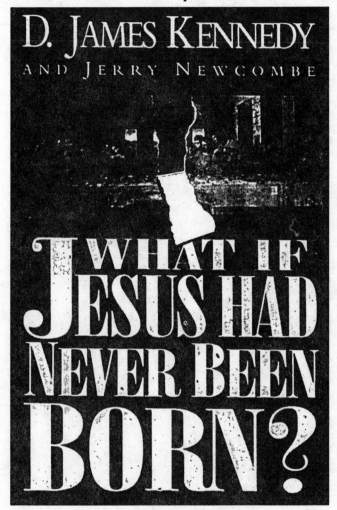